D1556913

KNOWLEDGE, PERCEPTION, AND MEMORY

PHILOSOPHICAL STUDIES SERIES IN PHILOSOPHY

VOLUME 5

CARL GINET

Cornell University

KNOWLEDGE, PERCEPTION, AND MEMORY

D. REIDEL PUBLISHING COMPANY

DORDRECHT-HOLLAND / BOSTON-U.S.A.

Library of Congress Cataloging in Publication Data

Ginet, Carl,
        Knowledge, perception, and memory

        (Philosophical studies series in philosophy ; 5)
        Bibliography: p.
        Includes index.
        1. Knowledge, Theory of. 2. Perception.
3. Memory. I. Title.
BD161.G54   121   75–8602
ISBN 90–277–0574–7

Published by D. Reidel Publishing Company,
P.O. Box 17, Dordrecht, Holland

Sold and distributed in the U.S.A., Canada, and Mexico
by D. Reidel Publishing Company, Inc.
306 Dartmouth Street, Boston,
Mass. 02116, U.S.A.

TABLE OF CONTENTS

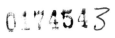

PREFACE

In this book I present what seem to me (at the moment) to be right answers to some of the main philosophical questions about the topics mentioned in the title, and I argue for them where I can. I hope that what I say may be of interest both to those who have already studied these questions a lot and to those who haven't. There are several important topics in epistemology to which I give little or no attention here – such as the nature of a proposition, the major classifications of propositions (necessary and contingent, *a priori* and *a posteriori*, analytic and synthetic, general and particular), the nature of understanding a proposition, the nature of truth, the nature and justification of the various kinds of inference (deductive, inductive, and probably others) – but enough is covered, to one degree or another, that the book might be of use in a course in epistemology.

Earlier versions of some of the material in Chapters II, III, and IV were some of the material in Ginet (1970). An earlier version of the part of Chapter VII on memory-connection was a paper that I profited from reading and discussing in philosophy discussion groups at Cornell University, SUNY at Albany, and Syracuse University in 1972–73.

I do not like to admit how long I have been working on this book. I don't remember all the sources from which I have derived ideas, and I am fairly sure that I have forgotten with respect to some of the ideas used here that they did come to me from others. I have, of course, acknowledged the sources I do remember. I have also tried to mention treatments by others that are significantly similar to my own, arrived at independently, where I am aware of them. My apologies to those whom I should have remembered or known about but didn't.

I am grateful to many teachers, colleagues, students, and friends from whom I have received valuable stimulus relevant to this book. My thinking on matters I treat here has had especially great help, through their discussions with me and their writings, from Keith Lehrer, Norman Malcolm, Sydney Shoemaker, and the students in several epistemology courses I have given, at the University of Michigan, the University of Rochester, the University of Washington, and Cornell University. I appreciate the special encouragement that the editors of the Philosophical Studies Series in Philosophy have given me in getting the book to publication. I am grateful to Vanda McMurtry for the bulk of the work in preparing the Index.

I thank my children, Lisa, Alan, and Greg, for the encouragement I've derived from their interest in the fact of this project and for their never-failing tolerance of my fits of abstraction.

Finally, I want to express my gratitude to Sally McConnell-Ginet. I've gained much from the many times I've discussed points in the work with her. She has read the entire manuscript, made a large number of suggestions for stylistic improvements, and saved me from more than one error in the content. In this as in all my endeavors I have been supported and inspirited by her love and her example.

CARL GINET

Ithaca, New York
March 1975

CHAPTER I

INTRODUCTION

1. What is it to *know* that something is the case? What am I saying when I say, 'I *know* that the temperature outside is below freezing' or 'I *know* that the money was in my pocket when I left the house' or 'Now we *know* that the moon has a great deal of dust on its surface' or (to my son while helping him with his arithmetic) 'Now, you *know* that six tens are sixty'? What sort of thing would make one of these propositions, or any other of the form 'S *knows* that p'[1], true? What will constitute a case of knowing that a certain proposition is true, that is, a case of *propositional knowledge*?

I intend this as a philosophical question. Thus the sort of answer I want will be an *a priori*, conceptual truth. How do we understand knowledge claims like those mentioned above? What do we mean by 'know' in such constructions? The answer to the question of what constitutes a case of propositional knowledge is, at least in part, an elucidation of the *concept* of knowing.

One way of going about answering the question would be to say 'This sort of case, that sort of case, and this other sort of case are all cases of propositional knowledge', specifying for each case the factors in it that seem to make it a case of knowledge. Case by case, one could try to delineate minimally sufficient conditions for particular varieties of propositional knowledge. (A condition sufficient for the truth of some set of instances of 'S knows that *p*' is minimally sufficient if nothing weaker – entailed by the given condition but not entailing it – is sufficient.) Although such detailed analyses of particular cases or kinds of propositional knowledge could be extremely interesting, they would not adequately answer the *general* question of what it is to know that something is the case. When we have finished the inventory of special cases, we are still unsatisfied. We want to construct a unified account of what it is to know that something is the case that will embrace all the special instances, an abstract definition of propositional knowledge that will be satisfied by any adequate account of particular cases.

Belief that such a general account can be given is wide-spread and deeply rooted, but I am well aware that it is not shared by all philosophers. Many have doubted that the construction 'S knows that p' has a sense for which there is an interesting general analysis (even given the restriction that 'p' must express a true or false proposition). Some suggest that although our uses of that construction in various cases interconnect and overlap in such ways as to prevent our saying that the construction is simply ambiguous, those uses are so diverse that it is futile to try to specify a set of conditions that will in general be necessary and sufficient for a person's knowing that a proposition is true.[2] One can make a case that a general definition is possible, and make clear what it is supposed to define, only by offering one and defending it against objections. This is what I propose to do.

There are two major dichotomies within the whole of propositional knowledge that I will distinguish: that between inferential and non-inferential knowledge and that between fallible and infallible knowledge. I will discuss at some length each of two more specific categories of propositional knowledge: perceptual knowledge, which is one's knowledge that one perceives a certain sort of thing, and memory knowledge, knowledge that p that one can justifiably claim to have because one remembers that p. These are important because one's knowledge in these two categories contains virtually the whole basis of one's knowledge of contingent truths about the world beyond the present content of one's consciousness. (I am confident that this is true of every actual person; whether it is *necessarily* so is another question, to which I think that the answer is no.) Trying to say what perceptual and memory knowledge are will naturally involve me in trying to say what perception and memory are, what it is to perceive something and what it is to remember something.

All these categories of knowledge have been distinguished and much discussed, in one guise or another, by other philosophers; but my definitions of them (like my general definition of propositional knowledge) will not necessarily be the same as anyone else's. On my account, the division between inferential and non-inferential knowledge does not coincide with that between fallible and infallible knowledge, contrary to the way in which some philosophers have viewed those divisions. Perceptual and memory knowledge are both species of fallible knowledge; and, while all memory knowledge is non-inferential, perceptual knowledge does not fall entirely on either side of that divide. (Perceptual knowledge is peculiar in that it is distinguished by the kind of proposition known, rather than, as with the other categories I've mentioned, the kind of justification one has for claiming that one knows.)

2. 'Know' is the main verb in many forms of proposition other than 'S knows that p'. For instance:

(1)   'S knows whether or not p'
       'S knows what/who/when/where ... is'
       'S knows which . . . is - - -'
       'S knows why p'

(2)   'S knows R' where 'R' is a name or definite description of someone or something.
       'S knows what it is like to ...'
       'S knows what it would be like to ...'

(3)   'S knows how to ...'

In confining my investigation to conditions for the truth of propositions of the form 'S knows that p' am I ignoring all these other forms of proposition? No, not most of them, not entirely.

Propositions of the forms indicated in (1) all ascribe to S knowledge of the truth of some proposition of a certain sort or range without specifying which particular proposition it is. To assert a proposition of the form 'S knows whether or not p' is to assert that either S knows that p or S knows that it is not the case that p. A proposition of the form 'S knows what/who/when/where... is' is true if and only if S knows to be true some proposition that is a satisfactory answer to the question 'What/who/when/where is...?'. Similarly a proposition of the form 'S knows which... is - - -' is true if and only if S knows to be true some proposition that is a satisfactory answer to the question 'Which... is - - -?', and a proposition of the form 'S knows why p' will be true if and only if S knows to be true some proposition that answers the question 'Why is it that p?'.

Which classes of propositions will serve as acceptable answers to questions like these can not be determined without reference to the interests involved in raising them. For the questioner's concerns really determine what question is being asked, which of the formally possible answers are actually relevant. For example, one who asks 'Where is

Jones?' may want to find out 'In which room is Jones?' or 'In which country is Jones' or any of an indefinite number of other things; and one who asks 'Who is Jones?' may mean 'Which incident of my meeting someone was my meeting Jones?' or 'What unique and important position in the community does Jones hold?' or 'What role is Jones playing in the play?' or any of an indefinite number of other things. Likewise, which propositions are such that S's knowing one of them to be true will establish the truth of a proposition expressed by an utterance of any of the forms in (1) that contain blanks or 'why' will depend on the interest of the person entertaining that proposition, the corresponding question he has in mind; this really determines what proposition he would intend to express with such an utterance.

The forms indicated in (2) all have to do with the 'acquaintance' sense of 'know'. The first, 'S knows R', is found in such examples as 'Cindy knows chemistry', 'Brenda knows San Francisco', 'It is a rare father that knows his own child', 'Lucille does not really know her own husband', 'Sam used to know Nixon when they were students at Whittier', 'Do you know that French restaurant in McGraw?' The attributions of knowledge involved in these examples (whether asserted, denied, queried, or something else) imply that S is acquainted with R. But sometimes such a proposition implies more than mere acquaintance; sometimes, as in the first four of the examples just given, it implies that S knows a significant number of the significant truths about R. What 'significant' means here is, of course, rather vague and will depend on what R is and on the context of the utterance, especially the intent of the utterer.

What suffices for being acquainted with R will vary a good deal, depending on what R is. Being acquainted with a person is different from being acquainted with a restaurant. In general, S's being acquainted with R seems to require some sort of interaction with R (usually involving S's having perceived R, if R is a perceivable thing, but not necessarily: one can become acquainted with a person by corresponding with her). No matter how much I may know *about* George Washington, it is impossible for me to know him (or to have known him): the dates of his death and my birth preclude the required sort of interaction. Being acquainted with a person seems to require more than having merely perceived that person; one must also have had some sort of social interaction with the person, but how much and what sort is required would be hard to say. That not just any sort or amount will be enough is suggested by remarks like 'I have *met* him but I don't actually *know* him'. And perhaps being acquainted with a restaurant requires more than having perceived it once: perhaps one needs to have observed it closely enough to know some of the distinctive salient facts about it.

In order to know *R* in the acquaintance sense one must, besides having had a certain amount and sort of interaction with *R*, now recall a certain amount of this interaction from the time of its occurrence: a person suffering from amnesia for his experience prior to a certain time no longer knows the people with whom he was acquainted only prior to that time, no matter how much information he may have been given in the meantime about his experiences with those people. And this interaction cannot have been so long ago that *R* is likely to have changed significantly in the interval: I do not now know my childhood friends whom I have not seen since childhood, no matter how much I may recall of my childhood experiences with them. In these sorts of cases we can say that one used to know *R* but no longer does. All this suggests that knowing *R* in the acquaintance sense may always consist in a certain sort of propositional knowledge, knowing in a certain way certain sorts of truths about one's experience of *R*: one knows *R* (in the acquaintance sense) if and only if one has had experience of *R* that is of the right sort and knows that one has had this experience by remembering it from the experience itself. (There is a special use of '*S* knows *R*' – as in, for example, 'Even with my new beard he knew me at once' – that implies, not only acquaintance of the sort we have been discussing, but also an occurrent recognition of *R*.)

A proposition of the form '*S* knows what it is like to *VP*' where '*VP*' refers to some action or experience – for example, '*S* knows what it is like to feel the most intense kind of pain', '*S* knows what it is like to shoot down white-water rapids in a canoe', '*S* knows what it is like to snap the wrist in the proper fashion in the forehand squash stroke' – seems to imply that *S* has *VP*-ed, or else has done something else that is like *VP*-ing in the respect intended by 'what it is like to *VP*', and remembers what it is like to do it; that is, it implies that *S* is *acquainted* with the particular kind or property of experience intended by 'what it is like to *VP*'. Knowing a *property* (of experience, or a perceivable property of external things) in the acquaintance sense is, however, *propositional* knowledge, even if the property known cannot be put into words but must be expressed with the aid of demonstration or oblique reference: '*That* is what it is like to *VP*' or 'What it was like to ... is what it is like to *VP*'.

A proposition of the form '*S* knows what it would be like to *VP*', seems to imply that *S* does not have acquaintance with the property in question but that he would be able to recognize the property should it occur in his experience. Though he's never had the experience itself, he has a well-founded accurate idea of it and, should he have it, he would be able to say honestly, 'Yes, that is what I thought it would be like'. Knowing how to recognize what it is like to *VP* is also propositional knowledge, though if one is asked to say what it is that *S* knows when he knows what it would be like to *VP*, the best one may be able to do is to say, '*S* knows that it would be like *this*: if *this* were to happen to him he would be able to recognize it as what it is like to *VP*'. How could one be justified in thinking that one can recognize a certain property of experience if one has never been acquainted with it? Well, one may have been acquainted with an essentially similar property: I may know what it would be like to have one's left leg in a cast if I have had my right leg in a cast. Or one may have a particularly vivid or informative description to which one's imagination is able to respond; I have never felt as if the upper half of my body were floating away from the lower half but I think I know what it would be like to have such a feeling.

3. With respect to propositions of form (3), '*S* knows how to...', I am inclined to think (although I am not perfectly confident) that they do nothing more than ascribe certain sorts of propositional knowledge to *S*. It does seem clear that such a proposition always *implies* that *S* has propositional knowledge of a certain sort. It implies that he knows the truth of some proposition that gives a satisfactory answer to the question 'How can one...?' or 'How should one...?', a proposition that will take the form 'A (the) way to... is to---'.[3] But it may also seem that at least some such propositions attribute to *S* certain *abilities* that are beyond any that are involved in knowing the truth of any propositions.

Ryle appears to suggest that this is the case.[4] But all that he actually brings out, as far as I can see, is that the exercise (or manifestation) of one's knowledge of how to do a certain sort of thing need not, and often does not, involve any separate mental operation of considering propositions and inferring from them instructions to oneself. But the same thing

is as clearly true of one's manifestations of *knowledge that* certain propositions are true, especially one's knowledge of truths that answer questions
of the form 'How can one...?' or 'How should one...?' I exercise (or
manifest) my knowledge *that* one can get the door open by turning the
knob and pushing it (as well as my knowledge *that* there is a door there)
by performing that operation quite automatically as I leave the room;
and I may do this, of course, without formulating (in my mind or out
loud) that proposition or any other relevant proposition.

Moreover, one may have and exercise knowledge of truths as to how
various sorts of things can be done or should be done without ever formulating those truths in any way or even being able to formulate them. It
may be that no one can – even that no symbols exist with which it would
be possible to – formulate a fully detailed description of the sorts of
things one must know to do in order to ride a bicycle (smoothly) or play
a certain piece on the piano (well) – all the complex and subtle responses
that one must know to make in the various subtly changing circumstances
and at the various points in the operation that one must be able to discriminate. Indeed, the nature of the moves, responses, features to be discrimi-
nated, etc. required in the successful performance of many operations is
very likely to be such that it is quite impossible to know what they are
without having done or experienced them; one must know what they are
like. In this case knowledge of such truths about how the operation is
performed, even if they could be expressed in symbols, could not be
learned by means of them alone but only by training and practice aimed
at becoming acquainted with the sort of thing one must do or recognize,
that is, training aimed at acquiring the ability to perform the operation.
For example, in order to know that a particular sounding of a certain note
on a violin is flat one's hearing must have been trained to discriminate the
difference; in order to know that pressing the string in *this* way, but not in
this other, slightly different way, will yield the sound one wants one must
learn to feel and demonstrate the difference.

When there is, at least in practice, no other way for a person to acquire
or show that he has knowledge of important truths as to how to do a thing
except by acquiring and showing the ability to do it (properly) then of
course we are not likely to think that he knows these truths – knows how
it is done, knows how to do it – unless he is *able* to do it. Thus, though we
are very often entitled to infer from 'He knows how to...' to 'He is able

to ...', and to think that he *cannot* know how unless he is able, it does not follow that 'He knows how to ...' ascribes abilities beyond what are involved in knowing sufficient truths about how to ....

Two further considerations support my inclination to deny that any such further abilities are ever required for knowing how to .... One is that in the case of every ability that I can think of with respect to which it is clear that there can be a case of a person who lacks that ability but knows all the same truths about how to do the thing as one who has the ability knows, it would sound very odd to characterize the difference between such a person and one who has the ability by saying that the latter *knows how* to do the thing but the former does not. For example, it would not be right to report the fact that I am able to lift a hundred pounds off the floor but my eight-year-old son is not by saying that I know how to do this but he does not know how. Insofar as there is any knowing how involved he knows how as well as I; he just doesn't have the strength to do it.

The other consideration is very similar. When someone knows how to ... and has the ability to ... (for example, ski expertly, play the violin well, read English, parallel park a car) but then suddenly loses the ability to ... through a cause that clearly cannot change (at least not immediately) the truths he knows about how to do ... (for example, he suffers a sudden paralysis or takes a drug that disturbs his muscular control or becomes blind) it would certainly not be right to report this sudden loss of ability to ... by saying that this person suddenly no longer knows how to .... An expert skier who in the course of a downhill run gets a bad case of stomach cramps and is able to complete the run only very clumsily still knows how to ski very well even while temporarily unable to do so. The only sort of case where '*S* no longer knows how to ...' is clearly appropriate is one where it is also appropriate to say '*S* no longer remembers what to do in order to ...'. If a violinist cannot be said to have *forgotten* (or otherwise lost his memory of) what all the subtle right moves are for fingering a certain piece, but he is no longer able to make them all simply because of damaged fingers, then he still knows how to finger that piece. Indeed, it may be because he knows how to finger it that he can tell from a few tentative movements of his fingers that he won't be able to finger it. Loss of knowing how to ... requires loss of memory of what must be done in order to ... and is not entailed by mere loss of physical ability to .... We should not be led to overlook this by the fact that very often one may not be able to show that one still knows how to do a thing except by doing it and may discover that one no longer remembers how to do it by trying and failing.

If, however, despite these considerations that suggest the contrary, there are some correct and strict applications of 'S knows how to...' that ascribe abilities to S beyond any entailed by his knowing sufficient truths about how to..., then there is a use of 'know' that will be neglected hereafter in this study.

4. I have set myself the (somewhat formidable) task of proposing and defending a general definition of the concept of propositional knowledge. Indeed, my claims in Sections 2 and 3 suggest that the restriction to propositional knowledge may be no real restriction at all. So to understand knowledge in general, it may be enough to consider a set of conditions necessary and sufficient for the truth of propositions expressed by sentences of the general form 'S knows that p'.

Before turning to that job in the next chapter, I need to introduce a stipulation as to how I will interpret such knowledge claims. I will take 'S knows that p' as equivalent to the claim that S knows to be true all of the *obvious content* of the proposition that p. The obvious content of p includes every proposition q such that p entails q and no one could understand p without understanding q and knowing that p entails q.[5] The most important consequence of this stipulation is that if the sentence replacing 'p' contains a name or definite description 'A' of a particular individual – so that 'p' could be represented as '$F(A)$' – then 'S knows that p' is to be taken to imply that S knows *that it is A* of which '$F(...)$' is true.

Usually it is taken for granted that if 'S knows that p' expresses a true proposition then 'I know that p', if uttered by S, expresses a true proposition, but this need not always hold. Given the right sort of context, one may say 'S knows that p' without misleading, even though, as one knows, S does *not* know all of the obvious content of the proposition that p in the sense spelled out above. For instance, if someone describing her sister's adventures in a foreign land says, 'This shopkeeper knew that my sister was an American', she will not be taken to be implying that the shopkeeper knew that it was her sister who was an American.[6] If she had said, 'The shopkeeper knew that this woman he was dealing with was an

American', we probably would take her to be claiming that the shop-keeper knew the obvious content of the proposition that this woman he was dealing with was an American. Her second report is from the point of view of the knower (that is, the shopkeeper), whereas the first was from her own viewpoint (that is, the speaker's). In its context the first utterance, 'This shopkeeper knew that my sister was an American' must be interpreted as a loose, convenient way of expressing what might more strictly be put in terms like 'Of this person, who was in fact my sister, this shop-keeper knew that she was an American', that is, as saying that the shop-keeper knew to be true some proposition in which being an American is ascribed to that person, without saying which proposition it is.[7]

Anyway, I will be considering only those uses of 'S knows that p' that are intended to imply that S knows the obvious content of the proposition that p to be true. And it will be useful to extend this stipulation to cover all sentences of the form 'S ATTs that p' where 'ATT' covers any verb or verb-phrase of positive propositional attitude or positive propositional act. Thus 'S believes that p', 'S claims that p', 'S wishes that p' will be taken to imply that S's belief, claim, or wish is with respect to all the obvious content of the proposition that p.

NOTES

[1] I shall use the phrase 'a proposition of the form "S knows that p"' as short for 'a proposition that could standardly be expressed by utterance of a sentence of the form "S knows that p"'; and a sentence of that form is one that is obtainable from the schema 'S knows that p' by replacing 'S' with some expression that designates a person (name, definite description, pronoun, demonstrative phrase) and 'p' with a sentence that would in the standard utterance of 'S knows that p' express a true or false proposition.

A *proposition* is what is true or false, also what one believes, desires, asserts denies, wagers, etc., to be true or false, and what one intends, offers, promises, requests some-one, etc., to make true or false. A proposition is the bearer of truth-value and the object of propositional attitudes and illocutionary acts. A proposition is distinct from any particular sentence, clause, or phrase used to express it and from any particular utterance in which it is expressed, since the same proposition may be expressed by different utterances of different sentences (where there may be no more reason to identify the proposition with any given sentence or utterance than with any other). (A detailed argument for distinguishing propositions, the bearers of truth-value, from sentences, utterances of sentences, and speech acts is to be found in Cartwright (1966).) What a proposition is would be explicated, I take it, by giving criteria for when an utterance of a sentence or sentence-part expresses a proposition and for when two different utterances of sentences or sentence-parts express the same proposition. I will not attempt such an explication here but will just rely on the understanding of the term 'proposition' that my readers already possess, hoping that what I have to say

does not depend on any mistaken assumptions about what exactly propositions are.
[2] On this view 'know' is, in Wittgenstein's phrase (1958, p. 44), one of the 'odd-job' words in our language. See also Saunders and Champawat (1964).
[3] The two forms of 'how' question are importantly different, as D. G. Brown (1970) brings out. 'How *can* one... [for example, prove this theorem, get this trunk open]?' inquires after some *means* to..., whereas 'How should one...?' inquires after the *correct* or proper or required *manner* to... where this is to be distinguished from other manners in which one might... Corresponding to each of these two sorts of question is a different interpretation of '*S* knows how to...' and '*S* knows that a (the) way to... is to---', that is, these constructions are ambiguous. If *S* does not know how to... in the sense of not knowing any correct answer to 'How can one...?' then it follows that *S* is unable to... ; but if *S* does not know how to... in the sense of not knowing any correct answer to 'How should one...?' then it does not follow that *S* is unable to... : he may still be able to... in some improper way. For the thesis that knowing how to... is always just knowing some correct answer or answers to a question of one of those forms, Brown offers arguments based largely on considerations of English syntax. While these arguments are welcome reinforcement, they do not seem conclusive. In the text I offer some inconclusive arguments of a different kind.
[4] Ryle (1949), Ch. 2.
[5] For the sake of brevity I shall permit myself to use the letters 'p', 'q', etc. not only as sentential variables (as in '*S* knows that p'), but also as variables for names of propositions (as in 'p entails q') and, combined with quotation marks, as variable names of sentences (as in 'the singular terms in "p"'). I shall also use quoted sentences or sentence-forms sometimes as sentence names or variable sentence names and sometimes as proposition names or variable proposition names. Which of these varied uses is being made will always be clear from the context. In contexts where different uses are made of the same variable letter or quoted sentence (or sentence form), the context will make clear whether or not they are dummy names or expressions of the *same* proposition or sentence throughout.
[6] This example bears significant resemblance to one given by Dretske (1970), which he uses to support the claim that a person's knowing the truth of a proposition does *not* necessarily require him to know the truth of every obvious consequence of that proposition.
[7] This is not to say that the speaker's use in this context of 'This shopkeeper knew that my sister was an American' was such that the position occupied by 'my sister' was *referentially transparent* in the sense of Quine (1953). If the speaker's sister was the long-lost daughter of the shopkeeper but the shopkeeper did not know this, then the speaker could not but have misled if she had uttered instead, in the same context, 'This shopkeeper knew that his daughter was an American'. It is hard to imagine any context in which this sentence could be uttered without seeming to imply that the shopkeeper knew that it was his daughter who was an American.

CHAPTER II

THE GENERAL CONDITIONS OF KNOWLEDGE: TRUTH AND CONFIDENCE

1. The general definition of propositional knowledge that I propose to defend is along traditional lines and can be expressed as follows:
   S knows that p if and only if

   (1) p,
   (2) S is confident that p, and
   (3) S's being so is supported by a disinterested justification for being so
   (4)   that is externally conclusive.

The traditional lines here are conditions (1), (2), and (3). They or some conditions very like them have long been thought necessary for knowing that something is the case (though the necessity of (2) and (3) has recently been disputed). Some philosophers have also thought that (1), (2), and (3) are jointly sufficient. Only since Gettier (1963) provided clear counter-examples to this claim has it been widely recognized that some fourth condition is needed; but there has been no general agreement as to what it should be.

I will explain each of the four conditions and argue that each is necessary to the definition. My reason for thinking that these conditions are jointly sufficient is, in the end, simply that I cannot see what else could be required. I am unable to think of any counter-example in which a proposition of the form 'S knows that p' would be disproved by something other than the absence of one or more of these four conditions. This is not a very interesting argument but it is, I think, the only sort of reason one can have for thinking that a proposed definition is adequate to an already established concept (where sufficiency cannot be just stipulated).

2. Condition (1) needs little comment. If anything is obvious about the literal use of 'know' it is that one cannot *know* to be the case what is *not* the case. This does not mean that it is always unacceptable and pointless for a speaker to say (of some person S and some proposition p) that S

knows that p when the speaker knows that his hearers know that it is false that p. But such uses of 'know' must be interpreted as ironic. In a magazine article about Christopher Columbus I encountered the sentence "In 1492 most people *knew* that the earth was flat". Here there is an attempt at wit that there would not be had the author written 'were sure' or 'confidently believed' instead of 'knew'. One would not have been surprised had 'knew' here been put in quotation marks. If one reads the sentence aloud it is quite natural to deliver 'knew' with a slightly mocking intonation. A similarly ironic use of 'know' might be made in another sort of case – for example, someone's ruefully declaring 'I *knew* he would come' after he has not come – not so much for amusing effect but to point up the fact that though the speaker's case resembled knowing in all the ways recognizable to him at the time it still fell short in one crucial respect: the suggestion conveyed by the irony would be: 'How silly/vain/poignant my thinking that I *knew* looks now'. In all such cases the point of the ironic ascription of knowledge depends on the hearers' being aware that, speaking literally and straightforwardly, one cannot *know* that something is the case unless it *is* the case.

3. One can see that condition (2), that S is confident that p, is necessary for S's knowing that p by considering the case of S's having an uncertain memory of what he once knew. Suppose A and B are doing a crossword puzzle and A goes to S with the question 'Do you know who was President between Cleveland's two terms?' It would be perfectly intelligible and natural for S to respond: 'I used to know that – used to know all the Presidents in sequence in fact – but I'm not sure I do anymore. Let's see now, was it Garfield? or was it Harrison? I'm just not sure anymore, but I'm inclined to think it was Harrison. Well, I'm sorry that I don't *know* who it was, but I *think* it was probably Harrison.' Suppose A returns to B and tells him that S thinks it was Harrison. B might well ask 'Does he *know* that it was Harrison?' to which it would be only honest and straightforward for A to reply 'No, he's not at all sure'. This demonstrates that a person's not being confident that p is conclusive ground for saying that he does not *know* that p (at least when one is called upon to be scrupulous in one's use of 'know'). For in this case the only reason that A has for denying of S, and that S has for denying of himself, that he *knows* that Harrison was the one is that his memory on the point falls short of being confident.

Curiously, the case of uncertain memory has been thought to show that being confident that p (or even believing that p) is *not* necessary to knowing that p. Colin Radford (1966), for instance, has pointed out that even in a case where a person's memory of what he once knew is a good deal more uncertain than in the case sketched in the previous paragraph (even where, for example, he doesn't know that he ever knew the answer to the question and thinks he is just guessing) it might be acceptable, in the right sort of context, to say that he knows, or still knows, the thing in question.[1] But to infer from this to the unqualified conclusion that being confident is not necessary to knowing is to overlook the difference between *strict* and *loose* uses of 'know'. This distinction explains why it is that S's not being sure gives us (and him) a conclusive reason in one sort of context to say that he does not know that p but that in another sort of context, without any change in him, it seems unobjectionable to say that he still knows that p. One can see how it is that the fact that S's present uncertain belief that p represents his *retaining to a degree his former knowledge* that p and the fact that his present state is *as good as knowledge* for some purposes – for example, for being able to give the right answer to certain questions – make it natural to speak loosely of his 'still knowing' that p. (And it will be still more natural, and perhaps speaking somewhat less loosely, if – as in one of Radford's examples – S's uncertainty represents a more or less *unreasonable* distrust of his memory: it seems to him that he clearly remembers that p but he is, for no good reason, unsure that this memory impression is correct.) But that it is a loose use of 'know' is shown by the fact that it will not bear emphasis. Though it would not be misleading in some contexts to say of the S of our previous example 'It's remarkable: although he hasn't thought of it for years, S still knows who was President between Cleveland's terms', one could not but mislead if one stressed 'know' and said of S 'He still knows – really *knows* – that the President between Cleveland's terms was Harrison'. (Where 'know' is used thus loosely and will not bear emphasis one can insert 'in effect' without really weakening the intended assertion. Compare: 'She did not really *say* that p but she in effect said that p' and 'She does not really *know* that p but she in effect knows that p'.)

It is plainly absurd to say 'I know that p but I am not sure that p' and this might be thought to be evidence that knowing entails being confident. But Radford thinks that this absurdity can be explained in another way, and indeed it can: since 'I know that p' obviously entails that p, if I am not sure that p I cannot be sure that I know that p and so cannot assert without reservation that I do while at the same time confessing uncertainty about p. But this does not explain why it is also absurd to offer, along with the confession that one is not sure that p, the uncertain conjecture that one knows that p. If our use of 'know' were such that the proposition that one knows that p, strictly understood, does not imply that one is confident that p, but would be made true merely by one's having known that p in the past and having a present uncertain memory that p, then it should be perfectly acceptable with nothing odd about it at all to respond to the question 'Do you *know* that p?' with 'Well, yes, I *think* that I know that p, but since I'm not sure that p I can't be *sure* that I know it.' But this is clearly not an acceptable response to that question, in which, as its emphasis indicates, 'know' is intended quite strictly and to which the only honest answer is 'Well, no, I don't *know* that p'. (This is different from the momentarily uncertain response to 'Do you know who was President between Cleveland's terms?' that I allowed in my example. Being unsure whether or not one knows something must, as in that example, be a matter of being temporarily unsure whether one can after reflection and effort come up with an answer that one can be sure of and claim to know.) So, in the strict sense, knowing that p requires being confident that p; and it is the strict sense that interests us here.

Some philosophers have suggested that knowing that p cannot imply believing that p because to say of someone that he *believes* that p is normally (at least outside epistemological discussion) to imply that he does *not* know that p.[2] Presumably, the same could be said of saying of someone that he is *confident* that p: normally one would not say this if one thought that the person in question knew that p; one would say instead that he *knew*. But the explanation of this is not that the proposition expressed by 'S is confident that p' or 'S believes that p' is incompatible with the proposition expressed by 'S knows that p'. It is rather that normally it is a reasonable presumption, given the sorts of purposes normally in view in discourse, that a person will not say less than what he knows if it is relevant. So that if someone says 'S is confident that p' without any indication that this is *not* the strongest statement he is prepared to make, his hearers may infer from his so saying that it *is* the strongest he is prepared to make, that he does not think that S knows that p. And in most con-

texts this is reason to think that the speaker believes that S does not know
that p and is aware that his believing this is likely to be inferred from his
saying (merely) that S is confident (or believes) that p. And this, that the
speaker believes that S does not know that p, will in turn normally give
his hearers good reason to think that S does not know that p; for if S did
know that p, then the speaker would, ordinarily, be in a position to know
it if he were in a position to know that S is confident that p. Thus in saying
merely that S is confident that p in a normal sort of context a speaker may
reasonably expect or intend his hearers to infer from his so saying that S
does not know that p and in this sense he may *imply* that S does not know
that p. He would be implying this in the same way that a speaker who
remarks 'S has completed two years of college' may, in a normal sort of
context, imply that S has *not* completed *four* years of college: this would
be implied, not in virtue of being entailed by what the speaker said (which
it plainly is not), but in virtue of the general conversational principle
mentioned, that in the absence of obvious reasons for doing otherwise
one says the strongest thing one knows that is relevant (and also the presumption that if the stronger proposition were true the speaker would not
be likely to be ignorant of it while knowing the weaker proposition). A
speaker's saying 'S is confident that p' or 'S believes that p' normally
suggests at least a doubt that S knows that p simply because normally
there would be no point in asserting the weaker 'S is confident that p'
rather than the stronger 'S knows that p' if one knew the latter to be
true.[3,4]

4. I want to call attention to two other circumstances that resemble the
circumstance that the speaker doubts or believes it false that S knows that
p in the respect that they are typically present when a speaker asserts of
someone that he is confident that p and are typically needed to give point
to his so asserting; namely: (a) the question as to whether or not S is
confident that p has somehow become relevant to the current interests of
the speaker and his hearers and the speaker thinks his hearers do not
realize that S is confident that p or need to be reminded of it; (b) the
proposition that p is such that it is at least conceivable that S should have
been in doubt or ignorant that p (even though it were true that p). Likewise, neither of these circumstances is entailed by the proposition that S
is confident that p. It may be that the presence of (a) and (b), or at least

the speaker's belief that such circumstances are present, is necessary for the act of *asserting* (or stating or telling someone) that S is confident that p. But from this it does not follow that the presence of either of these circumstances is required for it to be true of S that he is confident that p.[5] I have been uninterruptedly confident that my name is 'Carl Ginet' for some time now, even throughout long periods when neither (a) was true with respect to that proposition, nor anything else that could have given point to my asserting it or (as perhaps it should be put) given anything I might do the function of asserting it. And I am now confident that I am conscious even though (b) does not hold with respect to the proposition that I am conscious; and I can be so in a context in which my uttering the words 'I am confident that I am conscious' does not function as an assertion that I am confident that I am conscious, or even as an expression of that proposition (because not surrounded by the right sort of train of thought).

What is entailed by the proposition that S is confident that p – as distinguished from the proposition that someone has asserted or expressed or thought that proposition – is just what is necessary in order that, *if* circumstances were to arise making it possible (giving it point) to assert or express or think that S is confident that p, so asserting or expressing or thinking would be asserting or expressing or thinking a *true* proposition. In fact (2) may be regarded as equivalent in its truth conditions to the following:

(2′)   If there had now arisen any sort of situation that would make it possible for S to act confidently as if p (for example, by firmly asserting that p), then his doing so would be a sincere manifestation of his present attitude towards the proposition that p.

(2′) spells out a bit how I think we should understand (2). On this understanding, I am now confident that I do not have an intense pain in my leg, even though (b) is false of that proposition and (a) is false of it with respect to my present circumstances, because if occasion were now to arise for me to assert confidently that I do not now have such a pain then I could do so sincerely, and that is a fact about my *present* attitude towards that proposition.

5. From what I have said it is clear that being confident that *p* does not require being currently engaged in confidently asserting that *p* or otherwise confidently acting as if *p*. This is a feature that must also be shared by knowing that *p*. For all of us at any given time there are a great many propositions whose truth we currently know, and very likely even more whose truth we are currently confident of, that we are not currently contemplating or having anything to *do* with. Knowing and being confident of things, like capacities and abilities, are enduring *states* of persons that are manifested or used when occasion arises.

It may give some light on the nature of the state of being confident that a certain proposition is true to consider a bit further the sort of thing that manifests it. A situation that makes it possible for *S* to manifest confidence or lack of confidence that *p* will be a situation such that *S*'s other currently active beliefs and desires make the question of whether or not *p* relevant to the choice among acts then facing *S* and they do so in such a way that *S*'s doing some among the things open to *S* will manifest confidence that *p* (though perhaps insincerely) whereas *S*'s doing others will manifest the absence of confidence that *p*, *provided* that *S* then realizes the relevance of the question whether or not *p*. One such occasion, for example, would arise if *S* is asked 'Are you sure you mailed that letter?', *S* understands the question, has no desire at all to keep the questioner from knowing the answer, and takes 'yes' to be an affirmative and 'no' a negative answer to such a question; then *S*'s saying 'yes' with the intention of answering that question would manifest confidence, and *S*'s saying 'no' would manifest lack of confidence, that he mailed that letter. For another example, suppose that *S* wants to put sugar in his coffee. If the family sugar-bowl is before *S* and *S* unhesitatingly puts some of the white grains it contains into his coffee then *S* manifests confidence that those white grains are sugar but if *S* tastes some of the white grains first then *S* manifests lack of confidence that they are sugar, *if* it is also true that *S* dislikes sugar straight, thinks that there are substances other than sugar that look like it but taste different, and is not acting entirely automatically without awareness of what he is doing. On the other hand, if I fail to release the energency brake before driving off this may not manifest a lack of confidence that driving a car with the emergency brake on will result in damage to it; I may, even then, be quite confident, *know* perfectly well, that this proposition is true but just fail to think of it and its relevance to what I am doing. Or if I unhesitatingly sit on the sturdy looking chair that recently collapsed when I sat on it, this does not necessarily manifest confidence that this chair will not collapse this time if I sit on it; I may not be at all confident of that but just fail at the time to think about whether or not *this* chair will hold me.

When I speak of acts that manifest confidence that *p*, or acting confidently as if *p*, or the like, I do not mean just physical acts. One can act *mentally* as if confident that *p*. One might, for example, in the course of an unexpressed ('private', 'internal') train of thought raise the question whether the word 'oxymoron' has the meaning one wants in a sentence that one is composing and conclude to oneself after slight reflection that it definitely does not. That mental act would, obviously, show confidence in that proposition as much as an overt assertion of it would.

The factors relevant to determining that an act manifests confidence that *p* are, it is clear, often very complex, involving many facts about the subject's other beliefs, desires, conscious processes, and relations among them. And the relation between the *state* of confidence that *p* and its manifestations is no simple matter. It seems right to classify confidence, and belief geneially, as a *dispositional* state, taking that to mean merely that, according to the concept of it, the primary criteria by which its presence is determined are findings that the subject would in various circumstances do various (physical or mental) things that would manifest it.[6]

But confidence is not the simplest, most straightforward kind of dispositional state, not like the fragility of fine china or my allergy to cats. If we seek to construct a subjunctive conditional that is equivalent to the ascription of confidence that *p* and that specifies in its antecedent a certain sort of situation for the subject and in its consequent a certain sort of act that the subject would perform in that situation – a proper disposition-ascribing conditional – then we must come up with one essentially like the following:

(2″)   If there had now arisen any sort of situation that would make it possible for *S* to act confidently as if *p*, *S* realized the relevance of whether or not *p* to the choice of acts facing him in that situation, chose an act that manifests some doxastic attitude toward *p*, and in so doing had no intent to deceive, then he would have chosen to act confidently as if *p*.

There are some peculiarities to note about this conditional. For one thing, its antecedent is not limited to specifying circumstances that are quite separate from the act specified in the consequent; the antecedent also specifies a certain class within which that act must fall, one manifesting either confidence that p or lack of it. This marks confidence that p as a special sort of dispositional state, but not any more peculiar logically than the disposition of certain material to break *in a certain pattern* of fractures when struck hard enough to make it break at all.

Another peculiarity is the occurrence in both antecedent and consequent of the phrase 'act confidently as if p' which is synonymous with 'act as if confident that p', which (in turn) contains the predicate 'confident that p' the ascription of which the whole conditional is equivalent to. The variety of circumstances in which it is possible to act as if confident that p and the variety of such acts, each sort associated with a sort of circumstance that would give it that character, are so large – indeed uncircumscribed – that a broad characterization of this sort is the only sort that can logically guarantee that all possibilities are covered.

Because it employs this construction that contains the predicate 'confident that p', it may seem that (2″) gets us nowhere as an explication of the concept of the state ascribed by that predicate. But (2″) does advance the analysis. The concept expressed by 'being confident that p', when this is taken to be a predicate that a subject may satisfy at a time when he is acting in no way to which it is relevant whether or not p, is secondary and derivative relative to the concept expressed by 'acting as if confident that p' – or rather by 'acting as if confident that p while realizing the relevance of whether or not p to one's act and without intent to deceive' or, for short, 'knowingly and sincerely acting as if confident that p'. The latter is primary despite the fact that our expression of it contains a phrase that expresses the former, logically derivative concept. This is only an accident of our language that could have been otherwise though the concepts were the same. The primary notion here is of a kind of act in a context (of intentions, other beliefs, conscious processes, etc.) that endows that act with a certain kind of significance. We must grasp this concept, if we are to grasp the notion 'being confident that p', and not *vice versa*.

We do not first have the concept of the unmanifested state of confidence or belief that p, employing criteria for this that have nothing to do with how it is manifested, and then derive from that a concept, which we might or might not have had in addition, of ways in which that state can explain or cause or be evidenced in various sorts of (mental or physical) act. It is not like the relation between the state of a material object's being hollow and its hollowness being evidenced in such behaviors as floating in certain solutions or giving off a certain sound when struck. To *explain* a particular act of S's in a particular situation (or partly explain it) by reference to S's state of being confident that p is not to imply that there is a state of S's that is ascertainable independently of any of S's acts that it might explain and is linked by causal law to that sort of act. It is, rather, by suggesting a range of subjunctive conditionals that are true of S, to place his act in a certain sort of familiar *pattern* of dispositions to act. (Compare explaining an act by saying that it was a certain sort of move in a certain sort of game: the significance this gives the act consists not only in the kinds of categorical propositions, but also in the kinds of subjunctive conditionals, that such an explanation implies about the agent and surrounding events.)

We could not have the concept of the enduring *state* of being confident that p without having the concept of sincere and knowing action as if confident that p. But we could have had the latter concept without having the former, though we would not then have expressed it that way. We could have used 'is confident that p' or 'believes that p' to signify a property of actions ('There he was confident that p' 'There he lacked confidence that p'), in a way analogous to that in which 'intends that p' is often used, the property that, as things are, we can describe as the subject's showing or, perhaps better, *living* confidence that p. And then we might or might not have added the concept we could then have expressed by 'being dispossed, if circumstances were appropriate, to be confident that p'. Our actual language is misleading as to this relation among these concepts. It is as if we lacked a word for the concept expressed by 'breaks' and had only some expression for the notion 'behaves as if it fragile under such stresses as it is currently subject to'. If this possible arrangement of our language were the actual one, it would not make it any the less the case that the concept of the dispositional property of fragility under such-and-such stress was derivative from the concept of the occurrent behavior of acting as if fragile under such-and-such stress.

It ought to be pointed out that, contrary to first appearances, neither (2″) nor (2′) entails that a person's knowing *and sincere* action as if confident that p can never be *misleading* as to that person's state of confidence that p. Both allow us to make sense of such a remark as 'Though he confidently *says* that p and is quite sincere in so saying, this does not show his true state: he does not *really* believe that p (or he is not really as confident as that)'. What such a remark must mean is that, though he knowingly and sincerely acts as if confident that p in *this* situation, this bit of behavior is not an accurate guide as to what his knowing and sincere action would be throughout the whole range of situations that might arise in which it would be possible to manifest confidence or lack of confidence that p. There are some other situations of that sort such that, if one of them had now arisen and he made some choice of action for which he was aware that the truth of p was relevant and did so without intent to deceive, he would have acted as if lacking confidence that p. Of such a person one might be inclined to say that he is *in a way* confident that p and in a way not. Or one might think of him as like two distinct subjects with respect to being confident that p. But he is not a plain, clear case of having, *or* lacking, confidence that p. And he satisfies neither (2″) nor (2′), both of which begin 'If there had now arisen *any* sort of situation...'. In this context 'any' clearly means a universal quantification of wide scope, not an existential one. If (2″) were changed to begin 'There are at least some among the sorts of situations that would make it possible for S to act confidently as if p that are such that if one of them had now arisen, S realizedt he relevance... etc. [continuing as in (2″)]', then we would have specified a disposition that we could express as S's being *at least in some ways* confident that p.

None of what I have said implies that being confident that p requires at some time manifesting confidence that p or thinking of the proposition that p. The proposition that I do not own a giraffe is one that I have been confident of for a long time without (as far as I remember) ever having manifested that confidence or thought of that proposition until just now.

Nor does what I have said take us far in elucidating the concept of confidence in a proposition. This concept must be understood in terms of a whole system of concepts of psychological states and their capacity to explain and be manifested in behavior and conscious mental processes of saying to oneself, imaging, and the like. This is a system that we all do grasp, more or less, but an adequate philosophical elucidation of it would be a large task.

6. Let us return to the point that (2) does not entail either (a), that the question of whether or not p is somehow currently relevant, or (b), that the proposition that p is such that S might conceivably have doubted or been ignorant of its truth. If (2) did entail either of these it could not be entailed by S's knowing that p.

That (a) cannot be entailed by S's knowing that p is fairly obvious as soon as we see the distinction between conditions necessary for the truth of a proposition and conditions necessary for the speech act of asserting that proposition. Just as I do not cease to exist in circumstances that deprive me (or someone else) of the opportunity of telling someone that I exist, and it does not cease to be the case that I have never been on Mars in circumstances that deprive me of the opportunity of telling someone that (even though such circumstances are the norm), so also I do not cease to know that these things are so merely because circumstances usually or always deprive me (and others) of the opportunity of asserting that I know them.[7]

It is perhaps not so obvious that (2) should not entail (b) if (2) is to be entailed by 'S knows that p'. There do seem to be substituends for 'p' such that the sentence 'S *doubts* that p' (in the sense that S is uncertain whether or not p) fails to express an intelligible proposition or one that could possibly be true (if it is assumed that 'S doubts that p' entails that S understands the proposition that p, which seems plausible since the latter is, as we shall see, entailed by 'S is confident that p'). Such substituends for 'p' seem to include 'he [S] is conscious', 'he [S] feels an intense pain in his leg', as well as '$1 + 1 = 2$'. Some philosophers have inferred from this that for such substituends for 'p' the sentence 'S knows that p' also fails to express an intelligible proposition. Wittgenstein (1951), for example, remarks (I, 246):

It can't be said of me at all (except perhaps as a joke) that I *know* I am in pain. What is it supposed to mean – except perhaps that I *am* in pain?... it makes sense to say about other people that they doubt whether I am in pain; but not to say it about myself.[8]

The argument here seems to be that it is always pointless to say of a person that he knows that he is in pain (rather than just saying that he is in pain), because so saying never conveys *information* in the sense of ruling out alternatives that were possible *a priori* (other than the alternative that he is not in pain). But this reasoning overlooks another way in which saying 'I know that I have a pain' could have a point: namely, as part of a program of listing things one already knows that are, or might be, relevant to some particular question one is currently interested in (for example, the question as to whether or not one has a certain disease or bodily injury, or the question as to what can be deduced from such facts as one cannot possibly doubt). The point would be to assemble, not just a number of facts relevant to the question, but facts that one *already knows*, so as to see where what one already knows of the facts puts one with respect to the inquiry one wants to make and what further sorts of facts, if any, one might need to know to settle the question. This sort of purpose could give point to a person's saying 'I know that I feel pain in my leg' (or 'I know that $1+1=2$' or even 'I know that I still exist') or to someone else's saying such a thing of him. Hence, we do *not* want condition (2) interpreted in such a way that its being necessary for S's knowing that p would entail that S cannot be said to know such things as that he has a pain or that he is conscious.

7. Another feature of the meaning of (2) that should be noted is that S cannot be confident (or even believe) that p unless he *understands* the proposition that p. He need not understand it as fully as it might be understood. He might, for example, believe that the University owns a cyclotron without understanding very well what a cyclotron is. But he cannot believe what he does not understand at all. He must have at least enough understanding of the proposition to have some idea of how it may be determined whether or not it is true. It is perhaps enough to know that a cyclotron is some sort of instrument used by physicists (or just scientists) in some of their experiments. If he did not know whether a cyclotron is a scientific instrument or a vehicle with wheels or an animal, but only that it is some sort of material thing capable of being owned, then it would be very odd to say of him that he is confident that the University owns a cyclotron. To assert that he is confident that the University owns a cyclotron certainly suggests that he has a fuller grasp of what a cyclotron is than *that*. It is quite certain that if he also did not know whether a cyclotron was a material object or a kind of repeating decimal or what 'the University' refers to or what owning is, then he could not be confident that (or believe that or assert that or wonder whether) the University owns a cyclotron.

He could, however, believe that the proposition asserted by someone who has said 'The University owns a cyclotron' is true, because that is not the same thing as believing that the University owns a cyclotron. Here is an example from real life: I find in a mathematics textbook (Kelley, 1955, p. 146) after the word "THEOREM" the following sentence: "If X is a locally compact topological space which is either Hausdorff or regular, then the family of closed compact neighborhoods of each point is a base for its neighborhood system". I am quite confident, and with plenty of justification, that the proposition that the author asserts with that sentence, whatever it is, is true. But if I were to say in a confident manner (to someone who didn't know me well), "If X is a locally compact topological space... etc." or "I am sure (or I conjecture) that if X is a locally compact ... etc.", I would thereby pretend to a much greater comprehension of the concepts of topology than I in fact possess. Thus, although one can identify a particular proposition that one does not understand at all – say, by means of a sentence 'p' that someone has used to express it – and one can be confident that this particular proposition, the proposition that p, is true, one is not thereby confident that p.

Although being confident that p entails understanding the proposition that p (at least to a significant degree) it does not in every case entail being able to express that proposition in symbols of any sort. An animal that lacks altogether the capacity for putting things into symbols, for example, a dog, is yet able to show by his behavior that he confidently remembers or recognizes or expects certain things to be the case – for example, that stepping on glowing coals will hurt him, that someone is about to throw the stick he wants to fetch, that the stick is travelling through the air in a certain direction. And we ourselves know many things that we would be at a loss to put into words, for example, just how one must hold one's mouth and force air through it in order to whistle. I know what the characteristic appearance of a certain person is that one may go by in recognizing him, as I show by recognizing him, or pictures of him, very well; but if I am asked to *say* just what that characteristic appearance is I am able only to point to him, or a picture of him, and say, 'Well, it's what can be seen there' (though this *might* be fairly regarded as *saying* what he looks like). There are, to be sure, many sorts of propositions that a person could not be supposed to know or be confident of or understand unless he knows how to express them somehow in symbols, for example, propositions of higher mathematics or theoretical physics. But since this is not true of all propositions, the ability to formulate the proposition that p in symbols is not a generally necessary condition of being confident or knowing that p. Whether creatures altogether lacking in competence to symbolize *any* propositions can, nevertheless, *know* some truths (strictly speaking) is a different question. There is no reason in the necessity of (2) for knowing truths to deny that they can, but perhaps there may be in the conditions still to be discussed.

NOTES

[1] See also Woozley (1952) and Armstrong (1973), p. 141, where 'The Case of the Unconfident Examinee' is taken to show that knowing does not entail being confident.

[2] Moore (1962), p. 115, says, "There certainly is *a* common use of belief in which 'I believe' entails 'I don't know for certain'."

[3] The distinction between that which is implied by *what the speaker says*, by the proposition he asserts, and that which is implied by *the speaker*, in virtue of general conversational principles and his saying what he does in the particular circumstances, has been introduced and put to very good use in Grice (1961) and elaborated in Grice (1974). One test of whether we have a "conversational implicature" or a logical implication of what is asserted is whether or not the implication is "cancellable" (as Grice puts it). This test reveals that S's not knowing that p cannot be more than a conversational implicature of someone's asserting that S believes that p, as is made clear by Lehrer (1968), pp. 493–494.

[4] Vendler (1972), Ch. V, contends that the object of knowledge is never the same as the object of belief, that what one believes is a proposition but what one knows is a fact, and he appears to conclude from this that an analysis of knowledge that p in terms of belief that p must be mistaken, that (confidently) believing that p could not be a conceptually necessary condition of knowing that p. This inference, as far as I can see, is just a *non sequitur*. What reason is there to think that 'S knows that p' can entail 'S believes that p' only if 'that p' signifies the same object in both cases? Nor do I find Vendler's argument that knowledge and belief have different objects very convincing. It is based on such considerations as that, although 'I believe what you say' means 'I believe to be true the proposition you assert', 'I know what you say' does *not* mean 'I know to be true the proposition you assert' and that, although one can say 'I know what happened', one cannot say 'I believe what happened'. Some considerations that muddy the picture a good deal are ignored, however, such as the possibility of saying things like 'Is what you said at that point in your testimony something you know or something you merely believe?'

[5] Searle (1969), pp. 141–146, calls the failure to distinguish conditions necessary for *asserting* that p from conditions necessary for *its being true* that p the "assertion fallacy".

[6] Armstrong (1973), pp. 16–19, argues that the state of belief is not a disposition. But the considerations he offers have to do mostly with how belief differs from a simple disposition like brittleness and seem to me to show at most only that belief and britt-

leness are different kinds of dispositions. One argument he offers uses the premise that the belief state must have a *structure* that corresponds to the structure of the proposition believed, a contention that his remarks fail to make plausible to me.

[7] Contrast Wittgenstein (1969), 208, 260, 352, 464–468, 552–554, and elsewhere. But see also 431.

[8] Compare Wittgenstein (1969), 504–505.

CHAPTER III

THE GENERAL CONDITIONS OF KNOWLEDGE: JUSTIFICATION

1. To *know* that p it is not enough to be sure that p and happen to be right. One's confidence must be *justified* and that justification must be *disinterested.*

I shall take 'S has justification for being confident that p' (or 'S is justified in being confident that p') to mean 'S is in a position such that if he is, or were to be, confident that p then he is, or would be, justified in being so.' One is *justified* in being confident that p if and only if it is not the case that one ought not to be confident that p: one could not be justly reproached for being confident that p.

If one is justified in being confident that p, is it the case that one *should be* confident that p? In general, from its being false that one ought not to do something it does not follow that one ought to do it. But in certain cases the gap between these amounts to very little. Accepting a gift is (perhaps) such a case: if it is not the case that one ought not to accept a gift one has been offered (there is no reason why one ought not to) then one ought to accept it; exceptions to this are going to be rather special cases. Being confident is perhaps similar. Circumstances that justify a person in being confident that something is the case are generally also enough to oblige him to be confident in the sense that he will be open to a certain sort of criticism if he is not confident. When a person is justified in being confident that p but he is not so then he is being (at least a bit) unreasonable, unless there is some special explanation (perhaps he very much wants it not to be the case that p). A position is not generally considered to be such as to make it reasonable (to provide sufficient reason) to be confident that p unless it is also thought to be such as to make it unreasonable (lacking in any acceptable reason) not to be confident that p. Generally we think that confidence is not quite fully justified as long as there remains something that can rightly be regarded as a reason for still hesitating. But there are exceptions.

One clear sort of case that falls between being justified in being confident and not being justified in not being confident (where a person may be said to be justified whichever he is, confident or not) is that for which the distinction between interested and disinterested justification is useful. By a *disinterested* justification for being confident that p I mean one that does not involve wanting it to be the case that p. That is, S has a disinterested justification for being confident that p if and only if there is true a proposition that entails that S is justified in being confident that p but does not entail that S has reason to desire that p. If one can have a justification for being confident that p that is *not* a *dis*interested justification, then of such a case it could be appropriate to say that although one's special interest in p may justify one in being confident that p one is also, from a disinterested point of view, justified if one is not confident that p.

And one clearly can have (interested) justification for being confident that p although one lacks disinterested justification. Consider the following possible case: S regards R as his only close friend in the world. S is dismissed from his job by his boss who tells S that R has reported that S has been lifting cash from the till, although S has actually done no such thing. Now, if S has no good reason to think that his boss would want to lie about this particular matter then S has some reason to suspect that R did tell the boss a malicious falsehood about him; S now has some reason to doubt, to lack confidence, that R would never do such a thing. Indeed, we may suppose that, apart from S's strong desire that R should not have done this most unfriendly thing, S does not have sufficient reason for being sure that R has not done it. S does not have a case for confidence that will survive *impartial* scrutiny. Yet S's strong desire that R should be his trustworthy friend, and S's reasons for having that desire (of a sort most of us have for wanting dependable friends), may *justify* S, in a perfectly good sense, in maintaining his confidence that R would not do such a thing. As long as the case against R is not too overwhelming, who can blame or reproach S for this faith in R? One would not have to think S unreasonable to think that he would need much stronger evidence against R for his trust to waver. S's natural and reasonable dependence on the conviction that R is his friend makes it quite reasonable for S to maintain his trust in the face of some contrary evidence.

But it does not make it correct to say, even supposing that S is right in his belief that R did not do the nefarious deed, that S *knows* that R did not do it. For we may suppose that another person who was not thus emotionally related to R and who knew as much about R that is relevant as S

does might well *not* be justified (in any way) in being confident that *R* did not do it and thus certainly not justified in claiming to *know* that. A person who claims to *know* that *p* purports to give his hearers a special sort of assurance that *p*, a sort that he does not purport to give if he asserts merely that he is confident that *p* or even that he has reason sufficient *for him* to be confident that *p*. When I say of someone (whether myself or someone else) that that person *knows* that *p* I imply that that person's position is such that were my hearers (or anyone else) in such a position they too would be justified in being confident that *p*, regardless of whether or not they want it to be the case that *p*. In this way the assertion that someone knows that *p* – if the audience can believe the assertion is justified – can transfer the subject's warrant for being confident that *p* to that audience. It can transfer the subject's knowledge that *p*, provided that the receiver of the assertion knows that its maker asserts what he knows. But we can rely on another's justified confidence only if that person's justification for confidence is independent of his desires. *S*'s strong desire that *p* may properly weigh *for S* as a reason for believing that *p* but it cannot serve another person as a reason for doing that (unless, of course, this other person sympathizes with *S*); whereas, for example, *S*'s confidence that he has seen a certain thing can serve another (to whom this confidence is known) as well as *S* as a reason for believing that *p*. This is why *S*'s special desire that *p* (and *S*'s reasons for having that desire) cannot make the difference as to whether or not *S* is justified in claiming to *know* that *p*, although it can make the difference as to whether *S* is justified or to be reproached in being confident that *p*. If the disinterested person possessing all the same relevant evidence would not be justified in claiming to know that *p*, then neither would the interested person, despite the fact that the latter's special desire that *p* may be reason enough in the circumstances for that person to be confident that *p*.

So justification for being confident that *p* is justification for claiming to know that *p* only if it is disinterested.[1] I shall take up the question whether the converse of this is true as well, after I've said a bit more about the nature of justification for confidence. Hereafter, in order to make the prose a little easier on the eye, I shall frequently use 'justification' and its cognates, unmodified, as short for 'disinterested justification' and its cognates; it will be clearly indicated when the more general understanding of 'justification' is intended.

2. Incidentally, the features of assertion that S knows that p to which I have just called attention in order to explain why such assertions entail that S has a *disinterested* justification, are the features that have led some philosophers to say that 'I know that p' is like 'I promise that p' in being a performative utterance (roughly equivalent to 'I assure you, cross my heart and hope to die, that p'). To claim to know that p is, as noted, to give one's hearers a special sort of strong assurance that p, different from what would be given by simply asserting that p or that one is sure that p. But this is completely explained by the fact that to claim to know is to claim to have a disinterested justification for being confident that p, one that would justify that confidence whether or not a person has a special interest in its being the case that p. If one claims to know that p without really recognizing one's position as one that thus disinterestedly justifies being confident that p one is liable to special censure. For then, even if one is confident that p and it happens to be the case that p, one is still being deceitful in implying that one is disinterestedly justified in one's confidence when one has not recognized this to be the case. This is to try to lead someone else into confidence that p through misrepresentation, through implying, contrary to what one really thinks, that were anyone else in one's position he would (regardless of whether or not he desires that p) be justified in being confident too. Thus the act of *claiming to know* is an act of giving assurance that makes appropriate special censure should it be performed in the wrong conditions. In this it does resemble the act of *promising*, which is an act of giving special assurance that one will do something, making appropriate special censure should a promise be given in the wrong conditions (for example, without fully intending to do the thing or without being justifiedly confident that one will be able to do it). But from this similarity between claiming to know and promising it does not follow that 'know' is like 'promise' in being a performative verb, so that to say 'I know that p' is merely to perform an act of giving assurance. Promising and claiming to know are linguistic *acts*. But knowing is not an act (linguistic or otherwise); it is a condition or state that one comes into or achieves (perhaps by means of certain acts). 'I know that p' ascribes the same state to its subject as 'He knows that p', which clearly reports no act, ascribes to its subject. And, because knowing entails having disinterestedly justified confidence, the third-person report gives its hearers the same reason for being assured that p as does the first-person

report. But the act-reporting 'He promises that *p*', if it gives a hearer any reason at all for being sure that *p*, does not give him as much reason, or in the same way, as does 'I promise that *p*.' 'He promises...' differs from 'I promise...' with respect to purporting to give reason for assurance about as much, and in the same way, as 'He *claims* to know...' differs from 'He knows...'.[2]

3. Condition (3) resembles condition (2) in that loose uses of 'know' may, at first glance, seem to show that this condition is not necessary for knowing that *p*. Consider, for example, the case of the adulterous wife who overhears her husband express the suspicion that she is being unfaithful and hurries to tell her lover that her husband 'knows' of their affair. It must be admitted that it would be silly in such circumstances for the lover to object to her remark on the ground that, for all they know, the husband may not have evidence that disinterestedly justifies him in being sure that they are having an affair. For their purposes (we may suppose) the husband *as good as* knows it if he so much as suspects it and so it is quite natural for them to speak loosely of his knowing it. We can see that this is a loose use of 'know'. and that respect for condition (3) is required when 'know' is being used strictly, by considering the case of the friend of the husband who tries to restrain him from rash action by saying, 'You don't *know* that she has been unfaithful. All you really know is that that notoriously untrustworthy gossip down the street says that she has. You ought at least to have better evidence than that, to *know* that she is guilty, before you make up your mind to do something that you may later regret.'

Another sort of case that might be thought to show that being justified in one's confidence is not necessary to knowing is the case of creatures of whom we comfortably say that they know things but of whom it seems absurd to say that they are justified or unjustified in being confident of them. I may say of my dog, on the basis of her excited behavior as she sees me taking down her leash, that she knows that I am going to take her for a walk. But, since she altogether lacks, and is incapable of acquiring, the concept of being justified or not in believing such a thing and, so, the concept of being influenced in her belief by the consideration of justification, it makes no sense to raise the question whether or not she is justified in her belief, whether or not she merits reproach for having that confident belief. Owing to the limitations of her "form of life" (in Wittgenstein's sense) the whole category of appraisal in terms of being justified or reasonable or not in having a belief is simply inapplicable to her (as is also the category of moral appraisal as honest or dishonest, selfish or unselfish, conscientious or not, etc.). But I am inclined to say that my application of 'know' to my dog is in an extended sense of the term, based on similarities of my dog's case to those human cases where the term has primary application. This extended sense just eliminates consideration of the dimension of justification in which the dog cannot participate, but this dimension must be considered in the primary application. (The extended application of 'know' to my dog is, of course, encouraged by a counterpart in the dog's case to justification in the human case, the similarity between the fact that my dog's belief results from her having had several experiences of seeing the leash taken down and immediately thereafter being taken out for a walk and human justifications for claims to know what is about to occur that involve the subject's remembering that there has been a certain correlation of phenomena in his experience.) My interest here is in the primary sense, or application,[3] of 'know' – to human beings in the context of the human form of life.

Must creatures who do possess the concept of justification, and so can be appraised in terms of being justified or not in their beliefs, also be ones able to use language, to express things in symbols? It is far from clear that there is a logically necessary tie here.[4] It is, however, very hard to see how a being intelligent enough to have the notion of being justified or not in one's beliefs, to make judgments on that sort of question, could fail to be capable of acquiring some sort of language of roughly the same order of sophistication as ours. So it seems extremely unlikely that there ever have been or will be creatures possessing the concept of justification but lacking anything that could be called language.

4. What features must a person's position have if it justifies him in being confident that p? Many and various, of course, are the specific sorts of positions that do this. The features they need to give them this power will partly depend on the nature of the proposition that p. Some of them I will detail later for particular classes of propositions. But there are two quite general points about the nature of positions that justify confidence. I will discuss the first of these in this section and consider the second in the section that follows.

The first general point to be made is this: Every one of every set of facts about S's position that minimally suffices to make S, at a given time, justified in being confident that p must be *directly recognizable* to S at that time. By 'directly recognizable' I mean this: if a certain fact obtains, then it is directly recognizable to S at a given time if and only if, provided that S at that time has the concept of that sort of fact, S needs at that time only to reflect clear-headedly on the question of whether or not that fact obtains in order to know that it does. A fact can be part of what justifies S in being confident that p only if it is a fact that can *directly* influence S's doxastic attitude towards that proposition. That is, S's doxastic attitude at any given time towards any given proposition can be justified or un-justified only on the basis of what at that time requires only S's effort of attention or consideration in order to influence his attitude. It is not the fact that *there is* smoke rising from the forest that justifies S in being confident that there is fire in the forest but rather such facts as that S *is confident that he sees* smoke, S *has no reason to mistrust* his sight on this particular matter at this particular time, and S *seems to remember* that he has come to know that virtually always when there is smoke of the sort he sees there is fire. It is not the fact that the sum of the angles of a triangle is always 180° that justifies a person at a particular time in being confident that if two of the angles of this particular triangle are 90° and 45° then the third must be 45°, but rather such a fact as that he then confidently re-members having learned in some way (perhaps by having proved it, per-haps from a reliable authority) that the angles of a triangle always sum to 180°. The first sort of fact mentioned in each case cannot possibly influ-ence a person's doxastic attitude towards a proposition except through the influence of the second sort, to which the first sort may give rise. (In-deed it is not clear that an abstract, mathematical fact, such as that the angles of the triangle sum to 180°, can intelligibly be said to enter into the relation of *influencing* a person's doxastic attitude at all, directly or indi-rectly.) It is only what can directly influence a person's doxastic attitudes at a given time, through his then simply attending to it, that can be rele-vant to evaluating the reasonableness of his doxastic attitudes for him at that time.

This requirement of direct recognizability means that every fact be-longing to a set that minimally suffices for S's having justification for being confident that p must be such that if it obtains then the only possible way in which S could fail to know that it obtains would be through either (a) failure to consider sufficiently carefully the question whether or not it obtains or (b) failure to possess the concept of that sort of fact. A position that gives one justification for being confident of a proposition must be such that, given sufficient intelligence, one could acquire an ability to recognize that position whenever one is in it.

Thus, for example, the fact that S once came to know that Harrison was President between Cleveland's terms is not now directly recognizable to S because S may now fail to know of this fact through failure of memory and, in that circumstance, no amount of understanding of that sort of fact and clear-headed reflection on the question of whether it obtains could bring him to know that it does. Or, for another example, the fact that S now sees snow falling is one that S could fail to know owing to having good reason to think that what he sees that looks like snow falling is actually something else or that he is hallucinating, circumstances that no amount of clear-headed reflection on his position or understanding of what it is to see snow falling could remedy.

On the other hand, such facts as that S is now (at least in a way) confident that the President between Cleveland's terms was Harrison, or that it now seems to S that he remembers having come to know that Harrison was President between Cleveland's terms or that S's visual experience now is as if he were seeing snow falling *are* facts of a sort which S must know if he understands them and reflects sufficiently on the question of whether or not they obtain; they are directly recognizable to S. Facts directly recognizable to S will, pretty obviously, all be current mental states or occurrences of which S is the subject. 'It seems to S that he remembers...' and 'S is confident that...' express *dispositional* mental states of S that are directly recognizable to him. It is now true of S that he is confident that... (or seems to remember...) if and only if, were he now to consider carefully the question whether he is confident that... (or whether it seems to him that he remembers...) and try to answer it for himself, his answer would be 'yes'. (In light of the possibility noted earlier that a person's knowing and sincere action as if confident that... could be *in a way* misleading as to his actual dispositional state of confidence, 'confident' [or 'believes'] should be read here and in later chapters as 'at least *in a way* confident' ['at least in a way believes']. This reading makes no difference to the claims I make with respect to the relations among being confident, having justification for being confident, and knowing, if 'knows' is read similarly.)

The requirement of direct recognizability on justification for confidence (or justification for any other degree of belief) – that is, the requirement that any minimally sufficient condition for S's having justification for being confident that p be directly recognizable to S – can be seen to hold by the following argument.

Assuming that S has the concept of justification for being confident that p, S *ought* always to posses or lack confidence that p according to whether or not he has such justification. At least he ought always to withhold confidence unless he has justification. This is simply what is meant by having or lacking *justification*. But if this is what S ought to do in any possible circumstance, then it is what S *can* do in any possible circumstance. That is, assuming that he has the relevant concepts, S can always tell whether or not he has justification for being confident that p. But this would not be so unless the difference between having such justification and not having it were always directly recognizable to S. And that would not be so if any fact contributing to a set that minimally constitutes S's having such justification were not either directly recognizable to S or entailed by something directly recognizable to S (so that its absence would have to make a directly recognizable difference). For suppose it were otherwise: suppose that some part of a condition minimally sufficient for S's being justified in being confident that p were *not* entailed by anything directly recognizable to S. Then S's position could change from having such justification to lacking it without there being any change at all in what is directly recognizable to S. But if there is no change in directly recognizable features of S's position, S cannot tell that his position has changed in other respects: no matter how clear-headedly and attentively he considers his position he will detect no change. If it seemed to S before that he had justification for being confident that p then it must still seem so to him. So this sort of justification would be such that it would not always be possible for its subject to tell whether or not he possessed it, which is contrary to what we noted is an obvious essential feature of justification. So there can be no such justification. That is, there can be no set of facts giving S justification for being confident that p that has an essential part that is neither directly recognizable to S nor entailed by something directly recognizable to S.

The requirement on justification of direct recognizability does *not* mean that one who can recognize a certain sort of position as justifying confidence that p and discriminate it from any other sort of position that does not do so – who understands that such a position does justify confidence that p – must be able to describe all the features that go to make it a justifying position, or even that he must have concepts of them all. One can learn to recognize a characteristic complex of features without acquiring distinct conceptions of all the parts on which the overall characteristic depends. A child can learn to discriminate and identify square figures before he realizes that a square has to have four equal sides forming four equal angles, even before he has a concept of what an angle is. Similarly we can learn to recognize various sorts of positions that justify confidence in various sorts of propositions – to discriminate them and identify them as such, to back our confidence and our claims to know by appealing to the fact that we are in a position that puts to rest or prevents reasonable doubt – before we know (if we ever do) how to give any sort of interesting analysis of such positions.

5. Can we say anything interesting of a completely general nature as to what features make a directly recognizable position one that justifies its subject in being confident of a proposition? Just a little (and this is my other general point about the nature of such justifying positions).

Insofar as positions directly recognizable to a person can be *objectively* ranked as to how strong a belief in a given proposition, p, they justify that person in having – that is, insofar as we have a concept and practice of objective justification of degrees of belief – the ultimate authority for this ranking must be the concurring judgments of reasonable, experienced people who have the notion of and an interest in the practice of rational, objective justification of degrees of belief and who give the positions in question their thoughtful consideration. If we say of two sorts of directly recognizable positions that one would clearly justify a stronger belief in p than the other (or, as it may be, that clearly neither would justify a stronger belief in p than the other) we are right if and only if this would be the overwhelming judgment of reasonable, experienced people who knew what they were considering (so that their judgment would not be changed by their attending better to the nature of the positions in question or their having more experience or more rational intelligence). Similarly, to say of a certain sort of position that it clearly justifies confidence that p is to say that reasonable, experienced people when fully aware of the nature of the position will overwhelmingly agree in treating it as one in which lacking confidence that p is practically silly in normal circumstances (for a person with no particular desire that p be false). That is, aware and reasonable persons do, or would, share a policy of regarding such a position as offering no motive to hesitate about p, at any rate not normally, not unless, for example, far worse consequences than normal seem likely to ensue if one were to be confident that p and it turned out to be false that p.

According to such a general criterion for positions that justify confidence, I am, for example, justified in being confident that I see my younger son when my position is (roughly) the following: I am confident that I remember having seen that son's face many times before and that on those occasions it looked closely like the face that I am confident that I now see; I have no beliefs or impressions about this particular occasion that would, despite my having the visual and memory impressions implied in the preceding statement, give me reason to doubt that I see my son; I am confident that I remember having never seen nor heard of anyone else who looks so closely like my son and that I remember having come to know that such close look-alikes are very rare in general. Thus described, this position does not *entail* that I see my son, but it justifies me in being confident that I do. In the ordinary course of life, to lack confidence in a proposition of that sort when in that kind of position with respect to it – to follow a policy of hesitating over such propositions and protecting oneself against the possibility that they may be false even in such circumstances would seem to virtually anyone to involve an unreasonably great cost in inconvenience and unpleasantness. For a reasonable person could find no adequate motive to incur such costs. It would be *practically* absurd, indeed practically *impossible*; scarcely anyone *could* actually follow such a policy over a significant period.

This general criterion for positions that justify confidence – the criterion of the generally agreed judgment in practice of reaonable, experienced people who know what they are judging – is unquestionably a vague one. There are several ways in which cases can fail to fall clearly on one side or the other of the line it draws. Take the notion of general agreement. What proportion agreeing is enough to make agreement general? Who will count as reasonable, experienced persons? And some cases will be controversial or else generally agreed to be unclear (that is, not clearly ones where confidence is justified and not clearly ones where it is not justified). But we should not expect the concept of justification of confidence in a proposition, or the concept of knowing a truth, to be any less vague.

To reject this criterion in favor of some stricter or looser one is to make a recommendation that has no chance of being followed by reasonable, experienced people and one they could be given no motive to follow. For it would be a recommendation that they ought to respond to certain kinds of positions (those included by a looser criterion or excluded by a stricter one that are not included or excluded, respectively, by the criterion of general agreement among reasonable, experienced people) in a way different from that which in fact they are, or would be, led to respond to them by the fullest influence of their reason, experience, and attention to the nature of the positions. Such a recommendation cannot be taken seriously.

6. The following claim is suggested by my general definition of propositional knowledge: if one is (disinterestedly) justified in being confident that p then one is justified in claiming to know that p (provided that one is confident that p: one ought not to claim to know that p, even if one has justification for being confident that p, if one is not actually confident that p); everything that we should regard as reason for saying that a person who is confident that p should not have claimed (or thought) that he knew that p is also something we should regard as reason for saying that he was not, from a disinterested point of view, justified in being confident. How can this claim be made out?

Well, the only arguments there seem to be to show the possibility of a case in which a person is disinterestedly justified in being confident that p but is not justified in claiming to know that p appear to be seriously flawed. Many of them are arguments for thinking that the (directly recognizable) facts that justify a person's claim to know that p must also be such as to entail that p. From this it would follow that a person could have justification for being confident that p that was *not* also justification for claiming to know that p, since a justification for being confident that p need not entail that p, given the considered practice of reasonable people as the primary criterion of such justification.

One way in which one might be led to think that a justification for
claiming to know that p must entail that p would be simply through over-
looking the distinction between *knowing* and *being justified in claiming to
know*, between what is claimed and what justifies the claim. One might fail
to see that it is logically possible for someone to be justified in claiming to
know what he does not in fact know (because, for example, it is false). If
one fails to distinguish knowledge from justification for knowledge claims,
then one is in the position of having to say that most of the kinds of propositions that we ordinarily talk of knowing – for example, propositions entailing the existence of external objects or events in the past – are ones that
no one could ever conceivably know.[5] Since no facts that are directly
recognizable to a person at a given time could possibly entail such propositions and his having a justification at a given time for claiming or believing that he knows must, like justifications for doxastic attitudes
generally, consist in facts that are directly recognizable to him at that
time, one who insists that one is justified in claiming to know just when
one knows is forced to severe limitations on the class of propositions that
can be known.

But why embrace such an awkward consequence if we can account for
the actual use of 'know' by supposing that being justified in claiming to
know that p entails neither p nor knowing that p? We frequently do affirm
that a person knows a certain proposition to be true without hesitating at
all over the fact that no facts directly recognizable to him could entail
that the proposition is true, and we do so without any sense of looseness
or irony in our use of 'know'. I *know*, for example, that I am older than
my wife (whereas I merely *believe* that R. N. is older than his wife). Since I
must be entitled to think that I know this if I do know it and since only
directly recognizable features of my position can contribute to my being
so entitled, if such an ascription of knowledge is even possibly true, then
my being entitled to think that I know does not entail that I know. That
p and that S is justified in claiming to know that p are quite independent
entailments of 'S knows that p.'

One still might be tempted to think otherwise by the following sort
of reasoning: Since my knowing that p entails that p, how can I consis-
tently claim to know that p and at the same time allow that everything that
justifies me in that claim leaves it still *possible* that p is false? The apparent
force of this derives in large part from equivocation on 'possible.'[6] If one

uses, for example, 'It is possible that he will not come' (as such a sentence often is used) to mean that it is not out of the question that he will not come, not certain that he will come, his not coming is a possibility that one ought to be prepared for, his not coming is compatible with all that one knows (it is *epistemically* possible, as it is often put by philosophers nowadays), then of course one simply contradicts oneself if one adds 'but I know that he will come'.

The sentence 'I know that p, but it is possible that not-p' has other interpretations, however. It could mean the same as 'I know that p, but the proposition that not-p is logically possible (that is, the proposition that p is not logically necessary).' It is quite clear that sentences of this form can express logically possible states of affairs; consider, for example, 'I know that I am now conscious, though it is logically possible that I should (instead) have been unconscious now.' Or it could mean the same as 'I know that p, but the proposition that not-p is logically compatible with every fact that now justifies me in thinking that I know that p'. This does not seem absurd on its face, and in fact it expresses a common state of affairs.

But it is, perhaps, less clearly non-absurd than the preceding interpretation. Against its possibility the following might be claimed: if all the facts available to justify any of my beliefs – which, we have seen, are just those facts that are directly recognizable to me – are such that they are logically compatible with not-p as well as with p, then p and not-p are equally open possibilities as far as those facts go, and so, those facts cannot justify me in believing one to be true rather than the other or, therefore, in claiming to know one to be true rather than the other. Two things should be observed about this claim. (1) Since it entails that justification for any belief must entail what is believed it would, even if true, open no gap between justification for confidence and justification for thinking or claiming one knows. (2) It would be irrational, in a certain way at least, to try to satisfy the principle laid down by the claim, since to do so would require holding back at all times from believing anything beyond what is then directly recognizable to one or is entailed by what is then directly recognizable to one and that policy is one that fully rational, alert, experienced people have no adequate motive to follow, indeed, could not bring themselves to follow in practice. (I will return to this second point in the final section of the book.)

Another seemingly plausible argument leading to the conclusion that what justifies one in claiming to know that p must entail that p (and, hence, that one can know only what is entailed by what one can directly recognize) derives from the consideration that one who knows that p and who understands what it is to know that p needs only to reflect attentively and clear-headedly on his (directly recognizable) position in order to know that he knows that p. If I know that p and, hence, my directly recognizable position justifies me in claiming to know that p, then I need only to see this about my position in order to know that I know that p.[7] This observation is quite correct if properly understood, but it can easily be misunderstood and taken to imply that I can know only what is entailed by what I can directly recognize. For it may seem to say that whenever I know that p I can directly recognize that I know that p, simply through directly recognizing that I am justified in claiming to know that p; that is, the fact that I know something is a fact that I can directly recognize in all its components whenever it occurs. But actually that observation, when interpreted so as to be true, implies nothing of the sort. This becomes clear if it is paraphrased as follows:

> If I know that p, then I can, merely by attentive and clear-headed reflection (provided that I understand the proposition that I know that p), directly recognize that I am justified in claiming to know that p and, hence, that if I claim to know that p and this claim is true then this claim expresses something that I know.[8]

7. Further arguments for a gap between disinterested justification for confidence and justification for claiming to know arise from the thought that it might be possible to be justified in being confident of each of an inconsistent set of propositions. It might be said that, in contrast, it should not be possible to be justified in claiming to know an inconsistent set of propositions, since what one knows must be true and an inconsistent set of propositions cannot all be true. But this again fails to distinguish knowing from being justified in claiming to know. The set of all propositions that a person knows, or *truly* claims to know, must indeed be consistent; but from this it does not follow that all the propositions that he *justifiedly claims* to know must be consistent, since being justified in

claiming to know does not entail knowing. So something else must be adduced in support of the contention that one cannot be justified in claiming to know an inconsistent set of propositions.

I can think of nothing that would not also be an equally good reason for saying that one cannot be justified in being *confident* of an inconsistent set of propositions. We must distinguish, of course, between being justified in claiming to know (or being justified in being confident of) *each* of an inconsistent set of propositions and being justified in claiming to know the conjunction of an inconsistent set of propositions. What is true of the one may not be true of the other.

Could one ever be justified in claiming to know an inconsistent proposition? I don't see why not, *if* one could be justified in being confident of one. If a person arrived at confidence in an inconsistent or necessarily false proposition (one that was not obviously so) in such a way that we would not want to say that he ought not at the time to have been confident of it, we do not want to reproach him for having been confident in the circumstances then directly recognizable to him – for example, he has made an unnoticed slip in the course of calculation – then I don't see how we could say that he ought not to think that he knows the proposition, how we could reproach him for thinking that he knows it. Of course, if he recognizes the inconsistency or necessary falsehood of a proposition then he cannot possibly at the same time be justified either in being confident of it or in thinking that he knows it.

What about being justified in being confident of each consistent member of an inconsistent set of propositions while at the same time knowing that the set is inconsistent? This is not an obvious impossibility.[9] Consider the case of a large lottery.[10] Suppose one is justifiedly confident that there are a million tickets in the lottery and that out of them just one will be selected by a completely random procedure guaranteeing that each ticket has an equal chance of being drawn, that is, one in a million. Given this, it might be suggested, one has no reason not to be confident with respect to any single ticket that might be designated that it will *not* be the one drawn (since the chances are 999,999 to 1 against it). Yet at the same time one is hardly likely to fail to see that the million different propositions, each of which one feels justified in being confident of, plus the proposition that one of the million tickets will be drawn, which one is also justified in being confident of, form an inconsistent set.

However, I believe that there is a reason why the fact cited – that one is confident with justification that there are a million tickets in the lottery and that out of them just one will be selected by a random procedure that gives every ticket an equal chance – does *not* give one justification by inference for claiming to know that, say, ticket number 10 will not be the one drawn. This reason is connected with the notion of external conclusiveness – condition (4) of the general definition of knowing – and can be adequately explained only after that notion has been explained in the next chapter. (In outline, the point will be that the fact cited does *not* give justification by inference for claiming to know that ticket 10 will not win because it *does* give justification by inference for believing a proposition that entails that it itself is not externally conclusive justification for being confident that ticket 10 will not win.) But this reason is also, I claim, a reason why the fact cited does not give one justification for being completely confident that ticket 10 will not be drawn. And intuitively it seems right that it should not. Intuitively it does seem that if a person is confident with justification that the lottery drawing will be fair then (no matter how many tickets he knows are in the lottery) he ought not to be *completely* confident that a particular ticket will not be the winner: his justified conviction that there are *n* tickets and that the lottery will be fair does not justify him (by inference from it alone) in being sure, for example, that his buying ticket 10 out of no other motive than the hope of winning would be quite irrational or stupid (though this might be justified by the different conviction that the cost of the ticket to him is too high for the chance that it will win); it does not justify him in confidently regarding ownership of the ticket as of absolutely no value at all, of no more value than not owning any ticket; it does not justify him in taking no interest whatsoever in the announcement of the winning ticket on the ground that only the winning of ticket 10 would interest him. It does not, in short, justify him in taking quite the same rejecting attitude towards the possibility that ticket 10 is the winner as he would be justified in taking by such facts as would justify him in being confident that he has *seen* some other ticket drawn or has seen ticket 10 removed from the lottery before the drawing.

Or consider the question whether among all the propositions that you now justifiedly think that you know to be true there is not at least one that will turn out to be false. Does not what you know of your own experience and that of other men justly convince you that there must be? In this case,

I do not think the sort of argument I suggested for the lottery example applies. There is no apparent reason why the subject may not be justified in claiming to know or in being confident of each of the members of the inconsistent set of propositions in question, namely; the set containing (a) all those propositions he currently has justification for claiming to know and (b) the proposition that at least one of those propositions specified in (a) other than the one hereby being expressed is false.[11] So I am inclined to think that this is a specification of an inconsistent set of propositions such that a person can have disinterested justification for being confident of and claiming to know each member of the set while also knowing that the set is inconsistent.

Thus a limited examination of particular examples of inconsistent sets of propositions, concerning which it might seem *prima facie* plausible to think that a person could have justification for being confident of *or* for claiming to know each member of the set (while knowing the set to be inconsistent), gives one reason to think that in all such examples justification for claiming to know and justification for being confident will stand or fall together: as the one turns out to be possible or not in the particular case so will the other.

I can see no line of thought other than those I have considered that holds out promise of opening a gap between being justified in being confident that p and being justified in claiming to know that p (if confident that p). Since we saw earlier that the latter entails the former, I conclude that these two descriptions are equivalent.

8. Now for some classifications of positions that (disinterestedly) justify confidence that p.

There are conjunctions such that S can have a justification for being confident of the conjunction that is a *compound* of parts each of which is a justification for being confident of just one of the conjuncts. To put it another way, many conjunctions of logically independent propositions (for example, 'The switch is on but the light is not') are such that if S has a justification for each conjunct then he has, in that compound of justifications, a justification for the conjunction. S can have a similarly compound justification for being confident of a proposition that is not itself such a conjunction but is equivalent to one, provided that the equivalence is so obvious that one who understands both propositions must see it (as it is, for example, between 'S's hand is a straight flush' and 'The cards in S's hand are all of the same suit, and the cards in S's hand form a consecutive sequence', and as it is *not*, for example, between 'The number of people in the organization is equal to 4^3 minus 2^3' and 'The number of people in the organization is greater than the product of the smallest prime greater than 3 and the smallest prime greater than 7; and it is less than 3 times the greatest prime smaller than 20').

It cannot simply be assumed, however, that for any two propositions, p and q, if S has at the same time a justification for claiming to know that p and a justification for claiming to know that q then he has in their compound a justification for claiming to know that $(p \& q)$. There may well be pairs of propositions and justifications for them for which this does not hold. One thing that suggests this possibility is the product theorem of the probability calculus, according to which the probability that both of two events, a and b, will occur (relative to some body of evidence) equals the probability that a will occur *times* the probability that b will occur, provided that there is no reason to think that whether or not the one occurs has any influence on whether or not the other does. In this case, if the probability of a's occurence is less than 1 and so is the probability of b's occurrence then the probability of the occurrence of both a and b will be less than the probability of a's occurrence and also less than the probability of b's occurrence. If there were a situation in which S knew evidence relative to which such probabilities for such independent propositions were assignable, so that the product theorem applied, and in which these probabilities could correctly be regarded as measures of the degrees of belief in those propositions that S was justified in having by inference from that evidence, then it might be that the degree for p and the degree for q were each just enough for confidence but the lesser degree for $(p \& q)$ was not. For example, suppose that S knows that a certain test for detecting in people the incipient stages of a certain disease has proved correct in 99% of the thousands of cases to which it has been applied, and also that the test has given a negative result for 100 new cases to which it has just been applied. It is not very implausible to suggest that S might on this basis be justified in being confident and claiming to know, with respect, say, to any 15 of these 100 cases that might be singled out at random, that none of those 15 has the disease, but not justified in being quite confident or claiming to know this with respect to any 30 of them that might be selected. Or consider that it does seem plausible to suggest that a typical adult's (remembered) experience may give him good reason to believe that at least one among all the propositions that he now has justification for claiming to know is false. If he does, then the set of propositions that he has justification for claiming to know might contain two disjoint subsets such that each is a small enough portion of the whole set so that his well-founded belief that the whole set contains at least one false member would not be sufficient reason for him to lack confidence that all the members of that subset are true, but the union of the two subsets is a large enough portion of the whole that this belief *is* sufficient reason to be at least somewhat less than confident that all the members of the union are true. Although these observations hardly constitute a conclusive argument for the contrary, I think it wise to refrain from affirming that a justification for claiming to know that p and a justification for claiming to know that q together will *always* yield a justification for claiming to know that $(p \ \& \ q)$.

9. Non-compound justifications (to which I will confine attention hereafter, except where otherwise noted) divide into the inferential and the non-inferential. A non-compound (and minimally sufficient) justification that S has for being confident that p is *inferential* just in case it entails that there is another proposition q such that (i) S has justification for being confident that p can be inferred with confidence from q and (ii) S has justification for being confident that q. Otherwise it is *non-inferential*.

It is fairly obvious that condition (ii) is essential for inferential justification. The fact (i), that S has justification for being confident that p can be properly inferred with confidence from q, obviously cannot by itself suffice to give S justification for being confident that p. Nor can that fact *plus* the mere fact that S is *confident* that q. One's confidence in a given proposition can by inference from it *justify* one's confidence in another proposition only if one's confidence in the premiss is justified; and having justification for confidence in the premiss can give one justification for confidence in the conclusion even if one unreasonably lacks confidence in the premiss.

It is true that if I am confident that q and also confident that if q then p, then I am unreasonable if in addition I lack confidence that p. But what is unreasonable in virtue of the nature of the three propositions involved here, and hence not justifiedly held, is the *trio* of doxastic attitudes and not necessarily any single one of them. The logical relations among the propositions that are their objects entail that this set of doxastic attitudes is unreasonable, hence unjustified to hold all at once, without implying anything about which particular members of the set are unjustified in a particular case. It could be that, given all the facts directly recognizable to me, my lack of confidence that p is justified but my confidence that q is not; or it could be the other way around.

It is true also that in a case where S satisfies our definition of inferential justification, is confident of the conclusion p, but lacks confidence in the premiss, q, and has no other justification for being confident that p, there is a sort of relative, second-order unreasonableness: although S is entitled to be confident that q, given (ii), since he is not confident of it and has no other justification for being confident that p, there is something odd and out of joint about his being confident that p. Still we can say flatly that, were S adopting all the doxastic attitudes to which he is entitled, given the facts that are directly recognizable to him, he would be confident of both q and p. It would be misleading to say that this entails the simple proposition that S is entitled to be confident that p, if this were taken to mean that (given the facts directly recognizable to S) S's being confident that p would be irreproachable no matter what his other doxastic attitudes might be. But I recommend our taking it to mean instead that p is among those propositions that are such that S would be justified if he were confident of all of them, given the facts directly recognizable to S.

One may wonder why, given (ii), we must have (i) (S's *having justification for being confident* that p can properly be inferred with confidence from q) in order to get inferential justification for being confident that p. Why not instead simply the *fact* that p can be properly inferred with confidence from q? Well, the proposition that I owe the grocer \$ 6.85 can be properly inferred with confidence, because it is deducible, from the proposition that I owe the grocer \$ 1.49 for one item, \$ 2.75 for another, and 87 ¢ apiece for three others; but if I am confident without justification that the one is deducible from the other (perhaps I have unjustified faith in the hasty computations of my seven-year-old child), then, though I may be confident of the first proposition with justification, I am not justified in being confident of the second.

Or consider the case of the detective who has collected a number of pieces of evidence about the murder but as yet has failed to survey them, to fit them together, in the right sort of way to see that altogether they point very strongly to the conclusion that Professor X is indeed the murderer: he doesn't yet see that this conclusion can be (nondeductively) inferred with confidence from their conjunction. Clearly the detective is not yet justified in being confident of that conclusion merely by his justified confidence in the conjunction of his evidence and the fact (unknown to him) that the conclusion is properly inferrable from that conjunction. Nor would it suffice to make him justified in being confident of Professor X's guilt if it were added that he is confident of the inferential connection but is so *without* justification (for example, although he doesn't see it himself he has been told that his evidence clearly points to Professor X by a comparative stranger with a French accent who resembles Hercule Poirot and this, unreasonably, makes him sure that the stranger must be right).

The *fact* that p can be properly inferred with confidence from q is not only not sufficient, when accompanied by S's confidence with justification that q, it is also not necessary to give S inferential justification for being confident that p. If, for example, S is confident that p is deducible from q and is so with justification – based, for example, on his having been told this by an authority whom he is justified in trusting – then, whether or not p is in fact deducible from q, S has inferential justification for being confident and claiming to know that p, provided that he has justification for confidence in q. But he won't thereby *know* that p, even if p is true, if it is not a fact that p is deducible from q; for then his justification will not be externally conclusive, as will be seen.

Note that my characterization of inferential justification does *not* entail that S has justification for being confident that p when S has justification for confidence that q_1, justification for confidence that $q_2, \ldots$, and justification for confidence that q_n, and also justification for confidence that p can properly be inferred with confidence from 'q_1 & ... & q_n'. This is as it should be in view of the possibility of cases where S's having justification for confidence that 'q_1 & ... q_n' is true does not follow from the conjunction 'S has justification for confidence that q_1 & ... & S has justification for confidence that q_n', such as the sorts of cases mentioned in Section 8.

In order to have an inferential justification for being confident that p it is not necessary to have gone through a corresponding process of inference, any more than it is necessary for being confident of a proposition that one have formulated it for oneself. My inferential justification for being confident that I now see my younger son before me may lie in my having justified confidence that I have seen my younger son close up many times before, that on those occasions he looked closely like the person I now see close at hand, that I have never seen nor heard of anyone else who looks so closely like this son, etc., without my ever having put to myself those propositions and thought 'therefore, this is, for sure, my younger son that I now see'; because I *would* appeal to my justified confidence in those propositions *if* I were to try to justify my confidence that I now see my younger son: that is what I have to offer should the question of my justification for that confident belief arise.

The study of the sorts of relations between two propositions that make it the case that one can be properly inferred with confidence from the other is a main concern of logic, deductive and non-deductive. Deducibility is, of course, one of these relations, extensively studied and fairly well understood, but it is only one among others.

The non-deductive inferential relations almost certainly include a number of significantly different sorts, some different from the paradigms of what is properly called *induction*. Consider the sort of inference that takes a person from justified confidence in the proposition that he sees and hears something that looks, sounds, and behaves as would a human being having sense-experiences, beliefs, intentions, etc., to justified confidence in the conclusion that he sees and hears something that *is* a human being having sense-experiences, beliefs, intentions, etc.; or the inference that takes one from justified confidence that in the vicinity of a certain metal bar iron filings behave as they would if the bar were magnetized (and that many other such consequences of the theory of magnetism have been borne out) to justified confidence that the bar is magnetized; or the inference that takes a person from justified confidence that someone has asserted that *p* in a confident and sincere manner to justified confidence that *p*. Clearly none of these inferences is deductive, and none seems to fit the inductive pattern of inference from a correlation in observed instances to a like correlation in unobserved ones. (The last example could be forced into the inductive mold by the addition of the premiss that in the subject's extensive experience of such testimony it has generally turned out to be truthful; but the question whether it could possibly have turned out otherwise raises a doubt as to whether this is genuine induction.) But what precisely is involved in such inferences and how (if at all) they do differ from induction proper are matters of much difficulty and controversy. Even working out the nature of clearly inductive inferences, and the properties of them that determine the degree of confidence they properly transfer from premiss to conclusion, is an enormous problem.

I will not try to sort out, characterize, and analyze the various sorts of inferential relations. I will only try to state what must be true of any relation between two propositions if that relation is to make it the case that one can be properly inferred with confidence from the other, that is, that a person's justified confidence in one can, in virtue of his justified confidence in this relation, be justifiedly transferred to the other. One might be tempted to say simply this:

> A relation between two propositions, p and q, is such as to make it the case that p can be properly inferred with confidence from q if and only if one who has justification for confidence both that this relation obtains and that q, thereby has justification for being confident that p.

But this will not do, because, although p's being deducible from q nicely satisfies the *definiens* here, not all the non-deductive inferential relations that justifiedly transfer confidence will satisfy it. It is a well-known fact about non-deductive inference that there can be three propositions, p, q, and r, such that p can be non-deductively inferred with confidence from q but not from the conjunction of q and r. (For example, let p be 'Cornell lost its game to Columbia last night,' q be 'Today's newspaper under the heading "Last Night's Scores" carries the line "Columbia 89 Cornell 56",' and r be 'The coach of Cornell's team has just told me that the newspaper made an error and the scores were actually the other way round'.) In such a case, one who was confident with justification that q and that p can be non-deductively inferred with confidence from q would *not* thereby be justified in being confident that p *if* he also happened to believe justifiedly that r, or to have justification for believing that r (whether or not he did believe it). We may, however, obtain a characterization that captures all the non-deductive inferential relations we want, as well as deducibility, if we complicate the one given above in the following way:

A relation R between two propositions, p and q, is such as to make it the case that p can be properly inferred with confidence from q if and only if one who has justification for confidence both that $R(p, q)$ and that q, needs to *have* no justification for any other particular sorts of beliefs, though he may need to *lack* justification for certain sorts of beliefs, in order thereby to have justification for being confident that p.

The points of the last few paragraphs can be incorporated in the following fuller definition of inferential justification:

> S has *inferential* justification for being confident that p if and only if there is some other proposition q such that S has justification for confidence that q and either
>
> (a) S has justification for confidence that p is deducible from q, or
>
> (b) (i) S has justification for confidence that p can be non-deductively inferred with confidence from q and
> (ii) there is no set of one or more propositions $\{r_1, ..., r_n\}$ such that S has justification for believing that r_1, that $r_2, ...$, and that r_n, and p cannot be non-deductively inferred with confidence from the conjunction of $q, r_1, ...$, and r_n.

Note that the *definiens* here could be true although it were false that q or false that p *is* deducible or non-deductively inferrable with confidence from q. Clearly, in such a circumstance such an inferential justification for being confident and claiming to know that p would not make it the case that S knows that p, even if it happened to be true that p. This is because such a justification is not externally conclusive.

We shall see later that non-deductive inferential justification is not the only sort of justification that requires a condition like (b) (ii), the absence in the subject of any countervailing justifications. So also do all non-inferential justifications that are *fallible* (a term to be explained in the next section).

Inferential justifications can, of course, be linked together in chains: S is justified in being confident that p_1 by inference from p_2, is justified in being confident that p_2 by inference from p_3, and so on. It is a cardinal point about any such regress of inferential justifications, however, that it cannot come round in a circle and cannot have more than a finite number of different links: it cannot, in short, have no beginning. It would be absurd to say, for instance, 'I know that p_1 because I know that it follows from p_2, which I know because I know that it follows from p_3, which I know because I know that it follows from p_4, and so on without end: I know every one of a beginningless sequence of propositions just by knowing that it follows from the preceding one in the sequence which I know in the same way.' This is absurd whether or not the beginningless sequence is circular, and for essentially the same reason (which has nothing to do with the finitude of human cognitive capacity). A beginningless sequence of inferential justifications is impossible because it gives no *source* or *origin* for the justification. Inference can only *transfer* justification of belief from one proposition to another; it cannot *create* justification. So a beginningless chain of inferential justifications (circular or not) would contain nothing to create justification for anything in the chain. The impossibility here is analogous to the impossibility of a beginningless regress of desires for things only as means to other things – desiring x_1 because it is a means to x_2, which one desires because it is a means to x_3, and so on – which would never come to anything that explains *why* anything in the chain of means is desired.[12] Similarly, a beginningless regress of inferential justifications would never come to an explanation of why any belief in the chain is justified.

Hence, if a person has inferential justification for being confident that p then he must also have *non-inferential* justification for being confident of some other proposition. There can be no inferential justifications unless there are non-inferential ones. Every justification is either non-inferential or part of an inferential chain that goes back to non-inferential justification. It is compatible with this that actual processes of inquiry and inference probably seldom appeal to non-inferential justifications but usually begin well up in the inferential structure of the inquirer's justifications.

10. Let me now explain my other major division among justifications: between the fallible and the infallible. A kind of justification for being

confident that *p* is *fallible* just in case it is possible to have the same kind of justification for being confident of a proposition that is false. Otherwise, it is *infallible*.

If a person is confident that *p* with an infallible justification then it follows that he knows that *p*. For an infallible justification for being confident that *p* cannot obtain unless it is true that *p*, and if it is infallible it must also be externally conclusive, as will be clear when we come to explain that condition. Whereas if a person is confident that *p* with a fallible justification, though it follows that he is justified in claiming to know that *p*, it does not follow that he does know it; since it could still be false that *p* or, even if it is true that *p*, the fallible justification could fail to be externally conclusive.

It is possible to have an *infallible* justification only for certain special sorts of propositions. These all fall into (but do not exhaust) one or the other of two classes: (a) *a priori* truths[13] and (b) contingent propositions about the intrinsic nature of the subject's current conscious state. In each of these classes there are propositions for which it is possible to have an infallible justification that is non-inferential, and also an infallible justification that is inferential. The inference involved in any inferential justification that is infallible must, of course, be deduction, since it is the defining mark of non-deductive inference that it is logically possible for it to lead from a true premiss to a false conclusion. In each of classes (a) and (b) there are also propositions for which ordinary mortals, at any rate, can have only *fallible* justifications.

An *a priori* truth is one for which one can have an infallible and non-inferential justification just in case it is so simple and obvious that no one could be said to understand it who does not see and fully accept that it is true (with a remotely possible exception to be noted below), the sort of truth of which one can say 'I can see just by grasping the content of this proposition – getting clearly before my mind what it is – that it is true: understanding it and seeing its truth cannot be separated.' It seems clear that there are such self-evident truths. If a child, say, is seriously inclined to deny or doubt the proposition he takes to be expressed by 'A triangle has three sides' or 'A sister is a female' or 'If your birth happened the day before mine then mine happened the day after yours' or 'Every integer has a successor,' then that is an absolutely sure sign that he does not understand that sentence to express the proposition that it would be standardly used to express. (Perhaps he takes it to express a different proposition; perhaps he has no clear understanding of it at all.)

To the dictum that to understand truths like these is to be confident of them it is no objection that it is (apparently) possible to profess sincerely that one is not certain of anything. Such professions are usually based on an unsound argument to the effect that certainty can never be justified (for example, the argument in Descartes' First Meditation). But sincere profession to doubt is not the same thing as genuine doubt. The philosophical skeptic who, without intending to deceive, *says* that he is certain of nothing nevertheless manifests an attitude of confidence that $2+2=4$ when he is checking the addition on the grocery bill, or figuring out what he has left in his checking account, or measuring for his carpentry, or in any practical context where something more than what he says hangs on his attitude. Then he does not hesitate or refuse to proceed because he fears that $2+2$ may not, after all, be 4. Anyone whose behavior convinced us that he really was reluctant to proceed as if $2+2=4$ would rightly be regarded as one who needs to have that proposition, the fundamentals about numbers and addition, explained to him. (One could no doubt imagine such cases where therapy might need to involve more than arithmetic lessons.)

It may be wondered, however, whether a person would not have reason to lack confidence in an *a priori* truth that he well understands and that is among the simplest and most obvious, if he thinks that he (or someone else) has deduced a contradiction from it and other equally obvious *a priori* premises by apparently self-evident steps. Of course, it is not logically possible that there should be a valid deduction of a contradiction from such self-evident *a priori* truths if they are true; and we all (infallibly) know that they are true and, hence, that no such deduction is possible. But suppose that someone *believed* that he or someone else had constructed just such a deduction, would not that belief provide an explanation for his lacking confidence in a self-evident *a priori* truth, an explanation compatible with his understanding it? Perhaps so. Yet it seems to me that if we were confronted with a person who in every pertinent situation really acts, without intent to deceive, as if he were not sure of the simplest truths of arithmetic then, no matter what reason he gives for acting this way, it would always be at least an equally plausible explanation that he no longer really understands those truths. If he is not disposed to act confidently in the ways that assume them, then it is hard to see what else could show that he is nevertheless still sure what those propositions are. Certain simple obvious, *a priori* truths seem to be such that in order for it to be beyond any reasonable doubt that S understands them S must be confident of them in practice. At any rate it is clear that S cannot understand such a proposition without at least having fully accepted it at some time. If S has never been disposed to act confidently in the ways that assume it, then there has never been any ground for saying that he understands it. So, more cautiously, we can say this: there are simple, obvious *a priori* truths such that any one who fully understands one of them must be confident of it, unless, as may be possible, he was at one time confident of it but now believes that it and other apparently equally obvious propositions constitute a deduction of a contradiction.

If it is in the nature of a self-evident necessary truth that one who understands it (and, perhaps we should add, does not believe that a contradiction can be deduced from it and other equally self-evident propositions) must be confident of it, then confidence in it on the part of one who understands it (and satisfies the other condition) can never be unjustified, can never be confidence that he ought not to have. To say a person ought not to be confident of such a proposition, ought despite his understanding it (and satisfying the other condition) to withhold full confidence in it, is to say that he ought to be doing what is, in the nature of the proposition, impossible, which is absurd. This means that, with respect to an *a priori* necessary truth of this extremely simple and obvious sort, merely to understand it (and, perhaps, to satisfy the other condition mentioned) is to be non-inferentially justified in being confident of it. And we must regard *this* sort of justification for being confident of a proposition as an infallible sort because we cannot allow it to be possible to have just this sort of justification for being confident of a false proposition: only with respect to propositions we take to be self-evident *a priori truths* can we allow that merely uderstanding them (and, perhaps, not believing that a contradiction is deducible from them) is sufficient to give justification for being confident of them. My certainty that it is impossible to have such a justification for being confident of a false proposition is, really, just the same as my confidence that it is impossible for those propositions, with respect to which I am confident that we have such justification, to be false.

What of those *a priori* truths that it is possible to understand fully without yet seeing that they are true? Must a justification for claiming to know any such truth be fallible? No. Such a justification must always be inferential – either one by deduction from self-evident truths or one by non-deductive inference from the testimony of a reliable authority (or calculating machine). But a *deductive* justification for being confident of an *a priori* truth will be infallible if it consists in the subject's having before his mind all at once – actually seeing clearly all its parts at the same time – a thoroughly self-evident proof of the truth in question; that is, a proof that proceeds entirely from self-evident premises by steps each of which is validated by a self-evident conditional But when he has such a deductive justification, the subject, in understanding all the parts of the proof, having the premises and the conditionals representing the steps therefrom clearly before his mind, *ipso facto* sees all at once the truth of the premises, the conditional steps, and (by a certain 'movement of the mind', as Descartes puts it) the conclusion: his doing the latter cannot be separated from his doing the former. So we can no more allow that a person might have such a deductive justification for confidence in a proposition that is false than we can allow that a person should have the justification of mere understanding for confidence in a false proposition. To postulate the possibility that a subject sees all at once such a proof for a proposition that is false would be to postulate the possibility that some proposition that is part of the proof could be self-evident to him, necessarily seen to be true in the mere understanding of it, and yet false.

A deductive justification for confidence in an *a priori* proposition will clearly be fallible, however, if it essentially involves confidence that has only justification that is itself fallible: for instance, confidence in the testimony of others as to the truth of some of the premises or some of the conditionals that validate the deductive steps, or confidence in either of these things that depends on the subject's *memory* that he has previously proved them. Memory is fallible. A person could be the victim of an erroneous memory-impression that he has constructed a thoroughly self-evident proof of a certain proposition (he may actually have proved something else and be misremembering the conclusion or he may be deluded in seeming to remember having done anything of the sort at all) and thereby be (fallibly) justified in being confident that he has proved it, and what he now sees to be a consequence of it, when in fact both are false. But even supposing that the proof the subject has in mind is based

on correct memory-impressions of what he has already proved, his justification will be just as fallible, since the same possibility for the justified
conclusion to be false – namely, through an incorrect memory-impression
– is allowed by the directly recognizable facts of the justifying position
whether the memory-impression is in fact correct or not, because the
correctness of a memory impression is not directly recognizable.[14]

Whether or not a given person at a given time relies on his memory in
going through the whole of a thoroughly self-evident proof depends, not
only on the length of the proof and the number of different ultimate
premises involved, but also on how much that person does in fact keep
in his mind and see all at the same time. Since this may vary from occasion to occasion and person to person we cannot say that the nature of
certain propositions is such that justifications for being confident of them
are always of the deductive but infallible sort. However, examples of
a priori truths, of which there are thoroughly self-evident proofs that it is
within the capacity of at least some people at least some of the time to see
all at once, can be found, perhaps, among the simpler propositions of
arithmetic or geometry that it is possible to understand without seeing to
be true, for example, 'The sum of any two odd numbers is an even number' or 'The sum of the internal angles of a plane triangle is equal to two
right angles.' These and others may be propositions for which it is possible
that there exist both infallible and fallible deductive justifications but no
non-inferential ones. There are, of course, many other *a priori* truths such
that it is hardly likely that any ordinary mortal can muster an infallible
deductive justification for claiming to know them. Many of these are,
however, truths that any schoolchild can easily come to know (fallibly),
for example, the proposition that $(5^2)^2 + (4^2)^2 + (6^2)^2 = 2117$.

11. *The* other class that I said contains propositions that it is possible to
claim to know with infallible justification was (b) those that are about the
subject's *own current* conscious state. Hence, no two people, and no
single person on two different occasions, can have infallible justification
for claiming to know the same proposition of this sort. Examples of propositions about my own current conscious state that are also such that I am
infallibly justified in being confident of them are 'I am conscious', 'I am
having visual experience', 'I am thinking about infallible justification',
'I am confident that I was born more than 30 years ago',[15] 'I want the

weather to warm up'[15] 'My visual experience is as if I were seeing a surface the color of yellow ochre in good light'. Each of these propositions
is such that I can be justified in being confident of it if and only if it is true.
That is, it is such that if I am confident of it and it is false then my confidence must be unjustified and the only circumstance in which my being
confident of it could be unjustified is that it is false. Some of these propositions may be such that it is possible for me to be confident of them even
though they are false. (The last example is, perhaps, the most likely.)
But this is possible with such a proposition only through *avoidable* care-
lessness or inattention on my part and never through my being the unwit-
ting victim of unnoticed slips in calculation or delusory impressions of
sense or memory or misleading appearances or evidence. Hence, my confidence in such a proposition as 'My visual experience is as if I were seeing
a surface the color of yellow ochre in good light' cannot be *justified* if the
proposition is false; if I am justified in my confidence in it then it must be
true. A subject has justification for confidence in such a proposition about
himself only when the proposition is true, so justification for confidence
in such a proposition about oneself is infallible. Conversely, a person's
confidence in a proposition of this special sort about himself must be
justified if the proposition is true. Given that I am having visual experience as if seeing the color yellow ochre in good light and I am confident that
I am, what circumstance could possibly make it the case that, nevertheless,
I *ought no* to be confident that I am? Since all that is required for my
confidence in such a proposition to be justified is that it be true, its being
true gives me non-inferential (as well as infallible) justification for being
confident of it. Not all propositions about a subject's current conscious
state are of this special sort, but for those that are, justification of confidence in them is infallible and non-inferential.[16]

There is a possibility that could cause some confusion here. It is possible
for a person sincerely to say 'My visual experience is as if I were seeing
yellow ochre' and be expressing a false proposition, not through avoidable
and careless haste or inattention, but through erroneous but justified
belief as to what color 'yellow ochre' is standardly used to designate. But
this person does not have justified but false belief in the proposition
expressed by 'My visual experience is as if I were seeing yellow ochre' that
I claim it is possible to have infallible non-inferential justification for
being confident of. That sentence can be used to express a different propo-

sition, one that would be more strictly expressed by '"Yellow ochre" is standardly used to designate this color that my visual experience is as if I were seeing'. And this of course, is *not* a proposition for being confident of which anyone can have infallible justification. But his having (fallible) justification for being confident of *this* proposition – even supposing (as seems correct) that his being confident of it is necessary for his understanding and, hence, for his being confident of the other proposition (that his visual experience is as if he were seeing yellow ochre) – is *not* necessary for his having justification for being confident of the other proposition. If he is in a condition such that *if* he *were* to be confident that the color it is as if he sees is yellow ochre then he *would* be justified in being so – whether or not he actually is confident of or even understands that proposition – then he has justification for being confident that the color it is as if he sees is yellow ochre; and such condition is its simply being the case that the color it is as if he sees is yellow ochre.

Color-designating terms like 'yellow-ochre', 'red', 'magenta', etc., not only refer to a particular kind of color but *mean* that kind: that 'yellow' designates the color it does is a matter of meaning conventions. Whereas, in contrast, other terms that might be used to designate colors, such as 'no. 17 on Kemtone's chart of blues' or 'the present color of our house', *merely refer* to a particular kind of color: that 'the color of my true love's hair' refers to the color it does depends crucially on a fact beyond any meaning-conventions. Thus, unlike 'The color it is as if I am seeing is yellow ochre', the proposition expressed by 'The color it is as if I were seeing is approximately the same as the color of John's bicycle' is one that I could understand without having any idea as to whether or not it is true; in order to know that it is true I cannot rely merely on my understanding of it and my present visual experience but must also rely on my perception, or my memory of my perception, or someone else's report, of John's bicycle. (An expression like 'corn-flower blue' or 'robin's egg blue' might be imagined to have shifted from the status of merely referring to a kind of color to that of meaning it. This would involve a shift from using comparison to a particular object or sort of object (where 'sort' does not refer to color) as the conclusive criterion of application to using memories of *the color itself*, freed from reference to the particular samples from which they were acquired, whose identity and other natures may be forgotten. 'Robin's egg blue' has acquired the status of *meaning* a certain shade of blue if it is conceivable that all those who think they know what color the term designates and agree in picking out samples of it could discover, or even be led by plausible evidence to think, that robin's eggs are not and never have been of that color.)

The propositions about the intrinsic nature of a subject's current conscious state that are such that he could have justified confidence in them when they are false are ones in which confidence could be justified only by deductive inference. For example: 'I am having a visual experience as if seeing three distinct star-shapes, each with a different number of points, whose total number of points is 15' or 'I am having a visual experience as if seeing three distinct star-shapes, each with a different number of points and such that the sum of the squares of the squares of the three numbers of points is 2117.' For the first of these, it might be possible for someone to see all at once, without counting or adding, the total number of points on the three star-shapes and thereby be infallibly justified in his confidence in that proposition (one could not be justified in *that* sort of way in being confident of the wrong number). But nothing like that is possible for the second. In either case it is possible for someone to have a fallible deductive justification for being confident of the proposition – by going through a sequential process of counting and performing arithmetical operations on the numbers arrived at – when it is false.[17] There is then room for the justification arrived at to be misleading, through errors of memory or in other ways. When deduction is peformed, not by thinking the propositions and attending to the relations between them, but by the mechanical manipulation of signs – as it often is in arithmetical calculation – there intrudes another sort of possibility of error in one's justifying memory-impression that one has deduced certain consequences from certain premises, not an error of memory but error arising from unnoticed slips in the manipulations of the signs. In such a case the erroneous belief to which the slip immediately gives rise at the time it is made is not justified. It then could have been and ought to have been avoided. But the erroneous memory-impression with which it leaves the subject does *later* justify his erroneous belief that he has found a certain operation to yield certain results.

The classifications of justifications for knowledge claims that we have been discussing – inferential and non-inferential, fallible and infallible – can obviously be applied also to cases of *knowledge*, according to the kinds of justifications they contain: a minimally sufficient condition for a person's knowing that p is *inferential knowledge* just in case the justification for his claiming to know that p that it includes is inferential or compound with an inferential component; a minimally sufficient condition for a person's knowing that p is *fallible knowledge* if and only if the justification for his claiming to know that p that it includes is a fallible justification; and so forth.

12. There is one last thing to note about condition (3). The fact that it is phrased 'S's being confident that p *is supported by* his having disinterested justification for being so', rather than simply 'S has disinterested justification for being confident that p', is not without significance. This phrasing is required in order to rule out the following possibility[18]: S has two different justifications for being confident that p and only one of them is externally conclusive (for example, S remembers having been told, 'I know that p', by each of two different people whom he had no reason to distrust, but only one of these people was speaking the truth and the other really had no belief at all as to whether or not p); but the other justification is the only one on which S's confidence that p is based. If S's confidence thus fails to be based on a justification of the sort required for knowledge, then S fails to know that p.

What would it be for a person's confidence that p to be based on one but not on another justification that he has for being confident that p? This possibility is not as easily realized as one might at first think. Bear in mind that a person's having a justification means that the justification is directly recognizable to him, needing only clear-headed reflection or an effort at recall and no further calculation or investigation in order to be consciously recognized. It is not sufficient for realization of the possibility in question that the one justification be the only one the subject has explicitly articulated (out loud or to himself) or be the only one he would think to articulate if he tried to answer the question of how he knows. For if it is also true that he would come up with the other justification if the deficiency of the first, on the matter of external conclusiveness, were exposed to him, then his confidence that p is supported and sustained, in the relevant sense, by the fact that the other, externally conclusive justification is there in his field of direct recognizability. It is *not* supported by it, I think, only if it is the case that he *would not* move to the conclusive justification *if* the deficiency of the other one were exposed, but would instead lose his confidence that *p* (perhaps because of some more or less temporary confusion he has that would prevent him from recognizing the conclusive justification, or because of an unreasonable reluctance to trust that particular justification). If the subject's conclusive justification is inferential and he unreasonably lacks confidence in its premiss, then he could not coherently appeal to that premiss in order to justify his confidence in the conclusion; if his justification for being confident that *q* fails to make him confident of it, then he can hardly be taken seriously if he says that, because he knows that *p* can be properly inferred with confidence from *q*, his justification for confidence that *q* does nevertheless make him confident that *p*. So we can say *S*'s being confident that *p* is *supported* by a particular justification he has for being so if and only if he would turn to that justification, and could coherently do so, if he were trying to justify his being confident that *p* and had lost all other justifications he now happens to have for that confidence.

NOTES

[1] It might be argued that an exception to this must be made for justified claims to know arising out of *intention*. It might be said that if *S* fully intends to do a certain thing in certain circumstances it follows that (a) he is confident, and justified in being confident and claiming to know, that he will try to do that thing in those circumstances if further circumstances then permit him to try to do it and also that (b) he *wants* it to be the case that he will try... etc. So we seem to have a condition that both justifies a claim to know a certain proposition and also involves the subject's wanting that proposition to be true and, so, is not disinterested.

It may be correct to answer this by saying that a proper analysis of *fully intending* to do a thing will show that it is one part of this state that entails that its subject is confident with justification that he will try to do it... etc. and another independent part that entails that he wants it to be the case that he will try... etc.; so that the *minimally* sufficient condition here for being justified in claiming to know that one will try... does *not* entail the subject's wanting it to be the case that one will try... (I heard such an analysis proposed by H. P. Grice in a paper read at the University of Washington in Spring 1970, according to which fully intending to do a thing is broken down into something called *willing* to do it and confidence that one's willing will issue in one's trying to do it if circumstances permit. I am doubtful, however, that willing can be distinguished from mere wanting or desiring – as it must be if willing, in conjunction with the other condition, is to be necessary and sufficient for intending – except by importing into willing confidence or belief that one will (or would) try to do the thing if...) If, however, such an analysis is not correct and it must be allowed that there is a special *intentional* mode of confidence, and of being justified in being confident and claiming to know, that one will try to do a thing if..., then we seem to have a choice of two alternatives. We might just allow this sort of case to be an exception to the principle

that disinterestedness is necessary for a justification for confidence to be also a justification for a claim to know; or we might amplify the explanation of interestedness so as
to exclude this sort of case, by saying that in that explanation I mean by "*wanting* it to
be the case that *p*" something stronger than the sense of "wanting" implied by intending:
I mean "wanting" in that sense in which it makes sense to say "Although he intends to
do it, he does not *want* to do it". Since in this work I am not much interested in this
special sort of intentional confidence or knowledge it makes little difference here which
alternative I choose.

² Harrison (1962) gives a sound critique of the performative treatment of 'I know
that *p*'.

³ There may be good reason to object to talk of an 'extended sense' here and to think it
better to use 'sense' in such a way that 'know' does not have a different sense when
applied to my dog. If so, I would put my point by saying that I am interested in the
necessary conditions of knowing in those cases of the appropriate application of 'know'
where the question of the subject's being justified or not in his confidence is also appropriate, and in such cases justification is necessary for knowing. A somewhat analogous case: 'wants' & 'desires' do not, we are very much inclined to say, apply in a different
sense to a dog; nevertheless, their application to a mature human being differs from
their application to a dog in the respect that the question of what the mature human
being would *say* if giving an honest answer to the question whether he desires *X* or not
is applicable and, necessarily, relevant: that he would give an affirmative answer is,
necessarily, some reason to think (although not necessary for its being the case) that
he does desire *X*. Here would seem to be a clear example of a term such that, although it
is true *a priori* that certain considerations are relevant to its application in certain sorts
of cases and also true that they cannot be relevant in other sorts of cases where it is
sensibly applied, it does not follow that the term has a different sense in its application
to the two sorts of cases. 'Knows' and the consideration of whether or not the subject
is justified in being confident may be like that.

⁴ For argument that there is see Bennett (1964). For what looks to me like an effective
effort to describe what would be counter-examples see Kirk (1967).

⁵ Malcolm (1952a) has suggested, I think rightly, that the denial that it is logically
possible to know such propositions is either necessarily false or else fails to use 'know'
to express the concept that it is ordinarily used to express.

⁶ As Malcolm (1950) has effectively pointed out.

⁷ Cf. Prichard's (1950) well-known remark (p. 88) that "whenever we know something
we either do, or at least can, by reflecting, directly know that we are knowing it..."

⁸ We obtain a paraphrase of the incorrect interpretation of the observation, which
leads to the absurd conclusion that when one knows something one can directly recognize that one knows it, if we omit from the above paraphrase the words 'and this
claim is true' and replace the last occurrence of 'it' with 'this claim'. One might be
tempted to do this by the thought that the claim's being true has already been postulated in the initial clause, 'If I know that *p*', and it is redundant to say something of the
form 'If *q*, then if *q* then *r*'. But this overlooks the fact that the conditional 'if I claim
to know that *p* and this claim is true then this claim expresses something that I know'
is not asserted in the paraphrase to be itself consequent upon my knowing that *p*, but
rather it is *the availability of that conditional to my direct recognition* that is asserted to
be consequent upon my knowing that *p*. It involves no redundancy to say something of
the form 'If *q*, then I can directly recognize that if *q* then *r*'.

⁹ That it is not impossible has been argued by Kyburg (1965 and 1970). That it is

impossible has been argued by Hintikka and Hilpinen (1965), by Hilpinen (1968), by Swain (1970a), and by Lehrer (1970).

[10] This example, often referred to as "the lottery paradox," was suggested by Kyburg (1965).

[11] Why not here the simpler proposition that (b') at least one of the propositions specified in (a) is false? The assumption that (b') is either true or false, together with the assumption that it is a member of (a) and that no other members of (a) are false, (as Keith Lehrer pointed out to me) leads to a contradiction: (b') is true if and only if (b') is false.

[12] A point made by Aristotle: "... we do not choose everything for the sake of something else (for at that rate the process would go on to infinity, so that our desire would be empty and vain)..." (*Nicomachean Ethics*, 1094^{a}19–20, translated by W. D. Ross).

[13] I do not have a satisfactory characterization of what it is for a truth to be *a priori*, but I hope that one might be worked out along the following lines: a truth is *a priori* just in case it is necessary and either it can be demonstrated *a priori* or it is formally related to a truth demonstrable *a priori* in such a way (which I don't know how to define generally) as to make it reasonable to hope, in the absence of an *a priori* demonstration to the contrary, that it is demonstrable *a priori* if it is true. For example, Goldbach's still unproved conjecture that every even number is the sum of two primes (which mathematicians generally believe to be true) may or may not be demonstrable *a priori*, but it is a universal generalization every instantiation of which we know to be such that either it or its negation is demonstrable *a priori*; the proposition (if it is one) that never in the expansion of π would there occur the sequence '777' may or may not be demonstrable *a priori*, but it is the negation of a proposition that, if it were true, would be demonstrable *a priori* by the same method by which many truths as to what occurs in the expansion of π have been demonstrated *a priori*.

A proposition is demonstrable *a priori* just in case it is either self-evident, that is, such that merely understanding it is enough to be justified in being confident of it, or deducible from self-evident truths, where deducibility is defined as follows: p is deducible from q if and only if there is a sequence of one or more conditional propositions such that q is the antecedent of the first, p is the consequent of the last, the consequent of each is identical with the antecedent of the next in the sequence, and all the conditionals in the sequence are self-evident.

Where 'If p then q' is self-evident but neither 'p' nor 'q' is, it is natural to think of a justification for being confident that p as equally, and equally directly, a justification for being confident that q. The interesting thing, of course, is that 'self-evidently follows from' does not express a transitive relation: 'If p then q' and 'If q then r' may be self-evident when 'If p then r' is not.

[14] Descartes, in his discussion of Rules VI, VII, and XI of his *Rules for the Direction of the Mind*, finds important the difference between deduction that depends on memory and deduction that the understanding is "able to apprehend as a whole and all at once"; he affirms that to approach nearer the latter sort of deduction (through the rapidity and uninterruptedness of the mind's movement through the whole deduction, so that it becomes less clear that there is dependence on memory) "affords a more certain knowledge of the conclusion we have in view". (Kemp-Smith (1957), pp. 52–53).

[15] In counting these two examples as reporting current features of my conscious state I do not suppose that they report states or processes of which I could be said to be consciously aware throughout the period that they are states of mine, in the way that I am

consciously aware of a headache or a sequence of thoughts while I am having it. Yet I am aware that I am (at least in some ways) confident of this and that, that I want this and that, etc., in the sense that I could not, were I to consider the question, sincerely deny that these propositions are true. They report dispositional properties of mine that I can directly recognize.

[16] After I had arrived at this explication of how one's justification for confidence in certain propositions about one's current conscious state is infallible I discovered that Alston (1971, p. 234) offers the following as one plausible candidate for what might be meant by saying that a subject has 'privileged access' to his own current mental states:

> "Each person is so related to propositions ascribing current mental states to himself that it is logically impossible both for such a proposition to be true and for him not to be justified in believing it to be true; while no one else is so related to such propositions."

Alston says, p. 236, that he regards this version of the privileged access thesis as less defensible than a version that requires *all* of a person's beliefs about his own current mental states (not just those that are true) to be justified; but it is not clear to me why he does so.

[17] A justification for confidence in a proposition like the first that is arrived at simply by counting may be regarded as deductive: the premiss of the deduction is some such proposition as 'I have just completed a correctly executed process of counting all the points (that is, I correlated with each point in succession, omitting none and taking none twice, a number, beginning with 1 and successively taking the next in the standard order, omitting none and taking none twice) and the last number I arrived at was 15' and the subject's memory-impression that he has done so gives him his justification for being confident of this premiss.

[18] Which I thank William Alston for pointing out to me.

CHAPTER IV

THE GENERAL CONDITIONS OF KNOWLEDGE:
EXTERNAL CONCLUSIVENESS

1. If all justification of confidence had to be infallible then conditions (1), (2), and (3) of our general definition would be sufficient for knowing that something is the case. But the possibility of fallible justification for a claim to know brings with it the possibility that conditions (1)–(3) should be satisfied and yet S fail to know that p, because the facts giving him his fallible justification do so only because they are protected by his ignorance of, or false but justified beliefs about, certain other facts, ones such that were he to learn of them the question of whether or not p would be entirely reopened for him (if he were being reasonable), his justification for being confident that p would be wiped out. Condition (4) must rule out just all such possible circumstances in which (1) and (2) are satisfied and (3) is satisfied by a fallible justification for claiming to know that p and yet S does not *in virtue of that justification* know that p. Let us speak of a circumstance that falsifies condition (4) with respect to a particular justification for claiming to know that p as *defeating* that justification for claiming to know that p. Let us consider first kinds of circumstance that can defeat non-inferential justifications and then kinds that can defeat inferential ones.

A non-inferential justification that is fallible entails, besides some positive conditions, the negative condition that the subject lacks any justification for a belief that would give him reason, despite the presence of the positive conditions, to lack confidence that p. Suppose, for example, p is the proposition that I have come to know that Harrison was President between Cleveland's terms and the positive condition of my non-inferential justification for being confident that p is that it seems to me that I definitely remember having learned that. Then a good example of the kind of proposition that the negative condition says that I must not at the same time have justification for believing is the proposition that I have recently had a very great many strong and clear memory impressions as to facts I have learned about American history that turned out to be mistaken. Notice that the justifications the negative condition rules out must be such as to make confidence in the proposition in question *far* from justi-fied, definitely unreasonable, just on the basis of the positive condition; they are not merely such as to make a slight doubt reasonable (as would, in the example just given, the belief that lately I have confidently misre-membered one or two things about American history[1]).

Now the sort of proposition that the negative condition of a given fal-lible non-inferential justification says that the subject must not have justification for believing is also just the sort of proposition that if true will prevent that non-inferential justification from giving its subject know-ledge that *p* even if it is true that *p* and he is confident that *p*. For if such a proposition is true then it is too much of an *accident* that in having that non-inferential justification for being confident of *p* the subject has a justification for being confident of a *truth*.

Suppose, for example, that I am confident that I see something that looks as would an elephant on the snow outside my living room window and am non-inferentially justified in being so because I have a visual experience as if seeing something that looks as would an elephant... etc. and have no special reason to lack confidence that I see something of that sort. If it happens also to be true that I have (unsuspected by me) ingested a drug that typically causes hallucinations of animals then, even though it may be true that I see something of that sort, it is, *in that circumstance* (and having no other justification than the one mentioned), too much a matter of luck that what I have that justification for being confident of is true for my confidence backed by that justification to be said to be knowledge. Or consider again the example where *S*'s justification for being confident that he has learned that Harrison was President between Cleveland's terms is his strong memory-impression that he has learned that and this memory-impression happens to be correct (*S* does remember that he learned that). If a great many other similarly strong memory-impressions about similar matters that *S* currently has are incorrect then, even though this is un-known to him, it becomes too accidental that this one among *S*'s current memory-impressions is correct for his confidence justified only by this impression to be knowledge.[2] In general we can say that for any (fallible) non-inferential justification (that is, any condition minimally sufficient for such justification) condition (4) entails that there fails to be true any propo-sition such that the justification in question entails that the subject does not have justification for believing that proposition.

2. Consider now *inferential* justifications. S has an inferential justification for being confident that p, we said, if and only if there is a proposition q such that (i) S has justification for being confident that q and (ii) either (a) S has justification for confidence that p is deducible from q or (b) S has justification for confidence that p can be non-deductively inferred with confidence from q and there are no propositions $r_1, ..., r_n$ such that S has justification for believing each of $r_1, ..., r_n$ and p cannot be nondeductively inferred with confidence from the conjunction of q, $r_1, ..., r_n$. We may speak of q here as the *premiss* of the inferential justification and the proposition that p is deducible from q, or the proposition that p can be non-deductively inferred with confidence from q, as its *inference rule*; and we may speak of such a justification as justification for being confident that *p by inference from q*. It is easy to see that S's having a (fallible) inferential justification will not make his confidence that p into knowledge that p, even if p is true, if the premiss or the inference rule is false. It is clear, for example, that if S is confident with justification of the truth that R flew to California today by inference from the proposition (of which he is confident with justification) that R flew to Los Angeles, California, today, and the truth is that R flew to San Francisco and not Los Angeles, then S does not thereby *know* that R flew to California today.[3] If S is confident with justification that Harrison was President between Cleveland's terms by non-deductive inference from the false proposition (of which he is nevertheless confident with justification) that his friend A confidently remembers it (when in fact he was just making a lucky guess), then surely S does not thereby know that Harrison was President between Cleveland's terms. If S is confident with justification of the truth that there is a fruit tree outside his window (suppose there is an apple tree there) by deduction from the proposition that he sees an orange tree there, when he is (unknown to him) having a visual hallucination of an orange tree, then he does not thereby know that there is a fruit tree outside his window. To give an example involving a false inference rule: suppose a teacher of formal logic slips up and tells his students that a certain somewhat complex argument-form is deductively valid, when in fact it is not. Then one of his students may be confident with justification that a certain conclusion is true because he sees it is related by that argument-form to certain premisses he knows to be true; but he does not on that account know that the conclusion is true, even if it happens to be so.

If we ask *why* the inferential justification, in these cases where the premisses or inference rule is false, so clearly fails to give the subject knowledge, the answer is again that, given the actual facts, it is far too much a piece of pure luck that *that* justification is a justification for a truth. If *S*'s position giving him his justification were corrected to accord with the relevant facts (in the present case this would be a matter, not of adding justification for belief in facts in which *S* now has no reason to believe, but of replacing *S*'s justification for false belief in the premiss or the inference rule with justification for belief in the true contradictory), then his position would no longer come anywhere near to giving him justification for being confident that *p*.

3. Another possibility that must be ruled out, with respect to non-deductive inferential justifications, is this: although the premiss, inference-rule and conclusion of the justification are all true, there may also be true (unknown to the subject) a proposition such that the conclusion cannot be inferred with confidence from the conjunction of the premiss and this other truth. And this other truth may also (but need not necessarily) be such that if the subject's confidence in the conclusion is justified only by inference from that premiss then it is too much of an accident that he has justification for confidence in a truth for it to be said that he *knows* it to be true. For example, suppose that *S* is justified in being confident that *R* flew to Los Angeles yesterday by inference from the true premiss that *R*'s husband has just told *S*, with apparent sincerity, that *R* flew to Los Angeles yesterday. Now suppose that *R*'s husband does not, in fact, believe that *R* flew to Los Angeles yesterday; he was lying when he told *S* that she did. Given this circumstance, we cannot say that *S knows* that *R* flew to Los Angeles yesterday by inference from this testimony of *R*'s husband, even if it happens that *R* did fly to Los Angeles yesterday. The conjunction of the proposition that *R*'s husband lied in his testimony with the premiss of *S*'s inferential justification (that he gave such testimony with apparent sincerity) is not merely a proposition from which the conclusion cannot be inferred with *confidence*: it is a proposition from which the conclusion cannot reasonably be inferred with any significant degree of belief at all. If *S* were to acquire justification for believing that *R*'s husband lied in his testimony while retaining all the elements of this inferential justification that are compatible with his having justification for be-

lieving that R's husband lied (that is, justification for confidence in the premiss and the inference rule and his lacking justification for other beliefs such that the conclusion could not be inferred with confidence from the conjunction of their objects and the premiss) then those elements plus the new justification would be *very far* from giving him justification for being confident of the conclusion, would in fact give him no justification even for believing the conclusion.

By altering the preceding example slightly we may illustrate an interesting complication that may be described abstractly as follows: Although S's justification for claiming to know that p by *inference from q* may be defeated by a certain fact r (such that p cannot be inferred with any significant degree of belief from the conjunction of q and r) S may have another justification for being confident that p, by *inference from the conjunction of q and some other proposition t*, that is *not* defeated by the fact that r because p *can* be inferred with confidence from the conjunction of q, r, and t and S's justification for being confident that t is not defeated by the fact that r. Let p be, as before, the proposition that R flew to Los Angeles yesterday, but change the premiss q to the proposition that R's husband told S, with apparent sincerity, that he took R to the airport yesterday and put her on the plane to Los Angeles; then let the fact r (that defeats S's justification for claiming to know that p by inference from q) be the fact that R's husband did not go near the airport yesterday and let the proposition t (such that S is justifiedly confident of it and p can be inferred with confidence from the conjunction of q, r, and t) be the proposition that R's husband would not try to deceive S as to R's whereabouts. We must suppose, of course, that S's justification for claiming to know that R's husband would not practice *that* deceit is such as not to be defeated by the fact that he has deceived S about his own whereabouts, but this is entirely possible: S's justification for being confident that t may, for instance, be by inference from such a proposition as that R's husband would not lie without good reason and has no motive to deceive S about R's wherabouts that could equal in his mind the consideration that R's whereabouts are of great importance to S.

4. Let us now consider some importantly different examples. Suppose that thousands of people have a justification for claiming to know the truth that Cornell lost its game to Columbia by more than 30 points last

night, solely by inference from the true premiss that they see in today's newspaper under the heading 'Last Night's Scores' the line 'Columbia 93 Cornell 57.' But suppose also that Cornell's coach (unhinged by the magnitude of the defeat) is telling people, with apparent sincerity, that the newspaper has erred and that the score was really 58–57. Now the conjunction of the proposition as to what the newspaper says and the proposition as to what Cornell's coach is seriously telling people is not a proposition from which it can be inferred *with confidence* that the score the newspaper gives is the correct one. Yet it seems most implausible to suggest that the coach's irrational prevarications can render false the justified claims of all those newspaper readers to know the score.[4]

Or, for another example, suppose that I am justified in claiming to know that I was born on July 11 by inference from the premiss that my parents have, with apparent sincerity, said this on many occasions and they must have known the date of my birth. But suppose that someone in the County Clerk's office of the county where I was born has just prepared an official copy of my birth certificate on which my birth date is given as July 21. (Suppose also that this is the result of a copying error and that my parents were right in what they told me.) From the conjunction of the premiss mentioned and this additional truth as to the date appearing on a newly prepared official copy of my birth certificate it cannot properly be inferred with confidence that I was born on July 11: the date on the new copy of my birth certificate would, if I came to know of it, give me reason to doubt, to lack confidence, that what my parents told me was correct (or else that my memory of what my parents told me is correct). Yet it seems implausible to suggest that such an error in a copy of my birth certificate can, even though unknown to me. prevent its being the case that I know that I was born on July 11 by inference from the testimony of my parents (which was, in fact, testimony as to what they knew).[5]

Thus it seems that S's knowing that p by inference from q is *not* defeated by just any truth r such that p cannot be inferred with confidence from the conjunction of q and r. The important thing to notice in each of the examples just given is that the 'outside' truth r that, despite its satisfying the condition on r just mentioned, fails to defeat the subject's knowing that p by inference from q has the following property: even if the subject were to have justification for believing r, if he were at the same time to retain all the properties entailed by his inferential justification

(whose premiss is q) that are compatible with his justifiedly believing r –
that is, to continue to have justification for being confident of the premiss
and the inference rule and continue to lack justification for belief in any
other propositions (than r) such that p cannot be inferred with confidence
from the conjunction of the premiss with those other propositions – then
those elements would still make it reasonable for him to believe that p to
some degree, though not with confidence. In fact, in the examples given,
it would not be unreasonable for someone in the positions described to
choose to give more weight to the premiss and to believe fairly strongly on
its basis that the conclusion is true and that the conflicting evidence must
have some explanation compatible with that conclusion. No similar thing
could be said about the examples where an outside truth r does defeat S's
inferential justification for claiming to know that p: take the example
where S, having justification for being confident that R flew to Los Angeles today just by inference from the premiss that R's husband told S with
apparent sincerity that he put R on the plane to Los Angeles today, learns
that R's husband was never near the airport today: it would be most
unreasonable for S to continue to *believe* (though with less than confidence) *just on the basis of R's husband's testimony* (without any other
'backup' evidence) that R flew to Los Angeles today and that her husband's not having gone near the airport must have some explanation
compatible with that conclusion.

I venture to generalize that in every case of inferential knowledge that
p where there is an outside truth r that in conjunction with the premiss of
the subject's justification does not support confident inference to p but
also does not defeat this justification, this will be because the conjunction
of r and the premiss of the justification would still justify some degree of
belief that p: they are not such as to give little or no justification even for
believing that p. If this is correct, then we can say that the possibility with
respect to inferential justifications for confidence in p that condition (4),
external conclusiveness, must rule out is this: there is true some
proposition r such that were S to have justification for believing
that r and to retain all the properties entailed by his inferential
justification for confidence in p that are compatible with his having
justification for believing that r, then those properties plus the
justification for believing that r would be very far from justifying him
in confidence that p.

5. Indeed, the phrasing we have just used provides an accurate way of summarizing all the possibilities we have recognized so far, with respect to both inferential and non-inferential justification, that external conclusiveness needs to rule out. In all of them, S's justification for claiming to know that p fails to give S knowledge that p because there is a truth r such that were S to have justification for believing that r and to retain every property entailed by his justification for claiming to know that p that is compatible with his having justification for believing r, then those elements would be very far from justifying S in being confident that p. It is obvious that any *compound* justification for claiming to know that p will also be defeated by a fact r of that description. Whatever justification S may have for claiming to know that p, if there is a fact r of that description, then, though it may be true that p, it will not be true that S *knows* that p on the basis of *that* justification.

I see no way of giving any informative general criterion for *how* far from justifying confidence is far enough to count as *very far* for the purposes of this description. In fact this may vary depending on the sort of justification in question: the examples we have considered that involve non-deductive inferential justification suggest that, for that sort of justification, *very* far is so far as to give little or no justification for believing that p at all; but with respect to *memory* justifications the example given at the end of Section 1 (p. 68) suggests that very far need not be quite so far. But it does seem clear in general that, for any given justification for claiming to know that p, the crucial difference between a justification-weakening proposition r whose truth would clearly falsify a claim to know that p based on that justification and one whose truth would clearly not do this, is always that the former would weaken the justification much more than the latter, often to the point of wiping it out altogether.

In any case, the line is far from sharp and examples can be imagined where one cannot say with assurance that a given outside fact does or does not defeat a given justification for claiming to know that p. Suppose that S is in a market looking at what appears to be a large display of fruit. Looking at a particular piece, S is confident with justification that it is, as it appears to be, an apple. But suppose also that sprinkled randomly through the display at a ratio of about 1 to 10 there are very good wax imitations of pieces of fruit. It seems clear that this fact, were S to learn of it, would give S reason to doubt, at least very slightly, to be at least a little short of completely confident, if all he has to go on is visible appearance, that the piece he is looking at is an apple. Yet it also seems clear that this fact, as long as S is unaware of it, does not defeat his claim to know that he sees an apple on the basis of the visible appearances he sees and his knowledge of what apples look like and what is likely to be found in markets. The conjunction of this truth and S's premiss is still a proposition from which it can be inferred with a fair degree of belief that what he sees is an apple (although this is not a matter of evidence still having weight *against conflicting* evidence, as in the examples given in Section 4). On the other hand, if the display were 90% composed of wax imitations of fruit then, even though S happens to be looking at one of the few genuine apples, that fact is not only such as to ruin his justification for being confident that he sees an apple should be learn of it, but it also such that S clearly cannot *know* that the piece he is looking at is an apple just by looking at it: in the circumstances he could so easily have had just the same sort of visible-appearance justification for claiming to know that he sees an apple when not seeing one. It also seems clear that no precise answer can be given to the question of how large the proportion of imitations to genuine pieces of fruit must be before it does begin to defeat S's claim to know that he sees an apple based just on looking.

6. Even when all the possibilities so far canvassed are ruled out there remains another way in which a justification S has for claiming to know a truth p can be defeated by outside facts if this justification is inferential, or compound with an inferential component. Then it is possible that S's justification for claiming to know the *premiss* should be defeated by an external fact in one of the ways already discussed although S's justification by inference from this premiss to p is not. If so, then this latter justification cannot give S knowledge that p, since, of course, one can know that p on the basis of a justification by inference from q only if one knows that q. Suppose that S has justification for claiming to know that (p) Bertrand Russell was born in 1873 just by inference from the premiss that (q) N is confident that he remembers having read that Russell was born in that year in Russell's autobiography; and S has justification for claiming to know this premiss q, just by inference from the premiss that (t) N has just told S that he confidently remembers that. Now suppose

that somehow this latter premiss, t, is false but the former, q, is not (for example, N wishing to mislead S, actually said "1872" but S misheard it as "1873"). Now not-t does not defeat S's justification for claiming to know that p by inference from q: it is *not* the case that if S had believed the negation of t while still possessing justified confidence in q and in the inference rule from q to p and lacking justification for belief in any other propositions such that their conjunction with q would not support a confident inference to p, then in those elements he would be far from being justified in being confident that p: those elements would in fact still give him justification for being confident that p. But the fact that t is false clearly does defeat S's inferential justification from t to q.

Now, in order to rule out this possibility that S may have no undefeated justification for claiming to know the *premiss* of his inferential justification for claiming to know that p, we do not really need to take account of any new basic possibilities. For if any of the justifications that S in fact has for claiming to know the premiss is defeated by some external fact it will be so in one of the ways already considered; and if any of his justifications for claiming to know some other proposition that he must be justified in claiming to know in order to be justified in claiming to know this premiss is defeated by an outside fact it will be so in one of the ways already considered; and so on.

Let us say that the ways we have already considered are ways in which a justification may be *locally* defeated. The summary of these given above (Section 5) defines this expression: A justification S has for being confident and claiming to know that p is *locally defeated* just in case there is a truth r such that were S to be justified in believing that r and to retain every property entailed by the justification in question that is compatible with his having justification for believing that r then those elements would be very far from justifying him in being confident that p.

Now what we want to say is this: S has justification for being confident that p that is undefeated *tout court* – globally undefeated – just in case he has the right sort of hierarchy of justifications none of which is locally defeated. The right sort of hierarchy must have a non-inferential base and be sufficient to give S justification for claiming to know that p. Such a hierarchy, which we can call a *global* justification for claiming to know that p, will exist just in case the following condition obtains:

(G)   There is a sequence of one or more sets of propositions $\langle \Sigma_1,$ ..., $\Sigma_n \rangle$ such that $\Sigma_n = \{p\}$, S has non-inferential justification for confidence in each member of Σ_1, and each Σ_i, where $i > 1$, satisfies one of the following conditions:

(a) Σ_i is a unit set and S has justification for being confident of its member by inference from some member of some set earlier in the sequence,

(b) each member of Σ_i is the sole member of a unit set earlier in the sequence, or

(c) Σ_i is a unit set whose member is a conjunction of two or more propositions, these conjuncts are the members of Σ_{i-1}, and the compound of the justifications that S has for being confident of each of the members of Σ_{i-1} constitutes a justification for the member of Σ_i.

It is obvious that if each justification comprising such a global justification for being confident that p is locally undefeated then, and only then, the global justification itself will, as a whole, satisfy the condition that defines local undefeat: that is, there will be no truth r such that, were S to be justified in believing that r and to retain all his properties entailed by his having the global justification in question that are compatible with his having justification for believing that r, then those elements would be very far from justifying him in being confident that p. So we can say that a locally undefeated justification that S has for being confident that p is also globally undefeated and, hence, *externally conclusive* if and only if it is part of a global justification that S has for being confident that p that contains no locally defeated justifications. And S has at least one such undefeated global justification if and only if there is no truth r such that, were S to be justified in believing that r and to retain all of his properties that are compatible with his having justification for believing that r, then he would be very far from being justified in being confident that p.

7. I am now in a position to give the explanation regarding the lottery paradox that I promised in Chapter III, Section 7.

Let L be the proposition that there will be a perfectly fair drawing of a single winning ticket from a lottery of one million tickets numbered from 1 to 1,000,000. Let $P_1, \ldots, P_{1,000,000}$ be the propositions 'Ticket no.1 will be the winner',..., 'Ticket no. 1,000,000 will be the winner', respectively. Thus the set of propositions $\{L,\ \sim P_1,..., \ \sim P_{1,000,000}\}$ is minimally inconsistent, that is, it is inconsistent and no proper subset of it is inconsistent.

Why is it, as we saw that intuition suggests, that a person S who is confident and can claim to know with justification that L is true can*not* by non-deductive inference from L have justification for being completely confident of or claiming to know the truth of any of $\sim P_1,...,\ \sim P_{1,000,000}$? My answer is this: although S's justified confidence in L gives him the premiss of an inferential justification for believing, say, $\sim P_1$ to some considerable degree, it also gives him the premiss of an inferential justification for being sure that *there is* a truth r such that, were he to be justified in believing that r and to retain all his properties that are compatible with his having justification for believing that r, then he would be very far from being justified in being confident of $\sim P_1$. What truth r? The truth that would be formed by disjoining P_1 (which is the proposition that ticket no. 1 be the winner) with that P_i such that i is the number of the winning ticket. It is obvious that L entails that there is exactly one truth of that description. If S were to acquire justification for believing *that* truth while retaining all his properties that are compatible with his having justification for believing it (including the property of having no reason to regard either of P_1 and P_i as more likely than the other), then, obviously, he would be very far from being justified in being confident that $\sim P_1$.

In general it seems to be the case that S can add p to the body of propositions that he has justification for being confident of and claiming to know, by non-deductive inference from a proposition q already belonging to that body, only if q does not support an inference to the belief that there is a truth r such that, were S to have justification for believing that r and to retain all his properties compatible with his having justification for believing that r, then he would be very far from being justified in confidence that p. It is not only the fact that it explains our prior intuition about the lottery example that suggests this general principle. It is also supported by the consideration that it seems absurd on the face of it to try to assert the following:

> I know that p, but I have – in the very justification I have for claiming to know that p – justification for thinking that there

is true a proposition such that were I to have justification for
believing that truth, while otherwise remaining as I am, then
I would be very far from justified in claiming to know that p.

Indeed this proposition remains just as absurd if 'justification for thinking that there is true' is replaced with 'no justification for being confident
that there is not true'.[6] The fact that *this* cannot possibly be true means that
if a person S has a justification for being confident and claiming to know
that p then he must therein also have a justification for being confident
and claiming to know that there is *no* truth r such that, were he to have
justification for believing that r while retaining all his properties that are
compatible with his having justification for believing that r, then he would
be very far from justified in confidence that p. That is, a justification for
claiming to know that p is itself a justification for confidence in its own
external conclusiveness. We can call this feature of a justification for a
claim to know its being *internally* conclusive. Although not every justification for a claim to know need be externally conclusive, every one must be
internally conclusive.

8. From the preceding considerations it follows that if S has justification
for claiming to know that p and is confident that he knows that p (from
which, obviously, it follows that he is confident that p) then S is also
justified in claiming to know that he knows that p; for then he will be
justified in claiming to know that all of the conditions of propositional
knowledge, (1)–(4), are satisfied.[7] This has just been shown for (4). It is
obvious for (1). As for (2) and (3), since they are directly recognizable to S,
his satisfying them by itself gives him justification for claiming to know
that he satisfies them.

It must be the case also that, if S knows that p and is confident that he
does, then he knows that he knows that p. For, first, his confidence that he
knows that p must be *supported* by the justification it follows that he has
for being confident that (1)–(4) are satisfied, the main substance of which
is just his externally conclusive justification for being confident that p. He
could not understand his claim to know that p and be unwilling to cite as
justification for his confidence that he knows that p what he is willing to
cite as (disinterested) justification for his confidence that p. Second, this
justification he has for being confident that (1)–(4) are satisfied (for claim-

ing to know that he knows that p) is externally conclusive with respect to each of (1)–(4), given that each of them is true (he knows that p). This is obvious in the case of (1)–(3). As for (4), it entails that there is no truth r that would defeat S's justification for claiming to know that p and the fact that this justification must be *internally* conclusive (which was argued in the last paragraph of Section 7) means that any truth r that would defeat his justification for confidence that his justification for claiming to know that p is externally conclusive would also defeat his justification for claiming to know that p: there could not be a truth r such that were he to acquire justification for belief in it he would be in a position to say, 'I am still justified in the way that I was in claiming to know that p but I am no longer justified in being sure that *that* justification is externally conclusive.'

9. Finally, note that condition (4) renders (1) redundant, since if it were not true that p then $\sim p$ would be a truth r that would falsify (4) with respect to any justification that S might have for being confident that p. So an adequate general definition of propositional knowledge could be stated as follows:

> S knows that p if and only if: S is confident that p, this confidence is supported by a disinterested justification that S has for it, and there is no truth r such that, were S to be justified in believing that r and to retain all his properties that are compatible with his having justification for believing that r, then he would be very far from justified in being confident that p.

NOTES

[1] Cases like this may provide further examples of positions in which a person would be justified if he were confident that p and also justified if he lacked confidence that p, ones of a different sort from those suggested in Chapter III, Section 1, which involved the subject's having reason to want it to be the case that p.

[2] That the circumstances that condition (4) must rule out can generally be characterized as those in which it would be too much of an accident that S's confidence that p on the basis of the justification in question is justified confidence in a truth, is, I think, a large part of the truth in Unger's (1968) interesting suggestion that a man knows that p (at a given time) if and only if it is not at all accidental (at that time) that the man is right about its being the case that p.

[3] This resembles an example given by Gettier (1963).

[4] This example resembles in the crucial respects one offered by Lehrer and Paxson (1969), pp. 228–229, to make an essentially similar point. In their example the conclu-

sion is that Tom Grabit stole a book from the library, the premiss is that the subject saw at close range someone looking just like Tom Grabit (whom the subject knows well) steal a book from the library, and the proposition that if conjoined to the premiss would not support a confident inference to the conclusion is that Tom Grabit's mother has averred that Tom was far away on the day in question and that Tom's twin brother John stole the book. In their example the mother is lying (pathologically) and there is no twin brother John, but these frills are not essential to the point.

⁵ I am indebted to Andrew Jameton for suggesting this example, which made me see that another formulation of the fourth condition that I had subscribed to in Ginet (1970) would not do.

⁶ But it will cease to be absurd if, in addition, 'be very far from' is replaced with 'not be'.

⁷ Though S could hardly be justified in claiming to know that he knows that p if he did not have *justification for claiming to know* each of (1)–(4), it does not follow that his knowing that he knows that p requires him to *know* every one of (1)–(4). As I pointed out earlier, a person may understand, and believe, the proposition that he knows that p without understanding all the components of our correct analysis of it.

CHAPTER V

PERCEPTUAL FACTS

1. Perceptual knowledge is knowledge that one sees or hears or smells or tastes or feels some specific sort of non-mental thing(s) or state(s) of affairs or event(s). A proposition of the form '*S* knows that *p*' reports perceptual knowledge just in case *p* is a perceptual proposition about *S*; and *p* is a perceptual proposition about *S* just in case *p* has the form '*S* perceives *d*', where 'perceives' may be replaced by a particular perceptual verb ('see', 'hear', etc.) or some conjunction of disjunction of such verbs, and '*d*' is replaced by an expression designating some non-mental thing(s) or event(s) or state(s) of affairs. Thus, for example, '*S* sees a house and a tree in the distance', '*S* sees and hears a galloping horse approaching', and '*S* feels a weight pressing on his stomach' would all express perceptual propositions about *S*.

The qualification 'non-mental' is included because some perceptual verbs (for example, 'feel') can take as objects terms denoting mental states ('I feel a sharp pain in my stomach', 'I feel depressed'). Such sentences do not report *perception* in the sense that interests me here. In this discussion, I am concerned only with sense-perception of things or events in space, in the 'external world'. (Neither do the verbs in such sentences as 'I hear that you are resigning', 'I see that Nixon has slipped in the polls', 'I smell trouble', 'He tasted defeat', and 'I feel that there is some sort of life on Mars' have the perceptual sense that interests me here. Of course, some such constructions are connected more or less closely with perceptual uses of those verbs.)

Even the perceptual uses of 'feel' are rather a mixed bag. Feeling the shape of an object in one's pocket and feeling the temperature of the bath water are *tactual* perceptions – perceptions by means of part of the perceiver's body coming into contact with the thing perceived (or whose property is perceived) – but rather different kinds of subjective experience (sensation) are involved. One can also speak of feeling the position or movement of various parts of one's own body relative to one another or the force that a part of one's body is exerting ('I feel my finger moving (relative to my hand)', 'I feel my arm bent at the elbow', 'I felt myself pushing strenuously with my hand against something before me') where this is quite different from tactual perception of those things, from feeling those states of one's body *with* another part of one's body (in the way that one might feel the relative positions or movements of parts of another person's body). Feeling *myself pushing* strenuously against something with my hand differs from feeling something pushing against my hand just in this non-tactual aspect of the perception. This *kinaesthetic* and *proprioceptive* awareness is not awareness of something outside the perceiver; but I classify it as a variety of perception because it is awareness of non-mental events in space (there is the possibility of kinaesthetic hallucination) and it is often integrated with tactual perception in an overall *haptic* perception of objects (for example, in feeling objects offering various sorts of resistance to one's movements or in feeling the shape of an object by feeling one's hand trace a certain path in moving over its resisting surface).

Usually, when we make an assertion with a sentence of the form '*S* perceives *d*', as defined above, we imply the existence or occurrence of something satisfying the description '*d*'. Normally, when someone says, 'I see a yellow-bellied sapsucker' or 'I hear a train in the distance' or 'I smell rubber burning somewhere near' or 'I taste garlic in this stew', or makes corresponding third-person statements, he means to imply that *there is* a yellow-bellied sapsucker in the vicinity, a train in the distance, rubber burning somewhere near, or garlic in the stew. In special circumstances, however, a speaker may use sentences of this sort without intending and without being understood to imply the existence of what he says he perceives. For example, he and his hearers may take it as understood that he is describing hallucinations; or the interest in his perceptual statement may be not at all in what it reveals to exist in his environment but only in what it indicates about the nature of his subjective experience, as it might be during a psychologist's experiment investigating perception. But I will regard an utterance of such a sentence as expressing a *perceptual proposition* only if the speaker intends the normal implication that the thing said to be perceived exists. And I will consider the proposition that *S* knows that he perceives *d* to be an ascription of *perceptual knowledge* only if the perceptual proposition it contains is understood to have this existential implication.

For visual, auditory, and tactual perception, the form of the perceptual proposition '*S* perceives *d*' can be further refined. The implications
of the scene-description '*d*', the description of what it is that *S* perceives
according to the proposition (suppose, for example, that the proposition
is '*S* sees a white marble statue, which covers a hole in the floor, a few feet
away behind grillwork in ordinary daylight'), all fall into one or both of
two categories: (a) some object or objects that '*S* perceives *d*' implies
that *S* perceives (*a white marble statue* and *grillwork* in the example given)
plus, perhaps, the relations of those objects to other things that '*S* perceives
d' does not imply that *S* perceives (*which covers a hole in the floor* in the
example); and (b) some relation or relations between the object(s) that
'*S* perceives *d*' implies *S* perceives and *S* that are such that they must affect
the appearance that those objects present to *S* (*a few feet away*
[from *S*], *behind* [on the other side from *S* of] *grillwork, in
ordinary daylight* [from *S*'s point of view] in the example). We can
indicate the division between these categories formally by using instead
of '*d*' the schema '*x* in *ϕ*', where '*x*' is taken to have just the
implications of category (a) and 'in *ϕ*' is taken to have just the implications of category (b).

Let me say more about the sorts of circumstances and relations I have
in mind for category (b):

S sees a thing in a certain *light*, from a certain *distance* and *angle* (perhaps on the other side of certain objects), and through certain *intervening
media*. For example, '*S* sees a house in daylight through clear air from the
front about 50 yards away'. Other intervening media through which one
can see things include water, haze, colored spectacles, windows, screen,
reflecting surfaces, binoculars, telescopes, and (perhaps) live television.
It is quite natural and non-figurative to say 'Glancing in my rear view
mirror, I saw a police car close behind' or 'Looking through my binoculars, I saw tears streaming down the coach's face' or (perhaps) 'I turned
on the television in time to see man's first steps on the moon'. That these
are natural is, I conjecture, at least partly because these special media are
sufficiently like other media through which things are unquestionably
seen (air, spectacles, windows, water, etc.) in immediacy of transmission,
in potential to distort, and in generally not distorting in ways that mislead
when the medium is known to the perceiver.

S hears something in a certain *direction* and at a certain *distance* and (sometimes) through a certain *intervening medium*: 'He hears voices fairly close on his right through a wall'.

S feels something in *contact with a certain part of his body* or in a certain *direction* from it and (sometimes) through a certain *intervening medium*. 'With his hand he feels through the rib cage something pulsating', 'He feels the heat of a fire behind him', 'He feels the coldness of the surface he sits on through his clothes'.

I stipulate that a description '*d*' fails to be of the form '*x* in ϕ' if it lacks implications in category (b). Thus the sentence '*S* sees a tree' fails to fit the form '*S* sees *x* in ϕ', but '*S* sees a tree in the distance' is of that form because 'in the distance' does imply a relation between the tree and *S* that is bound to affect the appearance that the tree presents to *S*. Here are some more examples of sentences of the form '*S* sees *x* in ϕ' with the part fitting '*x*' emphasized: '*S* sees *a horse standing on grass* in clear daylight about 50 yards away', '*S* sees a *large dog* about 10 yards away through the fog', '*S* sees *a small white bird circling* high above him *in a clear sunny sky*'. (In the last example 'in a clear sunny sky' has implications in both category (a) and category (b).)

2. In this chapter and the next I want to discuss the following two questions:

> What sort of complex of conditions constitutes a perceptual fact (that is, minimally suffices logically for the truth of a perceptual proposition)?
> What sort of complex of conditions constitutes perceptual knowledge?

An important point is the relation between these questions. There is a temptation to suppose that one needs to know the answer to the first in order to have the perceptual knowledge asked about in the second. But in fact the connection between the questions is not so strong. Only by seeing this can we deal satisfactorily with the much disputed question whether *sense-data* are part of a proper analysis of perceptual knowledge. We can admit something from both sides of the dispute. Sense-data advocates are right in saying that subjective perceptual experience is part of a proper analysis of perceptual *facts*; but sense-data opponents are right in saying that one does not need to know that one has a certain sort of subjective perceptual experience, and to make inferences from this information, in order to know a perceptual fact about oneself.

Throughout this and the next chapter I take vision as illustrative of perception in general. Conclusions parallel to most of those that I reach about seeing will, I believe, hold equally well for other modes of perception, including combined modes, but I shall not try to show this. I will concern myself largely with propositions that can be expressed by sentences of the form 'S sees x in ϕ'; but in so doing I will not be ignoring any cases of visual perception, for any true proposition that can be expressed by a sentence of the form 'S sees d' that cannot be expressed by a sentence of the form 'S sees x in ϕ' will be entailed by some other true proposition that can be expressed by a sentence of the form 'S sees x in ϕ'.

3. It is very nearly self-evident that the relation between a perceiving subject and an external thing that is signified by a perceptual verb must entail an ascription to the subject of a certain state of consciousness, of a certain sort of *subjective* experience. An essential element in perception is a state *intrinsic* to the perceiving subject – intrinsic in the sense that it entails nothing about the relation between the subject and anything external to the subject (or any non-mental state of affairs). The relation 'x perceives y' is more nearly analogous in this respect to 'x is dented by y' than to 'x is touched by y'.

This is perfectly clear (as Berkeley noted in the *First Dialogue Between Hylas and Philonous*) in the case of perception by means of touch of such things as the high temperature of the bath water or the sharpness of a pin point. In such cases one can specify the location in one's body in which one feels the sensation (of heat or of sharp pain) that is an essential part of the perception. And the very same kind of sensation could, conceivably, exist without being an ingredient in a perception of any external state of affairs. If we do not admit that the situation is analogous for all modes of perception – at least to the extent of involving an intrinsic modification of the subject's conscious experience peculiar to the mode of perception (if not a sensation, strictly so-called, located in a perceptual organ) – then we shall find it difficult to explain why being *conscious in these modes* (not blind, not deaf, not anaesthetized, etc.) is necessary to perceiving in these modes. Also it will be difficult to describe the possibility of perceptual hallucination – of the sort of experience that might

II.   To understand a perceptual proposition one does not need to
          understand any proposition asserting the existence of a sub-
          jective perceptual sensation.
          Therefore, the former sort of proposition does not entail the
          latter sort.[3]

Here the conclusion does not follow from the premiss. One could as
well argue that, since in order to understand the proposition that the
number of days in a week is seven one does not need to understand the
proposition that the number of days in a week is the cube root of 343, then
the former proposition does not entail the latter. It often happens that the
application of a more sophisticated concept is entailed by the application
of a less sophisticated one. Sophisticated concepts are often originally
fashioned so that they will be entailed by some already existing, more
common concepts. It is not part of the unsophisticated person's notion
of a *stone* that a stone contains neutrons if there are such things as neutrons,
but it is part of the sophisticated concept of a *neutron* that a stone (or any
matter) contains neutrons if there are such. It is part of the notions of internal angles and degrees of angles, though not part of the unsophisticated
notion of a triangle, that the internal angles of a triangle sum to 180°. It is
part of the sophisticated notion of *perceptual sensation*, though not of the
unsophisticated notions of seeing, hearing, etc., that perception contains
perceptual sensation. (In such cases it would often be misleading and
unnecessary to say that the new concept brings out a part of everyone's
prior understanding of the more primitive concept; rather it is a newly
discovered or *invented* implication perhaps only lately thought of by
anybody.) Thus it is perfectly consistent (and also true) to say (a) that the
concept of perceptual sensations is not possessed by everyone who understands ordinary perceptual propositions and (b) that it is necessary to
introduce this concept in order to elucidate what is essentially involved in
perceptual facts.

III. (1) At least for visual and auditory perceptions, the only way that
          the perceptual sensations allegedly involved in them could be
          reported by the subject would be by use of such forms of sen-
          tence as 'I seem to see (hear) *d*' or 'It is as if I saw (heard) *d*' or
          'It looks (sounds) to me as if *d*'.
     (2) But all proper uses of such locutions imply that the speaker

thinks that he does not see (hear) d or at least that he lacks confidence that he does.

Therefore, such locutions could not truthfully be used to report any subjective fact present in those cases where the speaker does perceive *and* is quite confident that he does. Therefore, no subjective perceptual sensations can be required in all cases of a person's perceiving something.

This argument suffers from the defect that both its premisses are false. Consider (2) first. It may be that ordinarily when one says something of the form 'It seems to me as if I were seeing d' or 'It is as if I saw d' one means to suggest either that one does not actually see d or that one has some doubt whether one does. But, as Grice (1961) has effectively shown, the ordinary implications of such remarks can be cancelled without falling into contradiction or absurdity. (They might be cancelled, for example, in the context of an experimental investigation of perception, or in a special game where one player is supposed to determine what, if anything, another player perceives on the basis of the latter's reports of his perceptual sensations.) The vehicle of implication is not *what* is stated in uttering 'It is as if I saw d' (the proposition) but rather the speaker's *act* of stating that rather than something else (say, 'I saw d') in the context; and the explanation of the implication is the general presumption in rational discourse that one does not say less than one knows that is relevant, the same principle that explains how a speaker who asserts a disjunction may thereby imply that he does not know which disjunct is true.

As for (1), there seems to be no logical obstacle to introducing a special terminology that is specifically intended for reporting the nature of one's perceptual sensations without implying any epistemic attitude whatever towards any perceptual proposition. In fact various terminologies of just this sort have been proposed.

4. One proposal would have us use the regular perceptual verbs with special modifiers and special sorts of objects. Thus the subjective sensory fact involved in the fact that I see a tree could be reported by 'I directly (inwardly) see a tree-like sense-datum (image, arrangement of colored patches)'.[4] (The adverbial modifier could be dispensed with as long as the object makes clear which use of the perceptual verb is intended.) The

trouble with this sort of terminology is that it suggests that one's awareness of the perceptual sensation is more analogous to perception (ordinarily so called, that is, perception of external things) than it actually is;
and in fact this sort of terminology has often been proposed by philosophers who have over-assimilated the two. They have been led to raise
such insoluble questions as whether the objects of direct perception can
exist unperceived, or whether thy have backsides. They have also been led
to postulate that perceivers must be aware of ('directly perceive') certain
sorts of things that, in fact, they are not necessarily or normally aware of
while perceiving. For example, it has often been insisted that one who
sees an arrangement of objects on a table as he moves round it must be
aware of a constantly changing two-dimensional mosaic of colored
patches that represents the unchanging external scene from the changing
point of view as a photograph would. And a number of properties com-
monly ascribed to external objects – the 'secondary qualities' of color,
sound, etc., – have been thought to belong, not at all to external objects,
but only to the objects of 'inner perception'; on this view, for example,
grass is never green (or any color at all) but rather what is green, strictly
speaking, is the visual sense-datum that a normal perceiver directly sees
when he indirectly sees grass.

Those are notorious pitfalls, but the main reason, from the point of
view of the analysis of perceptual knowledge, why one should avoid
thinking of awareness of sensations as analogous to perceiving objects is
that it naturally leads to thinking of one's knowledge of one's ordinary
('indirect') perceptions as inferred from one's knowledge of one's present
and past 'direct' perceptions – in the way that one infers fire from one's
perception of smoke and one's knowledge that smoke is usually caused by
fire. But to reject this terminology for describing perceptual sensations is
not to reject the whole idea that a subjective perceptual sensation is an
essential ingredient of a perception.

Other terminologies, free from such objectionable suggestions, are
possible. It has, for example, been proposed that we use sentences of the
form 'S is being appeared to d-ly' or 'S senses d-ly' or 'S senses in a d-
manner' for reporting the subjective ingredient of perceiving d.[5] This
terminology, in converting a description of an external thing into an
adverb modifying 'sense' or the possibe voice of 'appears', is intended to
be free from the implication either that the description fits the perceptual

sensation or that it fits a cause of the sensation or that the sensation consists of a 'direct' perceptual relation to an 'inner' object. All to the good. But this sort of terminology, though perhaps smooth enough when 'd' is 'red'. becomes awkward when 'd' is 'an evergreen tree' and quite hopelessly clumsy when 'd' is 'a two-storied blue house with a red door framed by evergreen trees'.

We can achieve the same advantages and preserve a natural mode of expression by adopting the following way of describing perceptual sensations:

> General: 'S's perceptual sensation is as if perceiving x in ϕ'
> Specific perceptual modes:
> > 'S's visual sensation is as if seeing x in ϕ'
> > 'S's auditory sensation is as if hearing x in ϕ' and so on,
> > where 'x in ϕ' is instantiated in the same way as it is in
> > perceptual statements.

Here what the subjective experience is like – what kind it is – is conveyed by likening it to that more or less specific kind of experience which, in the actual world, would normally occur as part of a perception of x in ϕ and which, in the actual world, perceptions of x in ϕ would normally contain.[6]

'A visual sensation as if seeing x in ϕ' will usually mean, then, a visual sensation of that kind that, in the actual world, the normal perceiver would have when seeing x in ϕ. Usually, but not necessarily always; for x and ϕ may be such that the normal visual preceiver could *not* see x in ϕ but an abnormally acute visual perceiver could. Someone with super-sharp eyes could see a small spot 20 feet away (in good light) that the person with only normal vision could not see at that distance. Someone with eyes more like those of a cat than is normal in human beings might be able to see things in light so dim that the normal human visual perceiver could not see those things in that light. In such cases the abnormally acute perceiver's sensation *may* be just like what the normal perceiver has when seeing the same thing in slightly more favorable circumstances, a slightly shorter distance away or in slightly better light. If so, then there is a normal-perceiver-way of specifying the kind of sensation that the abnormally acute perceiver has in his abnormally acute seeing. In all clear cases of this sort, the visual sensation that the abnormally acute perceiver has in seeing x in ϕ (which cannot be seen by the normal perceiver) can be described as of the same kind as the normal visual perceiver would have when seeing x in ψ, where ψ differs from ϕ only a little in its distance or lighting specification. (The possibility of cases of abnormal seeing that differ more radically from the normal in this way will be considered later, Section 11.)

But we should also allow for the possibility of an abnormally acute perceiver who, in seeing x in circumstances in which the normal visual perceiver cannot see x, has a visual sensation of a kind that a normal visual perceiver would never have. Any possible case of this sort must, however, be one in which the abnormal perceiver's visual sensation very much resembles that of a normal visual perceiver when seeing x in ψ where ψ differs from ϕ only a little in its distance or lighting specification.

'A visual sensation as if seeing x in ϕ' should, therefore, be interpreted in the following way: if the normal visual perceiver could see x in ϕ then it refers to the kind of sensation that the normal visual perceiver would have when seeing x in ϕ; if the normal visual perceiver could not see x in ϕ but ϕ differs only a little in its distance or lighting specification from circumstances in which a normal visual perceiver could see x, then it refers to the kind of sensation that an abnormally acute visual perceiver would have when seeing x in ϕ; otherwise, there is no kind of visual sensation to which it refers.

In most circumstances one could infer the truths as to what a person sees, and what his visual sensations are, that are of the plain sort that interest us here, just from the fact that the person is a normal, mature visual perceiver who is conscious with eyes open and working normally, together with sufficient information about his environment, about the lighting and what lies in the direction in which his eyes point. There is, however, one sort of circumstance in which whether or not a person sees x in ϕ, towards which his open eyes are directed, depends on a subjectively determined factor that may vary from one occasion to another of normal, mature visual perception. It may be that x is difficult to *pick out* visually from its surroundings. One normal visual perceiver may see and another may fail to see the elephant shape in the tangle of lines of a puzzle picture, the only difference being in a *gestalt* feature of the subjective experiences involved. Thus 'the kind of visual sensation the normal visual perceiver has when seeing x in ϕ' must be taken to refer to the kind that the normal perceiver has when he is conscious, directs his open eyes towards x in ϕ, *and visually picks out x.* This last phrase is, of course, a virtual synonym for 'sees *x*', but it has the advantage of making it explicit that seeing *x* requires this subjectively determined *organizational* feature of the visual experience.

(There is the possibility that visual sensations of a given description of the form 'as if seeing *x* in ϕ', however determinate the description may be, still vary among normal perceivers seeing *x* in ϕ in further respects that are dependent solely on differences in the individual perceivers and not on further differences in the external scenes they are seeing (differences not ruled out by the description '*x* in ϕ'). The features of a visual sensation of a given description 'as if seeing *x* in ϕ' that do *not* vary among normal perceivers seeing *x* in ϕ and do depend on its being *x* in ϕ that they are seeing – the features that justify the description – also, of course, depend partly on factors in the normal perceivers, as the case of abnormal visual perceivers (for example, the color-blind) makes clear; and it is more than likely that some of these subjective factors in turn depend partly on the normal perceiver's having had a normal sort of background of perceptual experience.)

The 'as if seeing (visually picking out)...' way of describing subjective visual experience is free from the unfortunate temptations that we noted in connection with speaking of the 'direct' seeing of special objects. For instance, in order to characterize the changing aspect of one's visual sensation as one moves around an unchanging scene we do not need to posit a changing two-dimensional object (which cannot be identified with anything in space). Instead we simply say that one's visual experience is as if one's *point of view* while seeing a three-dimensional scene were changing: no need for a changing object of seeing. (One can, of course, *make* one's visual experience more like what it would be if one were seeing a two-dimensional representation of the scene, perhaps by something like squinting or just by being keenly interested in what it would be like if one were seeing such.) Also, in not positing special, directly seen objects we do not permit the view that 'secondary' qualities like color really belong only to such special objects and not to external three-dimensional objects. It is still possible to think that external three-dimensional objects do not really have color, but this is perhaps a less attractive position if it entails that *nothing* really has color.

The 'as if seeing (visually picking out)...' mode of describing the subjec-

tive experience necessarily involved in visual perception leaves as much
room as one could want for further discovery of its nature. It leaves room,
for instance, for the account of what enables our visual experience to
prompt correct beliefs as to the spatial relations among objects we see
(for example, the belief that one sees one object in front of, or nearer than,
another) worked out by the psychologist James Gibson. According to
him, what is crucial are certain rather abstract features that remain invariant through certain sorts of *changes* in the subjective visual experience,
especially the changes that can be described as its being as if the perceiver's point of view were *moving* relative to the objects seen. This is my
own way of putting Gibson's idea, which he puts by saying that seeing is
the "pickup of information" directly from invariant features of the "am-
bient optic array" (the changing pattern of light rays converging on the
eyes as they move with respect to the seen environment) and by denying
that seeing entails having visual sensations, which he thinks of as awareness of two dimensional arrays of color patches or of excitation at the
retinas.[7]

This denial is surely right if it means only that visual perception does
not entail the interpretation or cognitive processing of *such* visual sensations. Its being as if one were seeing a penny standing vertically on a
horizontal surface while moving round it is *not* a matter of having an
impression of a two-dimensional array of color patches subtly and rapidly
changing their shapes and going by some mental operation from this to
the impression of an unchanging three- dimensional layout. Or, to consider another mode of perception, its being as if one were tracing with the
other end of a stick in one's hand the shape of a solid block is not a matter
of one's interpreting, or inferring from, one's awareness of sensations in
one's hand and arm, even if one could not have this experience without
having such sensations. The 'as if seeing...' and 'as if feeling...' descriptions of these subjective experiences are as *brute* descriptions of them as
can be given.

But Gibson's denial is surely wrong if it means that visual perception
does not entail a kind of subjective experience peculiar to seeing. Perception in any mode requires a kind of subjective experience more specific to
that mode than is implied in Gibson's phrase "picking up information
about the environment". (And it does not really *entail* the subject's
acquiring *knowledge* of his environment, as we shall see, though it nor-

mally is the means to this.) If one closes one's eyes and moves about a familiar room one can at each position easily think how the surfaces in the room are laid out with respect to that position (vertical white wall near on my left, vertical yellow wall further away on my right, horizontal red rug beneath my feet, sofa immediately behind me, etc.). One can have a kind of active awareness of the arrangement of one's environment that does not involve even *visualizing* it, much less having visual experience. Having this kind of awareness of the environment would not be *seeing* it, no matter how one came to have it, even if it somehow resulted from light striking one's retinas.

If we adopt 'visual sensation as if seeing x in ϕ' as the standard mode of describing the subjective experience ingredient in seeing external things, as I think we should, there will be circularity in our analysis of seeing. Since one component of the analysis will be specified by an expression of that form, someone who did not already understand 'seeing' well enough to be able to identify instances in his own experience to which 'seeing' applies could not be given this understanding by this analysis. But this does not mean that the analysis will be trivial and uninformative. For one thing, as we have already noted, in implying that seeing external objects necessarily involves subjective sense-experience, which could occur in the absence of any seeing of external objects, the analysis makes a substantive and controversial point.[8] For another thing, as we will see, there is plenty of room for error in stating how the subjective visual experience must be related to the subject's environment if his having that experience is to count as his seeing some of that environment.

As far as I can see, we are in any case compelled to describe subjective visual experience by referring to the kinds that would be ingredient in the normal seeing of this or that external scene. There seems to be no way of describing visual experience that is not parasitic on the language of seeing external things. Consider the following visual-sensation description: 'My visual sensation is as if I were seeing in clear sunlight an expanse of wild flowers of various bright colors stretching out before me towards a large stand of evergreen trees under a cloudless sky'. This, though fairly succinct, is richly informative about the nature of the sensation. Even if one tried to describe the same visual sensation by speaking only of the shapes, colors, relative sizes and spatial relations of the *surfaces* that it is as if one were seeing – and such a description would have to be very long to be as informative about the visual sensation as the one just given – one would still be relying on the 'as-if-seeing-such-and-such-an-external-scene' recipe for describing visual sensations. Even if one supposed (with, for example, Berkeley) that one could convey the nature of this visual sensation by speaking of the subject as 'directly seeing' (or 'visually sensing') a two-dimensional mosaic of variously colored patches, one would still be relying on this recipe. We really have no other.

Why do we have no way of specifying the kinds of sensations that are ingredient in our perceptions that does not depend on our language for specifying the objective appearances we perceive? The reason, I think, is this: the only reactions we make to our perceptual sensations that can serve as criteria of their various kinds,[9] with the specificity necessary to explain the specificity and accuracy of our perceptual beliefs prompted by those sensations, are the reactions that show the kinds of external things those sensations prompt us to believe we perceive. The only dispositions to react to our various perceptual sensations that we have or acquire that could serve as our basis for discriminating so many various specific kinds among them are the dispositions to react to them by forming certain perceptual beliefs or at least finding certain perceptual propositions tempting to believe (dispositions without which one could not be said to understand the perceptual propositions involved). It is difficult to imagine any other sort of reactions that could count as our discriminating such various and specific kinds among our perceptual sensations. We get our purchase on concepts of kinds of perceptual sensations through our grasp of kinds of perceptions, and it is hard to see how it could be otherwise.

5. For S to see x in ϕ it is necessary for S to have a visual sensation of one of a limited range of kinds and necessary also that his having that kind of sensation should result in a certain way from there being x in ϕ. What one sees are those things in one's environment that affect one's visual sensations in the right sort of way. So much is easy. It is more difficult to spell out the right sort of way in which a thing must cause one's visual sensations in order to be seen. It is obvious that not everything that plays a part in bringing it about that S has a visual sensation of a certain sort is thereby seen by S. The condition of S's optic nerve may affect the nature of all of S's visual sensations without his ever seeing his optic nerve. When S sees a train coming down the track, he does not see the fire and water in

the locomotive although they are factors in causing the smoke and steam and motion of wheels that he does see, and thereby the visual sensation ingredient in his seeing the train come down the track. The problem is what to add to the account of the relation obtaining between a visual sensation and a non-mental thing that obtains just in case the subject of that sensation sees that thing.

It seems plausible to think that the description of what S sees, in having a certain visual sensation, must, besides specifying a thing that plays a part in producing that sensation, also *match* in a certain way the correct description of the sensation. (This suggestion is reminiscent of, though not the same as, Descartes' and Locke's view that the ideas of sense *resemble* the properties of the objects whose causing of those ideas constitutes our perceiving those objects.[10]) Suppose S can be said to see a locomotive issuing steam and smoke several hundred yards down the track in clear daylight because such a locomotive (in conjunction with other factors) is causing in S a visual sensation as if seeing a locomotive issuing steam and smoke... etc. Here we have a matching in the fact that the description of what S sees, 'a locomotive issuing steam and smoke... etc.', also serves when prefixed by 'as if seeing' to describe S's visual sensation rather definitely: his sensation is as if he were seeing a locomotive... etc. But, supposing that the locomotive has water inside it, S could also be said to see something that has water inside it several hundred yards down the track in clear daylight, although no very definite visual sensation is described by 'a visual sensation as if seeing something with water inside it... etc.' So it seems that the required matching entails this: the description of what S sees must *pick out the same thing* as some description of what S's visual sensation is as if he were seeing that is sufficiently informative about the nature of the visual sensation. This it may do either by virtue of the fact that the two descriptions are the same or by virtue of the fact that what the latter description picks out is, as a matter of fact, identical with what the former picks out (the locomotive *is* something that has water inside it).

6. In order to develop a more precise analysis of the truth conditions for visual perception propositions that incorporates these ideas, I want first to distinguish what I shall call the pure and the impure among such propositions. *Pure* visual perception propositions include just those proposi-

tions of the form '*S* sees *d*' in which the scene-description '*d*' is such that it could not be altered (for example, by deleting components or replacing components with less specific components) in such a way as to produce a more general scene-description '*d**' (that is, '*d**' is entailed by but does not entail '*d*'), without its being the case also that the description 'a visual sensation as if one were seeing *d**' is more general than the description 'a visual sensation as if one were seeing *d*', that is, the range of kinds of visual sensations to which the former applies includes *and is greater than* that to which the latter applies. *Impure* visual perception propositions are just those that are not pure.

Consider the visual perception proposition '*S* sees the front of a large red house, which contains a purple closet off one of its upstairs bedrooms in clear daylight about 50 yards away at roughly a right angle to his line of sight'. Here the phrase 'which contains a purple closet off one of its upstairs bedrooms' represents an obvious impurity from the point of view of reporting just what *S* sees and no more, because it describes a fact about what *S* sees that makes absolutely no difference to the sort of visual sensation that what he sees produces in him in this seeing of it. That is, the description 'a visual sensation as if one were seeing the front of a large red house, which contains a purple closet off one of its upstairs bedrooms, in clear daylight about 50 yards away at roughly a right angle to one's line of sight' would not fit any more (or fewer) kinds of visual sensations if the clause 'which contains a purple closet... etc.' were deleted entirely.

But the visual perception proposition that remains after deleting that clause is still not pure. It is true that if we were to take the description 'a visual sensation as if one were seeing the front of a large red house in clear daylight about 50 yards away at roughly a right angle to his line of sight' and delete 'large' or 'red', or replace 'house' with 'building' or 'structure' or 'thing', we would obtain a description that would fit more different kinds of visual sensations than would the original. But suppose we replace all of 'the front of a large red house... etc.' with 'something that presents to one's view surfaces that are (in their shapes, colors and spatial relations to each other) such as the front of a large red house in clear daylight about fifty yards away at roughly a right angle to one's line of sight would present to one's view'. The result is a description that fits exactly the same kinds of visual sensations as the original, no more and no less. But the *scene*-description obtained from 'the front of a large red house... etc.' by making the replacement just mentioned is clearly more general than the original, since it is quite possible that something that is *not* the front of a large red house... etc., should present to one's view *surfaces* that are just like those presented by the front of a large red house ... etc. (and the contrapositive is not possible).

Do we, then, arrive at a *pure* perceptual proposition in '*S* sees something that presents to his view surfaces that are... etc.?' I am afraid not. There is still one more device – and a very important one for our subsequent discussion – that we can use to increase the generality of the scene-description without increasing the generality of the visual sensation description that results from prefixing to the scene-description 'a visual sensation as if one were seeing...' We can add to the beginning of the scene-description the phrase 'something that from *S*'s present point of view looks (has the same appearance) as would...'.

Here, 'from *S*'s present point of view looks as would x in ϕ' means the same as 'from the point *S* occupies and in the present appearance-affecting circumstances looks as x would look in ϕ'. This ascribes a certain *objective* appearance to that of which it is predicated; something that is never actually seen may, nevertheless, look as would x in ϕ, from certain points of view.[11] Something in the appearance-affecting relations it has to *S* – suppose it is y in θ – looks as x would look in ϕ just in case y in θ looks *to a normal visual perceiver* as x would look in ϕ. And this will be so just in case y in θ would have the same effect on the visual sensation of a conscious normal perceiver who directs his open eyes towards it and visually picks it out as would x in ϕ. That is, the range of kinds of visual sensation a conscious normal perceiver would be caused to have when directing his open eyes towards and visually picking out y in θ falls within the range he would be caused to have when directing his open eyes towards and visually picking out x in ϕ. (If the first range overlaps but does not fall entirely within the second, then y in θ *sometimes* looks as would x in ϕ and sometimes does not, depending on further factors not implied in those scene-descriptions.)

Thus, for example: a puddle of white gasoline on the pavement a few feet away in ordinary daylight looks as would a puddle of water in the same circumstances; a piece of canvas painted in a certain way standing about 50 feet away in stage lighting looks as would the front of a bookcase full of books in the same circumstances; full-sized cars 1000 feet below look as would tiny models of cars only 20 feet below; white lattice work 100 feet away looks as would a solid white surface 10 feet away; a pink surface in ordinary light looks as would a white surface in red light; a circular surface at a certain angle to one's line of sight and far enough away looks as would an elliptical surface perpendicular to one's line of sight at the same distance.

Note that 'y in θ looks as would x in ϕ' is vacuously true when y presents no appearance at all in θ and x presents none in ϕ; that is, when the normal perceiver *could not see y in θ or x in ϕ.* Thus, in utter darkness a stalactite presents the same appearance as a stalagmite or anything else in utter darkness, namely, no appearance at all; and a stalactite in utter darkness looks the way a penny in clear light 500 yards away looks, namely, no way at all. And if a normal perceiver cannot see x in ϕ then he cannot see something that from his present point of view looks as would x in ϕ, that is, looks no way at all.

A satisfactorily general criterion for when 'x in ϕ' is visually vacuous in this way – for when x and ϕ are such that the normal perceiver could not be said to see x in ϕ, though directing open eyes toward x in ϕ – is not as straightforward as one might at first think. It would be too simple to say it is a matter of whether or not being in ϕ would permit x to have any effect on the visual sensation of the normal perceiver facing it with open eyes. The water and fire inside the locomotive ultimately have an effect on the visual sensation of one who sees the locomotive's wheels move, but that perceiver does not on that account see that water and fire. The shape of a cardboard box completely wrapped in bright paper contributes to the kind of sensation the perceiver has in seeing the parcel, but the perceiver does not thereby see the cardboard box itself.

The main factors that determine whether x in ϕ affects the visual sensation of the normal perceiver (facing it with open eyes) in the right sort of way for it to be said that the perceiver thereby sees x seem to be these: (1) how distinctive x's shape is and (2) how various the shapes are that could be substituted for x's without varying the effect in ϕ on the visual sensation of a normal perceiver (facing it with open eyes). Thus a normal perceiver could perhaps be said to see a *football* completely enclosed in a tight-fitting cover a few feet away in good light, but hardly a *basketball* or a *brick*. One can see a boat enclosed in a *tight-fitting* opaque cover, but not one enclosed in an opaque *box*. One can see a light source (which must have a more or less definite shape) when it is in front of one and there is nothing but air intervening, but not when it is behind one or on the other side of an opaque screen.[12]

When we prefix the phrase 'something that from one's present point of view looks as would ...' to the scene-description 'something that presents surfaces that are ... etc.' we produce a more general scene-description, because it is possible that there should be a kind of external scene that does not satisfy the original description (without the prefix) but that has the same objective appearance as one that does – perhaps something rigged up with special lighting or mirrors or clever use of perspective. Yet the description 'a visual sensation as if one were seeing something that from one's present point of view looks as would something having surfaces that are ... etc.' must apply to precisely the same kinds of visual sensations as does 'a visual sensation as if one were seeing something having surfaces that are ... etc.'

We can generalize the point. Given any scene-description 'd' that is not visually vacuous and that does not itself begin with the phrase 'something that from one's present point of view looks as would ...' (or an equivalent phrase), the prefixing of that phrase to that scene-description yields a new scene-description that is more general than 'd', since it is always conceivable that there be a kind of scene that is not d but that looks as would d; but the description 'a visual sensation as if one were seeing something that looks as would 'd' must be satisfied by just the same kinds of visual sensations as satisfy 'a visual sensation as if one were seeing d'. So, for any such scene-description 'd', the proposition that S sees d must be perceptually impure. (If 'd' is visually vacuous then it cannot be shown impure by attaching that prefix, as we saw. But there will always be another way in which any visually vacuous scene-description 'd' can be made more general without making 'a visual sensation as if one were seeing d' more general. For example, 'stalactites a few feet away in utter darkness' could be changed to 'mineral objects a few feet away in utter darkness' and 'a small nail in clear light 500 yards away' could be changed to 'an object smaller than a golf ball in clear light 500 yards away.')

In propositions of the form 'S sees something that looks from his present point of view as would something having surfaces that are ... etc.' we finally reach examples of pure perceptual propositions. In fact, *any* proposition expressed by a sentence of the form 'S sees something that looks from his present point of view as would d' must be pure. For no matter what 'd'' is and no matter how perceptually impure 'S sees d'' is, the scene-description 'something that looks from his present point of view as would d'' cannot be made more general without becoming one that, when prefixed by 'a visual sensation as if one were seeing...', would yield a more general visual-sensation description than would the original. The prefix 'something that looks from his present point of view as would...' neutralizes the impurities of a scene-description 'd'' so that their remaining or being removed can make no difference to the range of scenes that fit the resulting description 'something that looks from his present point of view as would d'' and, hence, can make none to the range of visual sensations that fit the description 'a visual sensation as if he were seeing something that looks from his present point of view as would d''.

7. An impurity in a visual-perception proposition 'S sees d'' is an implication of the scene-description 'd'' that components of the scene have properties that are not themselves seen. We have illustrated one way in which this can happen: the description of what the subject sees implies that the subject is not in a position to see certain parts of it that make it satisfy certain implications of the description. A different way in which impurity may intrude is for the description of what is seen to imply a property that is *not a proper object* of sight.[13] The proper objects of sight do not include qualities of sound or taste or odor, so that the emphasized phrases in 'S sees billowing, black, *acrid* smoke', 'S sees a round, red, and *deliciously tart* apple', and 'S sees a *loudly roaring* jet airplane' all represent explicit impurities in these *visual* propositions. And 'S feels a *shiny* smooth stone in his pocket', 'S hears *brightly colored* parrots chattering', 'S smells *billowing, black* acrid smoke', and 'S tastes *bright red flakes* of paprika in the soup' give examples of explicit impurities for perceptual propositions in other modes.

   To say that these descriptive terms are impurities in those perceptual propositions is not to deny that a subject's knowledge or belief or thought that, for example, a freshly bitten apple is deliciously tart may affect in a special way the quality of his visual experience as he sees the apple. To say that an apple *looks tart* to a subject may mean nothing more than that he is inclined to infer that it is tart from certain properties of it that he sees in a perfectly strict and straightforward sense, for example, its coloring. But something else, something about his *visual experience*, in a broad sense, could be meant by saying that the apple looks tart to him, or, better, by saying that he *sees it as* tart. Many experiments of psychologists as well as common incidents in ordinary life show that the interests, beliefs, and the like that a subject has with respect to what he thinks he perceives can affect, not merely the inferences he is inclined to draw from what he thinks he perceives, but the nature of his perceptual experience. A fire can, in this special sense, *look* hot, and an air conditioner can, perhaps, *sound* cool. The visual experience of one who sees an apple and wants very much to eat it may be, because of that desire, different from the visual experience of one who sees the same apple but is not at all interested in eating it. The visual experience of one who stares at a painting trying to determine who painted it may be different from that of one who stares at it trying to determine whether it is a painting or a photograph. The visual experience of one who sees an ambiguous drawing as a picture of one thing is different from that of one who sees it as a picture of a different thing.

All such differences and qualities in perceptual experience depend in some way on the subject's having concepts or beliefs or desires or the like that originate outside the perception and that he brings to it. One who had no idea of what a rabbit is could not see an ambiguous drawing as a picture of a rabbit, and one who had no idea of what a tart taste is could not have the peculiar visual experience (if there be such) of seeing an apple as tart. Such qualities belong to an *extra* dimension or level of the description of perceptual experience. I have discussed it this much, not in order to investigate it, but merely to indicate what is ignored in the narrower, plainer sort of descriptions of perceptual facts, and of sensations ingredient in them, that I am concerned with in investigating the questions of what a perceptual fact is and how a subject knows perceptual facts about himself.

Descriptions falling within this special extra dimension of perceptual experience are such that when one is true of a subject he must think that it is. He cannot see lines on paper *as* a drawing of a rabbit unless he *thinks* he sees them as a drawing of a rabbit. An apple cannot *look tart* to him, in the sense that implies something special about his visual experience, unless he thinks that it looks tart to him. Whereas descriptions of the sort I am concerned with (of the form 'S perceives x in ϕ', 'S perceives something that appears as would x in ϕ', and 'S's perceptual sensation is as if he were perceiving x in ϕ') can be true of a subject without his thinking that they are. A small boy may see a Boeing 707 jet airliner on the ground in clear daylight at about fifty yards away on his left on a line of sight forming a 45° angle with a line running from its nose to its tail, and have a visual sensation as if he were seeing that, while at the same time he may be ignorant that either of these descriptions is true of him because he understands scarcely any of the expressions that make them up. The specifications of visual perceptions and their ingredient sensations that I am interested in here are the ones whose applicability do not depend (logically) on any special knowledge, desires, thoughts, attitudes, and the like, that the particular subject may then have with respect to what he sees.

8. With this understanding of the notion of a visual proposition, and of how to distinguish the pure from the impure, let us turn to the task of giving the truth conditions for such propositions.

For the impure case, matters are not too difficult:

> If 's sees d' expresses an impure perceptual proposition, then S sees d if and only if there is a description 'x in ϕ' such that 'S sees x in ϕ' entails 'S sees d' (and is thus impure) and S sees x in ϕ.
> If 'S sees x in ϕ' is impure, then S sees x in ϕ if and only if
> (i) S sees something that from S's present point of view looks as would x in ϕ and
> (ii) this something is x in ϕ.

Thus impure visual perception entails pure visual perception: a subject sees something of visually impure description if and only if it is identical with something of visually pure description that he sees. Condition (ii) is essential, of course, because, although it is always true that if S sees x in ϕ then S sees something that looks from S's present point of view as would x in ϕ, the converse does not always hold: facing a well-made wax imitation, S sees something that looks from his present point of view just as would, but is not, an apple a few feet away in ordinary light.

9. The pure case will be more complicated. We can start by listing the already clear requirements of sensation, external object, and causal

connection. S sees something that looks from his present point of view as would x in ϕ only if

(i) S has a *visual sensation* as if seeing x in ϕ (or some recognizable distortion of that sort of sensation),

(ii)   *there is something* that looks from S's present point of view as would x in ϕ, and

(iii)   this something specified in (ii) *contributes to causing* the sensation specified in (i).

Condition (i) implies that 'x in ϕ' is not visually vacuous, that a normal or abnormally acute visual perceiver could see x in ϕ and, hence, something that looks as would x in ϕ. For if the world is such that the normal or abnormally acute visual perceiver could *not* see x in ϕ then it is such that there is no kind of visual sensation that is as if one were seeing x in ϕ. I do not mean merely that there are no *instances* of that kind (in the way that there are, perhaps, no instances of the kind of visual sensation that is as if seeing a short distance away in ordinary daylight an animal with the body of a large frog and the head of a small anteater). I mean that there is no *concept* of that kind, no possibility that any sensation should count as one of that kind, that whatever sort of visual sensation one might *imagine* there is nothing to make it count as imagining an instance of that kind. In a similar way, since there is in fact no such thing as *seeing sound* pitched at middle C, there is in this world *no kind* of *visual* sensation as if one were seeing sound pitched at middle C: no one knows what to do in order to follow the instruction 'Imagine the experience of seeing sound pitched at middle C' (which is not to say that in no possible world is there seeing such a sound or that kind of visual sensation).

In condition (i) the parenthetical phrase 'or some recognizable distortion of that sort of sensation' is intended to cover such distortions of the sensation as would be produced by squinting, pressure on the eyeball, color blindness or other mild defects of the eye, drugs, and the like. (Unusual *external* distorters of a visual perception, such as properties of the intervening medium or the lighting, may appear in the 'in ϕ' component of the perceptual proposition.) This is pretty vague, but I think that such vagueness in the analysis is inescapable. The concept of seeing something just is pretty vague in that respect: the established use of 'see' does not reflect precise rules as to just how much abnormality (with respect to the shapes, colors, their spatial relations, distances, lighting, etc., it is as if one were seeing) there must be in the visual sensation produced in a subject by a scene towards which he directs his open eyes before we have to say that he does not see that scene.

Vague as it is, however, condition (i) still has the consequence that S may fail to see a thing that from his present point of view looks as would x in ϕ and that contributes to causing him to have a visual sensation, owing to the fact that the sensation is *not* as if he were seeing x in ϕ or some recognizable distortion thereof. If, for example, the scene towards which S directs his open eyes looks from his present point of view as would a field of varicolored wild flowers stretching out to a green forest under a blue sky in clear sunshine but, because of some unusual factor, it causes S to have a visual sensation as if he were seeing an endless expanse of snow under a leaden sky through frosted spectacles, then there can be no question that S does *not see* the scene before him. (In such a case it could be that the process by which the external scene *contributes* to causing S's sensation is the normal one (involving light reflected from the scene entering S's eyes and stimulating their retinas, which stimulus acts on S's brain through the optic nerve in the usual way) and the abnormal nature of the sensation thus caused results from an unusual additional influence in the brain or mind of the subject.)

In fact, it is an insufficiency of our three necessary conditions, as formulated so far, that they do not go far enough in the match they require between the objective appearance of what S sees and S's visual sensation. The analysis is so phrased that, at the most, only such very general, wide disparity as was just exemplified is ruled out. That this is not enough can be shown by an example. Suppose S has:

(1)   a visual sensation as if seeing in clear light a few feet away against a white background a bright blue sphere about the size of a basketball,

(1) entails the following more general description:

(2)   a visual sensation as if seeing in clear light a few feet away against a contrasting background a brightly colored object smaller than a breadbox.

Now suppose that S is caused to have sensation (1) by the fact that his open eyes are directed towards a bright red cube smaller than a tennis ball a few feet away in clear light against a green background (in combination with some strange influences in his brain). If this is the case it is clear that S sees no scene that looks from S's viewpoint as would a bright blue sphere... etc. A bright red cube... etc., in the circumstances mentioned does not look from S's viewpoint as would a bright blue sphere. There is no scene having such an appearance that S could be seeing. And it seems out of the question that in having sensation (1) a subject could ever be seeing a bright red cube... etc., or a scene that looks from the subject's point of view as would a bright red cube... etc. (The phrase 'or some recognizable distortion of that sort of sensation' will not stretch *that* far.) But if, in having sensation (1) as a result of there being a bright red cube... etc., S sees neither a scene that looks from his present point of view as would a bright red cube... etc., nor a scene that looks from his present point of view as would a bright blue sphere... etc., then he surely cannot, in having sensation (1), see a scene that looks from his present point of view as would a brightly colored object... etc.; this despite the fact that he has sensation (2) and the fact that a scene that looks from his present point of view as would a brightly colored object... etc., is causing him, by the usual channels, to have sensation (2).

These last two facts would, however, if the three conditions so far given were sufficient for pure visual perception, make this a case in which S sees something that looks from his present point of view as would a brightly colored object... etc. The difficulty is that at a sufficiently general level of description the visual sensation the subject is caused to have by the scene he faces may match the appearance of that scene (from the subject's point of view) but at a more specific level they may be so far from matching that we can hardly say that the subject sees that which causes his visual sensation. We can avoid this difficulty and secure a match at a sufficiently specific level if we complicate condition (ii) somewhat. Instead of requiring merely that the scene S sees match his visual sensation in the respect that it looks from his present point of view as would x in ϕ, we should require that it also match it in that way for every stronger description of the form 'as if seeing y in θ' that his visual sensation satisfies. That is, (ii) should read as follows:

for every description 'y in θ' such that it entails 'x in ϕ' and

S's visual sensation is also as if seeing y in θ (or some recognizable distortion of that sensation), there is something that looks from S's present point of view as would y in θ.

10. But even with this elaboration of (ii) our three necessary conditions still fail to be sufficient for S's seeing something that looks from his present point of view as would x in ϕ.

Consider the following possible case: S has the peculiarity that, no matter what sort of pattern of light enters his eyes, it always causes him to have exactly the same sort of visual sensation – say, as if seeing in ordinary light a uniformly blue surface that fills his field of view. The causal process leading from the light patterns striking his retinas to his visual sensation is such that it fails to preserve in the sensation any of the variation in the light patterns.

Clearly, S never sees anything external, not even when the three conditions so far specified are satisfied, that is, when his open eyes happen to be directed towards something that looks from his present point of view as would a uniformly blue surface in ordinary light filling his field of view.

The problem is with (iii), the causal condition. And the problem is that our peculiar S's visual sensation is, even when he satisfies (i)–(iii), not caused by a process such that its operation will make the caused sensation match the causing scene in the manner implied in (i) and (ii) through any relevant variations in the causing scene. For our peculiar S, no matter how the causing scene varies, with respect to such properties as the shape and distance of objects and the color of objects and lighting, it makes no intrinsic difference to the caused visual sensation.

The problem remains if we change the example so that S has this peculiarity only for a short time, the rest of the time seeing external things normally (that is, the light reflected from those things to his eyes causes his visual sensations by the normal process, one that makes the sensations vary in accordance with variations in the external things in the usual fashion). Still S does not see anything during this short period of his peculiarity, even if, by coincidence, his visual sensation and the scene towards which he directs his open eyes at certain points during that period happen to match in the manner implied by (i) and (ii). For another example of this sort, suppose an S who usually sees normally but on one occasion, when S's eyes happen for some reason to be insensitive to light striking them, the turning on of a beam of light at a little distance in front of S's open eyes causes something to fall on his head and thereby causes S to have a visual sensation as if seeing a beam of light a little distance in front of him. It is clear that, in obtaining that visual sensation in that manner, S does *not see* that beam of light (or anything else external). Yet S does satisfy the three conditions necessary for seeing such a thing that we have so far laid down.

What is missing, and what is essential in every instance of seeing something that looks from the perceiver's point of view as would x in ϕ, is the following: the sensation, specified in (i), must be caused by the matching scene, as specified in revised (ii), *by a match-ensuring sort of process*; that is, one such that the operation of that sort of process will generally make the caused sensation match the causing scene in the manner implied by (i) and (ii), no matter how the causing scene varies in the relevant respects. And this is, I believe, the only further restriction on the causal condition in pure visual perception that is needed.

There are, however, certain other restrictions that might seem necessary that we should examine. In the first place, it might be thought that the causal process from external thing to visual sensation must, in all seeing properly so-called, be the same as the one that occurs in actual normal vision. Suppose that neurological experimenters rig up to some person an artificial device that takes the place of the optic nerves that connect the eyes with that part of the brain on which vision depends. Given the same input from the eyes, this artifical device delivers the same output to the brain as would the optic nerves; but, let us suppose, the process by which it transforms the one into the other is very different from what occurs in the normal optic nerves. (We can imagine the device to be a large contraption, partly electronic and partly mechanical. which is outside the subject's body and attached to his head with wires.) Through this device the light striking the subject's eyes causes him to have the same sort of visual sensation that a normal perceiver would have were he directing his open eyes upon the same scene from the same point of view, and causes his sensation to vary in accord with variation in the scene in the same way that it would in a normal perceiver. The substantial difference here from the normal paradigm might incline some to say that this subject, with this artificial device in place of optic nerves, does not really see the external scenes that his visual sensations reflect; but I think that the more natural thing to say, on due consideration, would be that this subject *sees* all right, but by partly artificial means.

Another sort of addition to the causal condition, one that I have found more tempting, would require the match-ensuring causal process to operate over some suitably specified *significant portion* of S's visual experience if its operation in him on any particular occasion is to count as his seeing an external thing. Consider again our peculiar S whose inner mechanisms are such that any sort of light striking his eyes causes him to have a visual sensation as if seeing a uniformly blue surface that fills his field of view. Suppose that this S often has this sensation and for long periods of time, but that once in a great while something temporarily flips over in his brain and makes him for a short time like the normally sighted person, so that while in that temporary condition his visual sensation is being caused by the normal process that would ensure the normal sort of variation in the sensation as the external scene upon which his open eyes are directed varies. But on these few rare occasions when S is in that normal condition he happens to be directing his open eyes upon a uniformly blue expanse that fills his field of view. So S's visual sensation *never* varies. Can we, nevertheless, say that on those rare occasions when his sensation is caused via the normal process by something that looks as would a uniformly blue surface... etc., and only on them, he does see the scene before him? This case is so different from the paradigm of a sighted person, who relies on his sight to guide him around his environment, that it may seem wrong to say this. This sort of case – and others that can be imagined, such as a subject who has varied visual sensations that are like those of a normally sighted person but are only infrequently caused in the normal way by matching external scenes, usually being caused by a powerful demon bent on deceiving him – might make us think that *most* of S's visual sensations (or at any rate most of those not so discordant with the rest as to give him reason to suspect that he is hallucinating) must be produced by a match-ensuring causal process from the external environment, if any of his visual sensations so caused are to count as seeing. Otherwise, we might reason, S would have no way of telling, with any reliability, when he really sees and when he does not. He could not rely on his visual sensations for information about his environment without their misleading him more often than not. But one who sees, who has sight, is, surely, one who has in his visual sensations a *reliable guide* to his environment. This last dictum is true, I think, but only if it is taken to mean that one sees over a given period only if one's visual sensations *over that period* offer a reliable guide to one's environment. But this follows already from the three conditions, as amended, that I have admitted to be necessary. In order to yield an objection to the sufficiency of these three conditions, the dictum must be taken to mean something else, something false, namely, that one sees on any particular occasion only if one sees with sufficient frequency to be said to have in the totality of one's visual sensations a generally reliable guide to one's environment.

I am proposing to let the question whether S's having a visual sensation on a particular occasion counts as his seeing something be decided solely by the sort of process by which his sensation is caused *on that occasion*. Someone may still think it an objection to this to point out that a subject who satisfies my three conditions on a particular occasion, will be unlikely to have the *concept* of *seeing* things in his environment if his visual sensations as a whole (according to his current memory impressions) have been too much the same or, on the other hand, too chaotic; for then it would be unlikely that this subject would have the sort of expectations in response to his visual sensations that are necessary to understanding any visual perception proposition about himself. This may well be so, but if it is, my proposal is unaffected, for it does not seem necessary that a person, or other conscious creature, have an understanding of the proposition that he sees x in ϕ, or any concept of seeing at all, in order to see x in ϕ. It seems perfectly coherent to suppose a creature who occasionally sees things in his environment but is prevented, by the infrequency of his doing so or his having at other times too chaotic or too monotonous visual sensations, from ever realizing that he occasionally sees, from ever behaving (bodily or mentally) in ways that would manifest beliefs that he sees certain sorts of things, from over having so much as the *idea* of seeing.

I think, then, that we may consider that no further restrictions on our conditions are necessary in order to make them sufficient and that we may propose the following as a plausible analysis of the truth-conditions for pure visual perception propositions: S sees something that looks from his present point of view as would x in ϕ if and only if

(i) S has a visual sensation as if he were seeing x in ϕ (or some recognizable distortion of that sort of sensation),

(ii) for every description 'y in θ' such that it entails 'x in ϕ' and S's visual sensation is also as if he were seeing y in θ (or some recognizable distortion thereof), there is something that looks from S's present point of view as would y in θ, and

(iii) the sensation specified in (i) is caused by the thing specified in (ii) via a process of a sort whose operation would generally make the caused sensation match the causing scene in the manner implied by (i) and (ii).

11. I would like to be able to leave the analysis of visual perception at that (and perhaps I should), but there is a further question. It concerns cases in which no actual perceiver could see x in ϕ because x's being in ϕ, or the perceiver's failing to direct open eyes towards x, would prevent it. Is it not at least possible that there should be a *radically abnormal* visual perceiver who could see x in ϕ in such cases where no actual perceiver (whether normal or abnormally acute) could? Consider a few examples.

Suppose we know that S is (somehow) caused by the fact that his open eyes are directed toward a small white bird circling two miles away in a sunny, clear, otherwise empty sky to have a visual sensation as if he were seeing a small white bird circling about 50 yards away... etc. It is as if his eyes were powerful binoculars (at least at the time) – and, indeed, the explanation might be that his eyes do resemble binoculars, but that does not matter. If we know that this same sort of thing happens to S with significant regularity or over significant periods, are we not tempted to say in such a case that S sees a small bird circling two miles away... etc.?

Or suppose that S is (somehow) caused by the fact that his open eyes are directed towards some stalactites a few feet away in utter darkness to have a visual sensation as if he were seeing those very stalactites in their actual relations to him in good light. It is as if something other than light acts as light for his eyes. If we know that this same sort of thing happens to S with significant regularity or over significant periods, are we not tempted to say that S sees stalactites before him in utter darkness?

Or, finally, suppose that we know that certain scenes currently visible on a stage from a certain point in a theatre that is 2000 miles away from S, cause S (when he closes his eyes and tries to make his mind go blank) to have visual sensations as if he were seeing precisely those scenes from that point – it is as if he were viewing very large-screen, 3-dimensional, superbly realistic television transmission from that point in that theatre. Again, if we know that this same sort of thing happens to S with significant regularity or over significant periods, are we not at least tempted to say that S sees, with his eyes closed, scenes in a theatre 2000 miles away?

The analysis we have given of visual perception will not, however, permit us to succumb to these temptations. S sees x in φ, we said, only if S sees something that looks from his present point of view as would x in φ. But if the circumstances φ differ more than slightly from ones in which a normal visual perceiver could see x, as they surely do in these examples, then there will be no kind of sensation answering to the description 'as if seeing x in φ', no way in which condition (i) of the analysis of pure perception could be satisfied.

If we wished, we could recognize the possibility of these radically abnormal sorts of visual perception by replacing the preceding analysis with the following:

> For any description 'x in φ' such that a normal perceiver can see x in φ, S sees something that looks from some point of view (not necessarily S's present location or the appearance-affecting circumstances presently surrounding S or that thing) as would x in φ if and only if
>
> (i)   S has a visual sensation as if seeing x in φ (or some recognizable distortion thereof),
>
> (ii)   there is something and some point of view on it (not necessarily S's present location or the appearance-affecting circumstances presently surrounding S or it) such that, for every description 'y in θ' that entails 'x in φ' and is also such that the sensation mentioned in (i) is as if seeing y in θ, that something looks from that point of view as would y in θ, and
>
> (iii) the sensation specified in (i) is caused by the thing specified in (ii) via a process of a sort whose operation would generally make the caused sensation match the causing scene in the manner implied by (i) and (ii).

This analysis permits S to see x in circumstances ψ that are greatly different from any in which a normal perceiver could see x, provided, roughly, that x causes S to have the sort of visual sensation that a normal perceiver would have when seeing x in more favorable circumstances ϕ and this causal connection is no fluke.

But should we, after all, make this accommodation in our analysis of visual perception? Are any of the examples described really ones in which it would be quite literally true that the subject *sees* the scene to which his visual sensation corresponds and by which it is caused? Are the correspondence and the causal connection sufficient for that, given that it is not the normal sort of correspondence (reflecting the normal sort of influence of distance, lighting conditions, etc., on the perceiver) and the normal sort of causal process (by means of the kind and amount of light delivered from the scene to the subject's open eyes)? Isn't there also a temptation, given that there have never been any actual applications of 'see' in such cases, to deny that the subjects in those hypothetical cases quite literally *see* those scenes, and may not it be the sounder inclination? It seems to me that, as long as such cases remain only epistemologists' fancies and do not actually occur, we have no way to answer this question. Our concept of seeing has, in Waismann's term, *open texture* (like most of our empirical concepts, as Waismann says).[14] Whether or not 'see' should be applied in these sorts of cases has not been decided in our linguistic practice hitherto, and the speech-activities incorporating the decisions or judgments that would settle the question are not likely to be called forth until the actual occurrence of such cases demands them. We can say only how we think it likely that it would be settled, or how we think that it should be settled, not how it is settled.

So, in order to be faithful to the concept of seeing in its present state of development, we must be indecisive in our analysis. We have to say: it is not now determined whether the correct analysis of pure visual perception is the one proposed in Section 10 or the one contemplated in this section. We can say, however, that the former, conservative analysis gives a sufficient condition and covers all the cases that have any chance of actually occurring.

NOTES

[1] The term is used in this way, for example, in Price (1932), and in Grice (1961).
[2] The first two seem to be suggested in Ryle (1949), Ch. 7, and Ryle (1956). The third once persuaded me and is effectively criticized in Grice (1961); it is akin to reasoning suggested in Quinton (1955).

[3] The following remarks are from Ryle:
People without special theories or technical knowledge of physiology, optics, chemistry or psychology know well enough how to use the concepts of seeing, hearing and smelling, though not the concept of *sense-impression*... the concept of *perception* is on a more elementary or less technical level than that of *sense-impression*. We can know all that is a part of common knowledge about seeing and hearing, without knowing anything about these impressions. But from this it follows directly that the concept of sense-impression is not any sort of component of the concept of perception, any more than the concept of *vitamin* is any sort of component of the concept of *dinner*. (Ryle (1956), pp. 188–189)... the sophisticated concept of sensations or impressions is not a component of their [unsophisticated people's] concepts of perception.... People are ordinarily ready to tell what they see, hear, taste, smell, or feel.... But they are not ready, indeed they are not even linguistically equipped, to tell what impressions they are or have been having. So the notion that such episodes occur does not derive from study of what ordinary sensible people are found telling. They are not mentioned in the deliverances of untutored 'consciousness'. Rather the notion derives from a special causal hypothesis – the hypothesis that my mind can get in touch with a gatepost, only if the gate-post causes something to go on in my body, which in its turn causes something else to go on in my mind. Impressions are ghostly impulses, postulated for the ends of a para-mechanical theory. (Ryle (1949), pp. 242–243.)
Argument II is not explicit in these passages, but Ryle certainly seems to be taking his observation that the sophisticated notion of perceptual sensation is not part of the unsophisticated notion of perception as a reason for doubting, or viewing with suspicion, the thesis that perception necessarily involves sensation (in the sophisticated sense).
[4] See, for example, Moore (1922), pp. 168–196, Moore (1953), Ch. 2, and Moore (1952), pp. 629–630.
[5] See, for example, Ducasse (1951), pp. 259–260, Chisholm (1957), Chs. 5(3), and 8(3), and Sellars (1968), pp. 167–168.
[6] In a somewhat similar vein, Sellars (1963), p. 47, and (1968), pp. 21, 167, suggests an explanation of what is meant by '*S* has a sensation of red' or '*S* senses in a red manner' in terms of the standard result, or the result in normal circumstances, of a person's looking at a red thing.
[7] See Gibson (1972) and also Gibson (1950), Gibson (1966), and Gibson (1967).
[8] For one recent, extended controversion of it, see Pitcher (1971).
[9] Ginet (1968) expounds my understanding of the notion of criteria for kinds of sensations, and of how they are necessary for our having concepts of these kinds.
[10] See Descartes' *Sixth Meditation* and Locke's *Essay Concerning Human Understanding,* II, VIII, 15–16.
[11] Cf. J. L. Austin's remark (1962, p. 43) that "the way things look is, in general, just as much a fact about the world, just as open to public confirmation or challenge, as the way things are. I am not disclosing a fact about *myself,* but about petrol when I say that petrol looks like water."
[12] There is an interesting discussion of this topic in R. Firth (1967) and Caton (1967).
[13] The notion of a proper object of a given mode of perception was introduced by Plato, *Theaetetus,* 184B–185A, developed by Aristotle, *De Anima,* II, vi, and has been used by many philosophers since, for example, Locke, *Essay Concerning Human Understanding,* II, II, 1.
[14] Waismann (1945), p. 121.

CHAPTER VI

PERCEPTUAL KNOWLEDGE

1. Perceptual facts known to the perceiver immediately upon occurrence fall into two classes: those that he knows inferentially and those that he knows non-inferentially. This classification does not necessarily exhaust the domain of perceptual facts: it is possible for a perceptual fact to be unknown to its subject at the time it occurs.

Indeed, there are few kinds of perceptual facts of which it is necessarily true that every instance of one of them is known or believed or at least suspected by its subject at the time it obtains. For many propositions of the form 'S peceives d' (where 'perceives' is replaced by some particular perceptual verb, or conjunction or disjunction of perceptual verbs, and 'd' is replaced by some substantival scene-description), there are at least two ways in which it could happen that the proposition is true and yet its subject fails at the time to know or believe or even suspect that it is true. (1) He may be mistakenly convinced that he is currently having a perceptual hallucination, and thus think that he is not really perceiving anything at all; (2) he may fail to understand the proposition that he perceives d.

Confronted with the first possibility, a philosopher who wished to maintain that some epistemic attitude towards some perceptual proposition is essential to every perceptual fact[1] might retreat to the claim that if a person perceives d then he must believe or suspect either that he perceives d or that he would be doing so if he were not hallucinating or at least that he is having the sort of experience one has when one perceives d. But the falsity of this weaker claim is shown by the second possibility.

Let us again, consider seeing in particular. It is possible that a person should fail to understand *any* visual propositions, should fail altogether to have the concept of seeing, at a time when, nevertheless, he sees things. It is perhaps tempting to think that, on the contrary, a subject cannot be said to *see* things in his environment unless he is disposed to react to his visual experience (when he does not believe he is visually hallucinating) in ways that show that he is being given visual guidance to at least some features of his environment, that is, in ways such that he can be said to discern features of his environment by seeing them (for example, he is disposed to follow the movement of objects he sees with his eyes or to move to touch or avoid them). It must be agreed that if one who sees is so disposed then, whether or not he has the capacity to express them in symbols, he *understands* at least some visual propositions about himself, albeit perhaps only rather vague and general ones ('I see something moving toward me', 'I see something near enough and of a size for me to grasp', 'I see an object lying in the path of my movement (requiring me to go round, or step up, or step down)', and the like).

But the claim that one who sees must be so disposed will not hold up. There could be a case of which it would be right to say that a subject sees his environment even though he has not yet learned those reactions, or dispositions to react, to his visual experience that would show that he *grasps* that he sees his environment. It is possible, for example, that a person blind from birth should have his sight restored, that he should then take some considerable time before he becomes disposed to react to his new sort of experience in ways that show that he understands that he sees this and that in his environment, and that after doing so he should say, quite sincerely, that although he *now* realizes that he has been seeing various sorts of things in his environment for some time he did not at first realize he was doing so: it has taken him some period of seeing to realize what seeing things in one's environment is and that he has been doing it. I think that this would be a perfectly intelligible (and very likely true) remark in such a case. If it is, then we have a possible case in which a person was seeing a certain sort of environment – because he was having visual experience sufficiently like the normal perceiver has when he sees that sort of environment (this established by the person's remembering that he was) and caused by the environment in the way that it is when a normal perceiver sees that sort of environment – but did not understand, hence did not believe or suspect, that he was seeing any particular sort of thing or even that he was having the sort of visual experience one has when seeing a certain sort of thing.

There may be psychological limits to what can be seen by a person who as yet has no comprehension at all of what it is to see things in the environment. It seems quite unlikely, for instance, that such a person would ever be able to see certain things in surroundings that make those things difficult to pick out visually. It seems implausible to think that there may ever actually occur a case of a person who sees, say, an elephant shape in a puzzle picture but does not have the idea of seeing something that looks as would a definite shape in a mess of lines, does not understand even so much as the proposition that he could express to himself (if he knew the appropriate language) by saying, 'I see *that* [focussing his attention on the shape he sees]'. It seems plausible to suppose that creatures such as we are would never get to have the *kind* of visual experience that the normal visual perceiver has when he visually picks out a shape in surroundings that make it difficult to discern without having had a good deal of visual experience and visual belief, and having been guided in acquiring visual perceptions by beliefs as to what can be seen. But, as far as I can see, there is no reason to suppose that these limits are more than psychological ones, that they are logical limits, that it is conceptually impossible that a person who as yet has no idea that he sees should nevertheless have just the sort of visual experience that the normal perceiver has when he sees something that is difficult to pick out visually.

So it cannot be maintained that perception is essentially an epistemic affair, that to perceive is, necessarily, to make a perceptual judgment or to have some epistemic attitude towards some sort of proposition having to do with that perception.[2] (It remains true, however, that over a sufficiently long run of perceiving various things in various ways a subject's sense-experiences must be such that they would naturally (in a normal subject) give rise to some (true) perceptual beliefs: if a subject's sense-experiences over a sufficiently long and varied stretch are not such as would dispose him (eventually) to some (true) perceptual beliefs then they cannot be related to his environment (throughout that stretch) in such a way as to constitute perceptions of it, because then they could not be outcomes of a process that is match-ensuring in the way required by our analysis of visual perception (Chapter V, Section 10). Instead they would constitute either a prolonged perceptual hallucination or else no sort of *perceptual* experience at all.)

Of course, when a *propositional* construction is put as the object of a perceptual verb the resulting sentence, '*S* perceives that *p*', would in most contexts express a proposition implying that *S* knows (or at least believes) that *p*. But this proposition also implies more than a mere perception. It implies that there is true some perceptual proposition that obviously implies that *p and* that *S* knows (or believes) that proposition (and thus knows, or at least believes, that p). The proposition that S *sees that* the thing on the wall is a photograph has epistemic implication because it implies the conjunctive proposition that S sees a photograph on the wall *and* in addition (not implied by the first conjunct) that S knows (or at least believes) that he sees a photograph on the wall and, hence, that the things that he sees on the wall is a photograph. On the other hand, the conjunction 'S sees a photograph on the wall and knows that he sees a photograph on the wall' does *not* imply that S *sees that* the thing on the wall is a photograph. It may not look anything like a typical photograph and scarcely anyone can *see* that it is one but has to be told that it is. Seeing a thing and knowing that it has a certain property do not make it the case that one sees that it has that property.[3]

It would be a natural way to use the phrase 'perceptual knowledge', although different from mine, to say that a person has perceptual knowledge that p just in case he perceives that p, assuming (I think correctly) that 'S perceives that p' entails that S knows that p. The preceding paragraph has indicated the relation between these two senses: from the premiss that S has perceptual knowledge that p in this other sense it follows that there is a perceptual proposition about S that entails that p in an obvious way (for example, in the way that 'S sees a photograph on the wall' entails that there is a photograph on the wall or, alternatively, that something S sees on the wall is a photograph) and that S knows to be true; so that any fact that S knows perceptually in the other sense will be obviously entailed by a perceptual fact that S knows perceptually in my sense. But the converse does not obtain: from the fact that S knows that he perceives d and that 'S perceives d' obviously entails that p, it does *not* follow that S perceives that p. S may know that he sees a photograph on the wall by having been told that what he sees is a photograph and not at all by seeing that it is. (Whether or not a person's knowing that p is a matter of his *seeing* that p depends on the extent to which his knowledge that p is derived from his knowledge of how what he sees looks or has looked (objectively) from his point of view and the extent to which how it looks or has looked (objectively) is how it looks or has looked *to him*.)

(There are other constructions that can be used after 'S sees...' to imply knowledge by S of a visual proposition about himself, constructions that are related in fairly obvious ways to the propositional construction 'that p'. For example, there is 'what x's color is' or 'the color x has' or just 'the color of x' or 'x's color'. Each of these phrases can be used after 'S knows...' to imply that there is some proposition 'p' that is a correct answer to 'What color is x?' and is such that S knows that p. Similarly, each could also be used after 'S sees...' to imply, for some proposition 'p' answering 'What color is x?', that S sees that p.)

2. Perceiving things is, of course, a very important means to knowledge about them. Many sorts of perceptual facts are, in the ordinary case, accompanied by their subjects' knowledge of them and, thereby, of the environmental facts that they obviously imply. They are *easy* for subjects to know. Subjects with normal capacities and normal backgrounds of experience are bound to know them.

Indeed, perceptual knowledge is *the* basic source of knowledge about the environment: all one's knowledge of contingent facts about the external world is either perceptual knowledge or inferred from perceptual knowledge. For example, consider the way in which the size of a planet is inferred from a variety of observations, or the way in which remote events are inferred from hearing or reading reports of them. But that perception provides the foundation for knowledge of the world around us is only a contingent fact itself. Conceivably, a person might deserve to be credited with knowledge of some external fact although he has not learned of it in any of the ordinary ways involving sense-perception. For example, on a number of occasions convictions about remote events might just 'come' to a person (from out of nowhere, as it were), and if these convictions always turned out to be right, we might begin to find it compelling to regard them as more than lucky hunches, as knowledge, even before we know why they arise and are always right. That is, we might be willing to say that in having these queer convictions this person *knows*, even if this person has not himself checked by ordinary means the general correctness of his queer convictions. But as things actually are, it seems quite likely that our senses are the only means by which we can *know* the way the world is.

How are current perceptual facts known by their subjects? How do different sorts of perceptual facts stand with respect to being known, at the time they obtain, either inferentially or non-inferentially? On this matter philosophers have sometimes gone to extremes. According to one strong tradition, a person can know any current perceptual fact about himself *only* inferentially. I will argue that this tradition is in error in not recognizing the possibility of non-inferential perceptual knowledge. But an opposing tendency, especially evident recently,[4] errs in underestimating the role of inferential justification in knowing current perceptual facts about oneself.

3. It has been widely held in the philosophy of perception that a person can know a current perceptual fact about himself only by inferring it from what he knows his sense-experiences to be or to have been. A major challenge for this view is giving a plausible account of how inferences from subjective sense-experience to objective perception are justified and what form they take. Descartes and Locke, who are among the more notable supporters of the view that current perceptual knowledge must be inferential, never really offered an analysis of the inferences involved. But it is not obvious what the account should be.

It cannot be said that the inference is simply a deduction, for it seems clear that no history of a subject's actual subjective sense-experience can logically entail that he is perceiving a certain sort of external scene. There is always the logical possibility that he is having an extensive hallucination. Simply having a certain sort of sequence of sense-experiences is not all that perceiving the external world amounts to. It requires also that the sense-experiences be caused by the external world and match it in the right sort of way. This has been acknowledged by virtually all who have held the view in question.

It is difficult to see how the inference could fit the strictly inductive pattern. How could it be an inference from a certain concomitance or proportion among properties in a set of examined cases to a similar concomitance or proportion among the same properties in some set of unexamined cases, since the perceptual conclusion *seems* to entail the instantiation of wholly different properties from any instantiated by the subjective sense-experiences of the premisses? But perhaps this is an illusion. Could the premisses and conclusion be understood in such a way as to be about the same sorts of cases, instantiating in the same way the same sorts of properties, with the only difference that the premiss cases are examined and the conclusion cases unexamined?

Phenomenalism attempts to offer this sort of account.[5] This view can be formulated as follows: A person can be in a position to infer by induction the proposition that he perceives a certain sort of external scene from what he knows his sense-experiences to be and to have been, because (1) such a proposition is equivalent in content to some proposition according to which (a) the subject is having a certain sort of sense-experience and (b) the subject will or would have, or would have had, certain other sorts of sense-experiences if he were to have, or had had, experience as if making certain movements of his body or sense-organs;[6] and (2) he can infer the (b) part of this proposition from the (a) part (which he knows non-inferentially) and certain general propositions about what sorts of sense-experiences are obtainable when certain sorts are had; and (3) he can know general propositions sufficient for that purpose by induction from his past sense-experiences.

Let us concentrate on point (1) of this phenomenalist thesis, using vision again as our illustrative sense. For any proposition of the form 'S sees d' (or 'S sees x in φ' or 'S sees something that looks from his present point of view as would x in φ') can we find an equivalent conjunction (or other truth-function) of propositions to the effect that S has (or has had) certain sense-experiences (visual or otherwise) and would have (or would have had) certain other ones if he were to have (or had had) experience as if making certain movements? The difficulties in the way of doing so may not amount to a proof that it cannot be done, but they are so great as to make it reasonable to despair.

The worst difficulty, it seems to me, stems from the possibility that a person could be the victim of an hallucination so extensive that all the sense-experiences he actually has *or could obtain* for an extended period might be such as to make him justifiedly confident that he sees a certain sort of external scene when, in fact, he sees no external scene at all. There could be an hallucination so extensive that it could not be discovered or reasonably suspected by the victim himself. That this has happened to someone might be discovered by others, who perceive the hallucinator acting as if he perceives a sort of environment that, as they perceive, is not there.

This sort of possibility might lead one to think that one can get an analysis that entails that S sees an external scene of a certain sort if one adds to the propositions about the sorts of sense-experiences that are present or obtainable *for S*, propositions about the sorts of sense-experiences present or obtainable for *other* subjects. But, in addition to the

fact that the problem of extensive hallucination would still be there
(several subjects could have agreeing sense-experiences that were all
hallucinatory), this suggestion encounters the difficulty of finding a way
in which descriptions merely of various subjects' sensations as if perceiving, say, a tree (assumed to be non-hallucinatory) can be made to entail
that those subjects are perceiving *one and the same* tree and not distinct
but very similar ones. I can see no way of doing this. No matter how
extensive the descriptions, as long as they are limited to intrinsic properties of various subjects' sensations, actual or obtainable, it will be a
logical possibility that those subjects are perceiving separate external
scenes. (If enough were included in the (non-hallucinatory) sensations
that each subject *could* obtain, then we could suppose them to be perceiving distinct objects only if we suppose an extensive duplication of
environments, perhaps even a symmetrical universe, that is, a universe
divisible into halves that are 'mirror-images' of one another.)

This possibility can be ruled out only by including some propositions
about the spatial relations among the subjects and the directions in which
they are perceiving. But including such propositions will defeat the point
of the phenomenalist analysis, which was to show how all perceptual
knowledge is equivalent to a combination of non-inferential knowledge of
actual sensations and inductive knowledge of obtainable sensations. This
objective obviously fails to be achieved as soon as the analysis of a subject's perceiving something is seen to require inclusion of facts not redu-
cible to the intrinsic features of sensations. For the subject will need to
know that these external facts obtain in order to know that he perceives
such-and-such a thing and the analysis does not explain how he can know
these facts by inductive inference from subjective experience.

In raising these difficulties for thesis (1) of phenomenalism, I have been
assuming that it would be true of a visual perception proposition if a
sense-experience equivalent for it could be found in which the kinds of
sensation are specified in the manner 'a sensation as if perceiving *d*'. But
on this understanding (1) would not support the idea, which some pheno-
menalists seem to have had, that the *concept* of seeing an external (mind-
independent) scene is derivative from (a logical construction out of, redu-
cible to) more primitive concepts of kinds of subjective sense-experience.
One could establish (1) in such fashion as to support this more radical
idea only if there existed a way of conceiving or describing visual sense-

experience that is not parasitic on the concepts and language of seeing external things. But, as we noted earlier, this there does not seem to be. It is more faithful to our actual practice of talking and thinking about vision to say that our concepts of various sorts of visual sensations are constructed out of, derived from, our concepts of various sorts of seeing of external things than to say the reverse. Likewise for perception in other modes and the sensations ingredient in them. So no one can hope to show that perceptual propositions, or their truth-conditions, could in principle be expressed without the aid of sentences (or clauses) expressing perceptual propositions.[7]

Given that phenomenalism fails, there seems little hope that the alleged inference from subjective sensation to objective perception can be made to fit a strict inductive pattern. However, the foregoing points against phenomenalism do not rule out the possibility of some other pattern of non-deductive inference such that whenever a person knows a perceptual fact about himself that fact will be related in the way prescribed by that pattern of inference to actual and obtainable sensations of his that he then knows of, or would know of if he understood the propositions that report them. In fact, in Chapter VIII I will indicate what I take to be such a pattern of inference.

But even if an account can be given of inference patterns that permit perceptual conclusions to be drawn from premises about one's sensations, the thesis that a person must know his perceptions by inference from his sensations would by no means be established. This thesis implies that a person must, in order to know that he sees a certain sort of external scene, know that his present and past sensations have been of a certain sort. However, Ryle's point that a person does not have to have the relatively sophisticated concepts of the various kinds of perceptual sensations in order to have the concepts of seeing, hearing, etc. is a knock-down objection to any such claim that perceptual knowledge requires that the subject have knowledge of his sensations (though, as we saw, it fails as an argument against the thesis that perception necessarily includes subjective sense-experience). If a person's knowledge of perceptual truths about himself had to be by inference from knowledge of the nature of his sensations, then no person who has an understanding of perceptual propositions while lacking understanding of the notion of subjective sensation ingredient in perception could possibly *know* that he sees or hears various sorts of things. For he could not know the premiss of the inferential justification supposedly required for knowledge of such truths. For one's claim to know that p to be justified and supported by inference from q, one must be justifiedly confident that q; and this one could not be if one did not even understand the proposition that q. But people who do not have the sophisticated concept of perceptual sensations are clearly not thereby barred from knowing that they see and touch and hear trees and tacks and trains.

4. Disabused, then, of the idea that perceptual knowledge must be by inference from sensations, let us try to give a correct account of its conditions.

I will deal only with visual knowledge, and I will undertake to give an account of the truth-conditions only for those propositions of the form 'S knows that he sees d' where 'd' is of the form 'x in ϕ'. This will not limit the generality of my account of visual knowledge. 'd' can fail to be of the form 'x in ϕ' only through lacking implications about the appearance-affecting relations of x to the perceiver, that is, all of 'd' goes into the 'x' slot of the 'x in ϕ' form. But if a person knows that he sees a certain sort of object – for example, a man, a rectangular surface – he must know something about its appearance-affecting relations to him, even if it is only something as non-specific as that the object is in at least dim light, at least not very far away, at least not very far from a right angle to his line of sight, at least not very far from the center of his field of view. And normally he will know much more specific facts about these relations. If a person knows that he sees x in ϕ, then, obviously, he knows that he sees x: *in* knowing the first he knows the second, what suffices for his knowing the first suffices for his knowing the second. Thus, whenever a proposition of the form 'S knows that he sees d' is true there is also true a proposition of the form 'S knows that he sees x in ϕ' that entails 'S knows that he sees d'. So to give a general account of the conditions under which propositions of the form 'S knows that he sees x in ϕ' are true is not to overlook any conditions under which propositions of the form 'S sees d' may be true.

As one might expect, the conditions that constitute a person's knowing that he sees x in ϕ differ according to whether the proposition that he sees x in ϕ is pure or impure. This division does not, however, coincide with the division between non-inferential and inferential perceptual knowledge.

I will argue that all cases of impure perceptual knowledge and some cases
of pure perceptual knowledge must be inferential (if not memory knowledge, an unlikely possibility that I will ignore); only knowledge of a certain special sort of pure visual perception proposition about oneself can
be non-inferential (and non-memory).

5. That S's knowledge that he sees x in ϕ must be inferential if 'he sees x
in ϕ' is impure can be seen by considering the nature of impurity in a
visual perception proposition. An impurity in 'S sees x in ϕ' is a property
of S's environment that is entailed by the description 'x' and is such that
in the perception reported by that proposition S cannot be perceiving that
property, because whether or not x has that property could not, given
that it is in ϕ, make any difference to the visual sensation that the subject
of such a perception would be caused to have. Thus, if 'he sees x in ϕ' is
impure then S can know that he sees x in ϕ only if he knows that what he
sees in ϕ possesses a certain property that he does not then see. There is
no way in which he can be justified in claiming to know that something
he sees possesses a certain unseen property other than by inference from
the conjunction of those objective appearances of the thing that he does
then see and other propositions he is then justified in claiming to know
that connect in some appropriate way this thing having those appearances with that unperceived property. By itself, a single perception can dis-
close to the perceiver only the objective appearances of the thing that he
then perceives. Anything else, anything not entailed by those appearances, that he knows about what he perceives he must know by
inference from his perceiving those appearances plus other information
about them.

What has just been said obviously holds for certain sorts of impure
visual proposition, namely, ones containing an *explicit* impurity in the
scene-description or ones such that scenes that do not satisfy the scene-
description but appear just like scenes that do satisfy it are fairly common.
An example of the first sort would be the proposition (that would normally be expressed by) 'I see a large oak tree *that my great-grandfather
planted*',[8] and an example of the second sort would be the proposition
'I see a solitary, small, brown shed on the hillside about 200 yards away
through fog and in the twilight'. None of the impurities in the latter scene-
description are explicit; but so many things that are not sheds could and

do look as would a solitary, small, brown shed on a hillside at that distance in those circumstances – a large rock, a tree stump, a rusting car body – that no one will want to deny that a person who claims to know that what he sees in those circumstances is a shed must rely for justification of his knowledge claim on other information besides what his present visual perception of that thing gives him in itself. And, of course, one who claims to know that the tree he sees was planted by his great grandfather must be relying on information other than what he can get just from his present seeing of the tree.

But the same thing holds for those *implicitly* impure scene-descriptions of the form 'x in ϕ' for which it happens to be true that it is extremely uncommon and unlikely that anything not x looks in ϕ just as x would look in ϕ. Consider, for example, 'I see an ordinary house in clear daylight about 50 yards away' or 'I see a stand of several large evergreen trees in clear daylight from within it'. Here, however, there may be a temptation to think that one who knows that he sees such a thing need not rely for his justification on information other than the appearances of what he then sees. Here it may seem that just the look of what he sees – namely, its looking as would x in ϕ – discloses to him what he sees – namely, x in ϕ – because that look is in fact seldom or never possessed by something that is not x in ϕ. But this last fact is a contingent one that the perceiver must know if he is, on the basis of knowing that he sees something that looks as would x in ϕ, to know that he sees x in ϕ. Suppose I see an ordinary house in clear daylight from about 50 yards away, but suppose also that, *for all I know*, things that are not houses, but look, from about 50 yards away in clear daylight, just as would a house (indeed just as would this house I now see), abound everywhere and that I have no reason other than the objective appearances that I presently see for thinking that I see a house. Then clearly I have no justification for claiming to know that I see a house; no one would allow that I did know it, under those circumstances. It is impossible to know *merely* from seeing what *looks* as would a house in clear daylight about 50 yards away that one sees a house; one must rely on other information as well, perhaps, for example, the information that what looks as would a house... etc. is virtually never anything other than a house... etc.

What holds for 'I see an ordinary house in clear daylight about 50 yards away' must hold for any impure perceptual proposition. No single perception of a scene can by itself give its subject knowledge that it fits a description implying properties not perceived in that perception of it. Such knowledge is obtained only if the single perception is supplemented by knowledge attained independently of this perception, either particular information about this particular scene or general information about scenes having the appearance this one does.[9]

In consequence, when 'S sees x in ϕ' is impure, the justification condition in the general analysis of what it is for S to know that he sees x in ϕ must be inferential, and the premiss of the inference must include the proposition that S sees something having a certain objective appearance plus some other proposition connecting what S sees with the unperceived properties of x implied in the impure proposition 'S sees x in ϕ'.

6. As with other kinds of propositional knowledge, I will fit my analysis of impure visual knowledge to the pattern of the four general conditions of knowledge introduced in Chapter II, Section 1. Doing this, together with illustrating the analysis of the specific kind, will help to give a better idea of what the general analysis means, especially in the third and fourth conditions, by showing what it generalizes. And, of course, showing that the general analysis holds up well in specific cases provides further support for that general account. Analyses of different kinds of propositional knowledge will differ importantly in the details of the third, justification condition. In presenting this condition I will rely on the general analysis of inferential and noninferential justification given in Chapter III, Section 9. This is the general strategy. Now for the detailed analysis of our present case.

> The conditions of impure visual knowledge may be stated as follows. If 'S sees x in ϕ' expresses an *impure* visual proposition, then S knows that he sees x in ϕ if and only if
> (1) S sees x in ϕ,
> (2) S is confident that he sees x in ϕ,
> (3) this confidence is supported by the justification that
>> (a) there is a description 'y in θ' such that S has justification for confidence that he sees something that looks from his present point of view as would y in θ,
>> (b) there is another proposition q such that S has justifica-

tion for confidence in the conjunction of q and the proposition that he sees something that looks from his present point of view as would y in θ and for confidence that from that conjunction there can be (nondeductively) inferred with confidence the proposition that what he sees that looks from his present point of view as would y in θ *is* x in ϕ and, hence, the proposition that he sees x in ϕ,

(c) there are no propositions $r_1, \ldots, r_n$ such that S has justification for believing each of $r_1, \ldots, r_n$ and the proposition that he sees x in ϕ cannot be inferred with confidence from the conjunction of q, $r_1, \ldots, r_n$, and the proposition that he sees something that looks as would y in θ,

(4) there is no truth r such that were S to be justified in believing that r and retain all his properties that are compatible with his having justification for believing that r then he would be very far from justified in being confident that he sees x in ϕ.

In typical cases satisfying these conditions 'y in θ' will have the same instantiation as 'x in ϕ'. A person's justification for thinking he knows, for example, that he sees a cardinal just outside the window in clear daylight will typically be by inference from a conjunction that includes the proposition that he sees what looks from his present point of view as would a cardinal just outside the window in clear daylight. But we need in (3) (a) to have 'y in θ', instead of 'x in ϕ' repeated from (1) and (2), in order to accommodate the following sort of case. It may be that a person who knows that he sees an astrolabe in a glass case a few feet away in good, ordinary light ('x in ϕ') does not rest this knowledge on his knowledge that he sees something that looks from his present point of view as would an astrolabe... etc. For it may be that he has just come to know how an astrolabe looks (in such circumstances) by coming to know that the thing he presently sees is an astrolabe. This latter knowledge may derive from his knowledge that it has certain other objective appearances – for example, that it looks from his present point of view as would pieces of brass of such-and-such shapes put together in such-and-such ways lying in a glass case a few feet away in good, ordinary light ('y in θ') – plus his knowledge that (q) the guide accompanying him has just pointed to the thing he sees and said (with apparent sincerity), 'That is an astrolabe'. (In this example the difference between 'x in ϕ' and 'y in θ' lies entirely in the 'x' and 'y' components. For an example where the 'ϕ' and 'θ' components also differ, let 'x in ϕ' be 'an astrolabe in a glass case a few feet away illuminated by a red light' and let 'y in θ' be 'pieces of pinkish brass of such-and-such shapes put together in such-and-such ways lying in a glass case a few feet away in ordinary light'.)

7. The proposition q (mentioned in (3) (b) and (c)), for which S needs to have justification for confidence if S's confidence that he sees x in ϕ is to be supported by a justification he has, may be any one of several different sorts. If it is the case that things that look (from some point of view) as would y in θ but are not x in ϕ are rarely or never encountered (so that people would rarely or never be mistaken if they were always to believe that they see x in ϕ whenever they see something that looks as would y in θ) then it may suffice if (a) S knows just that general fact about that sort of appearance. If, on the other hand, this is not generally true of that sort of appearance, or S does not know that it is, then it will need to be the case either that (b) S knows other appearances as well of what he sees, that is, appearances it presents from other points of view or in other circumstances – enough so that he does know (or at least has justified confidence) that what has all these appearances is always, or virtually always, x in ϕ – or else that (c) S knows other sorts of facts from which the fact that what he sees is x in ϕ can be justifiably inferred with confidence. Let me illustrate each of these alternatives.

(a) It may be that so few, if any, other actually existing things look (from any point of view) just as would a large mountain in clear daylight a few miles away that anything having that appearance is almost bound to be a mountain... etc. Thus S may need to know no more about the appearance of the particular thing he sees than that from his present point of view it looks as would a mountain... etc. in order to know, by inference from that appearance and that general fact about such appearances, that what he sees *is* a mountain... etc. It may be that all houses having a certain peculiar shape and arrangement of their front windows are houses that S's great-grandfather built. If S knows this and also that anything that looks (from some point of view) as would the front of a house with that peculiar shape and arrangement of its windows from fairly close in clear daylight is very unlikely to be other than the front of such a house, then S may know, by inference from those general truths about things having that sort of look plus the particular fact that he now sees something that looks from his present point of view as would the front of such a house... etc., that he sees the front of a house that his great-grandfather built.

(b) S may know that he sees a small shed on a distant hillside by inference from the facts that he now sees something that looks from his present point of view as would a small shed in sunlight on a distant hillside (a dark speck in a green expanse), that he was a short time ago looking at the same thing only a short distance away from it and then saw something that looked (from his point of view then) as would a small shed a short distance away in sunlight, and that things that look as would small sheds outdoors a short distance away in sunlight virtually always are small sheds.

How can S know that what he saw a short time ago that looked (from his point of view then) as would a small shed a short distance away in sunlight is *identical* with what he sees now that looks (from his present point of view) as would a small shed in sunlight on a distant hillside? One way would be by inference from his memory knowledge (if he has it) that in the interval he has moved his body in such a way that his point of view now is distant from his point of view then but he now faces and looks toward the same place he faced and looked toward then and that it is extremely unlikely that anything looking from his present point of view as would a small shed in sunlight on a distant hillside could in that interval have come into that place, or between that place and his present point of view, without a lot of commotion of a sort that he would have perceived had it occurred but he did not perceive.

S may know that he sees a small solid cube lying in his right hand by inference from the facts that he now sees something that looks from his present point of view as would a small solid cube lying on his right hand close before him in good light, that during a short period up to now he has been seeing something continuous with what he now sees in his right hand that looked from his point of view during that period as would a small solid cube being turned over on all sides in his right hand close before him in good light, and that during this same period he has been feeling with his right hand something that felt as would a small solid cube that he was turning on all sides in his hand. Here the generalization that anything having all those (seen and felt) appearances is a small solid cube may be non-contingent. With the right sort of description 'x', a thing's *objectively appearing* as would an x from a sufficient variety of points of view relative to it may exclude every possibility of its being other than an x, may entail its being an x.

(c) If S is ignorant of any such general truths connecting appearances of what he sees that he has perceived (plus, perhaps, a certain sort of circumstance in which it is being seen, such as its being outdoors rather than indoors or one part of the world rather than another) with properties of it that he does not see, he may yet know that what he sees has those properties by inference from other sorts of facts he knows. S may know that the house with the peculiar looking windows that he sees is a house that his great-grandfather built from the fact that his father has just pointed to it and said 'Your great-grandfather built that house'. S may know that the dark speck he sees on the distant hillside is a man (and not a rock or bush or small shed or something else) from knowing that his companion beside him has just said, 'There's Jonathan on the hill yonder, waiting where I left him'. Looking at a stage set, S may know that what he sees in the set that looks as would a bookcase full of books *is* a bookcase full of books from the fact that he, the director, instructed the stagehands to install in the set a real bookcase with real books.

If S knows that he sees x in ϕ only in way (c) and not in way (a) or way (b), then he does not *see that* what he sees is x in ϕ. If S knows that the dark speck on the distant hillside is a man only from knowing that his companion has just said, 'There's Jonathan on the hill yonder...', then clearly S does not *see that* the thing he sees is a man. All ways of being justified in thinking that he knows that he sees x in ϕ that will also support S's claiming that he *sees that* what he sees is x fall under (a) or (b). In seeing x in ϕ a person *sees that* what he sees is x only if he sees, or has seen, enough details of its appearance for it to be true that he knows that virtually always when something has that sort of appearance it is x.

8. Condition (3) (c) rules out the circumstances that would spoil S's justification for claiming to know that he sees x in ϕ, insofar as that justifica-

tion is given him by (3) (a) and (b). Condition (4) rules out the circumstances that would defeat S's claim to know that he sees x in ϕ, insofar
as that claim is justified by condition (3). Here are some examples of
how these negative conditions work.

Let 'x in ϕ' be 'a small shed built by S's great-grandfather, a short
distance away in good light', and let 'y in θ' be the same except for deletion
of 'built by S's great-grandfather'. Let q be the proposition that someone
has just told S (with apparent sincerity) that the shed S now sees was built
by S's great-grandfather. Condition (4) would be falsified in this case, of
course, if it were false that S sees something that looks from his present
point of view as would (y in θ) a small shed a short distance away in good
light or false that (q) someone has just told S that the shed he sees was
built by S's great grandfather. For then the premiss of the inferential justification ascribed to S in (3), which premiss is specified in (3) (b), would be
false. A proposition r, whose truth would falsify (4) and S's having justification for believing which would falsify (3) (c), but whose truth and S's
having justification for believing which, would not falsify (1) or (2) or the
premiss of the inferential justification (indicated in (3) (b)), would be the
proposition that the person who told S that the shed he sees was built by
S's great grandfather did not believe what he told S (which proposition
does not entail that what he told S was false).

Another illustration: Let 'x in ϕ' be 'a three-story wooden frame building in clear daylight about 50 yards away', and let 'y in θ' be the same.
Let q be the proposition that what S sees that looks from his present
point of view as would a three-story frame building... etc. is among things
that taken together look to a motorist passing through them as would a
small town and are, in fact, located on a mid-western prairie, and something of which all that is true is rarely anything other than a three-story
frame building... etc. Again, condition (4) would be falsified if it were
false that q or false that S sees something that looks from his present
point of view as would y in θ. An example of a proposition r whose truth
would falsify (4) and S's having justification for believing which would
falsify (3) (c), but whose truth and S's having justification for believing
which would be compatible with (1), (2), and the premiss of S's inferential justification, would be the proposition that what S is passing through
that appears to be a small town is actually a movie set and the great
majority of what look to the passing motorist as would buildings are

actually excellent canvas representations of the fronts and sides of build-ings. (But S happens to be looking at one of the few actual buildings that are mixed in with the canvas representations.)

In these examples we see how it is possible for S to see a certain sort of thing, be justified in claiming to know that he sees that sort of thing by inference from a premiss he knows to be true, and yet, because of unusual circumstances of which he is ignorant, fail actually to know that he sees that sort of thing. About the earlier example, where the premiss is S's hearing apparently sincere testimony, it seems right to say that the in-ference goes through a false intermediate step, but not so with the latest example.

9. S knows a pure visual fact about himself when, for some description of the form 'y in θ', S knows that he sees something that looks from his present point of view as would y in θ. This knowledge *can* be *non*-inferential, and normally will be so, if certain conditions are met. It depends on the nature of the description 'y in θ' and also on whether what S sees looks *to him* as would y in θ.

It can be the case (though normally it will not be) that S sees something that looks (objectively) from his present point of view as would y in θ but it does not look *to S* that way, that is, S's visual sensation is not as if seeing y in θ but rather some distortion thereof. Suppose, for example, that something S sees looks from S's present point of view as would a white rose in bright daylight but, because of some aberration in S's visual system, it looks to S as would a red rose in very dim daylight. If S never-theless knows that what he sees looks from his present point of view as would a white rose in bright daylight then, it seems clear, it is not just by means of S's present visual experience that S knows this and that S's justi-fication for claiming to have this knowledge would have to be by inference from (at least in part) knowledge that has come to S quite independently of S's present visual experience. Perhaps S knows that his present manner of seeing things is abnormal, and knows how to correct for the abnormali-ty in judging the visible properties of what he sees, by inference from his knowledge that he has taken a drug that he was reliably told would have a certain distorting effect on his visual sensations. Or perhaps the abnor-mality is permanent with S and S has learned how the way things always look to him deviates systematically from the norm (insofar as his experience permits him to understand this) by inference from much testimony of others as to how things really look. (A radically color-blind person, whose visual sensations record no differences in hue but only differences in intensity of the colors of what he sees, cannot know to be true, because he cannot understand, the proposition that he sees something that looks from his present point of view as would a reddish-orange surface...; but he could know that how what he sees looks (objectively) is different in respect of color from how it looks to him and that how it looks (objectively) in respect of color is what normal visual perceivers call 'reddish-orange'.) In general, it is clear that it is only by appeal to other things S knows that S can justify being confident that he sees something that looks (from his present point of view) as would y in θ, if that is not how it then looks *to him*.

But even if S is a perfectly normal visual perceiver he may still be barred from knowing *non*-inferentially that he sees something that looks from his present point of view as would y in θ by the nature of this description. S might know non-inferentially that he sees something that looks from his present point of view as would a *lavender* surface facing him in ordinary light a short distance away, but he could not know non-inferentially that he sees something that looks from his present point of view as would a surface *of Lisa's favorite color* facing him a short distance away in ordinary light.

The meaning of some descriptions of the form 'y in θ' – for example, 'a large red surface in ordinary light a short distance before one', 'a small square surface at roughly a right angle to one's line of sight in ordinary light a short distance before one' – is connected with how y in θ looks in a certain direct way. That is, knowing the meaning is directly connected with knowing what the appearance is like; whereas knowing the meaning of other descriptions of that form – for example, 'a surface the color of my true love's eyes a short distance before me in ordinary light', 'a surface of the same shape as the State of Wyoming a short distance before one in ordinary light' – is not connected in this way with knowing how y in θ looks. When knowing the meaning of 'y in θ' is connected in this direct way with knowing how y in θ looks let us say that 'looks as would y in θ' gives a *direct* specification of a visual appearance.

I have given some examples but now let me try to give a general characterization of this direct connection. If we had only color terms to deal

with, we could simply say that 'looks as would y in θ' gives a direct specification of a visual appearance just in case one cannot understand 'y in θ'
without knowing how y in θ looks. For the meaning of color terms must
be learned from visual experience; a person who does not know what
anything looks like (because, say, he has always been blind) cannot understand the description 'a *red* surface in ϕ'.[10] But if 'y' is instantiated with
'*square* surface' instead of 'red surface' then it will be false that one cannot
understand 'y in θ' without knowing how y in θ *looks*, because of the possibility that a person might learn what shapes are designated by certain
shape terms through tactual-kinaesthetic perception. Yet it seems clear
that a person's understanding 'square' requires him to know what *some*
sort of appearance of a square surface is like, and that a normal sighted
person's understanding of 'square' is *as* directly connected with his knowledge of what a square surface *looks* like as it is with his knowledge of what
one *feels* like. It is just that the meaning of simple shape terms, unlike that
of color terms, is directly connected not *only* to visual appearance.

I think that we can capture the class of visual-appearance specifications
that we want if we say this: 'looks as would y in θ' gives a *direct* specification of a visual appearance if and only if it is possible to understand 'y'
without having perceived y in any other mode than the visual one and
'y in θ' is such that one who has not perceived y in any other mode than
the visual one can understand the proposition that he sees y in θ only if he
knows how y in θ looks.

The following then are examples of direct specifications of visual
appearances: 'looks as would a red square surface perpendicular to one's
line of sight a short distance away in ordinary daylight', 'looks as would
a small blue cube a short distance before one in ordinary daylight', 'looks
as would a large tree some distance away in ordinary daylight', 'looks as
would a small bird circling a short distance before one in ordinary light',
'looks as would something that in ordinary daylight and the same orien-
tation would look as that object now looks to one'. None of the first four
of these would be direct specifications of visual appearances if 'ordinary
daylight' were replaced with, say, 'red light', for a person may know how
red or blue or brown looks (in ordinary daylight) and know what red
light is (and even how a beam of it looks) without yet knowing how a red
or blue or brown surface looks in red light. The last two examples in the
first four illustrate the fact that a direct specification may include a term

that is not a simple shape or color term (or a term like 'surface'), but the name of a kind of particular thing, if that term *implies* a characteristic shape or color in that kind of thing, so that a person could not be said to know what kind of thing the term denotes unless he knew what that characteristic shape or color was. This is true of many terms, some common and some not so common: for example, 'man', 'house', 'spoon', 'the letter A in Gothic script', 'rainbow'.

The last example in the list above depends on the fact that understanding one's demonstrative reference requires attending to what one demonstrates; this form keeps the propositions about directly specifiable appearances that one understands and knows to be true from being limited by one's descriptive vocabulary.

An example of a specification of a visual appearance that is *not* direct (is *in*direct) is 'looks as would an animal of the kind Melora likes least a short distance before one in the kind of light Roberta has in her room'. The meaning of this might be understood perfectly by someone who has no idea of what specific kind of appearance it refers to.

If 'looks from one's present point of view as would x in ϕ' is indirect then typically a person who knows that he sees something that looks from his present point of view as would x in ϕ will know how x in ϕ looks. S can know that he sees something that looks from his present point of view as would x in ϕ *without* knowing how x in ϕ looks only if S does *not* know whether or not the way x in ϕ looks (objectively) from his present point of view is the way it then looks *to him*. That S's knowledge in that case will have to be by inference from other things he knows is just as clear as it is in any case of abnormal vision where something looks to the subject otherwise than it really looks from his present point of view.

Typically, however, when 'looks from his present point of view as would x in ϕ' is indirect, S will know that he sees something that looks from his present point of view as would x in ϕ because he knows the following: x in ϕ looks as would y in θ (where this is a direct specification of a visual appearance) and he sees something that looks from his present point of view as would y in θ. Since no one who knows this conjunction to be true could avoid realizing that it entails that he sees something that looks from his present point of view as would x in ϕ, one who knows it to be true could be said to know by an obvious deductive inference that he sees something that looks from his present point of view as would x in ϕ.

Or, if we choose to say that *in* knowing that conjunctive proposition to be true S knows that he sees something that looks from his present point of view as would x in ϕ – the entailment is so obvious that the latter piece of knowledge cannot be separated from the former – then the latter knowledge will still be inferential because S's knowledge of one of the conjuncts, namely, that x in ϕ (indirect) looks as would y in θ (direct), must be inferential.

(This, the typical case of knowing that one sees something that looks from one's present point of view as would x in ϕ, when 'looks as would x in ϕ' is indirect, is also clearly a case where one sees *that* something looks from one's present point of view as would x in ϕ. And any other, atypical sort of case, where S knows that he sees something that looks from his present point of view as would x in ϕ without knowing whether or not how x in ϕ looks is how what he sees then looks to him, will clearly be a case where S does *not* see *that* something looks from his present point of view as would x in ϕ.)

10. S's knowledge of the other conjunct, that he sees something that looks from his present point of view as would y in θ (direct specification), can, however, be *non*-inferential. And normally it will be so, the only exceptions being either cases where S's vision is abnormal and what S sees looks to S otherwise than it really looks or cases where S has some reason to distrust his visual sense on this occasion but this is over-ridden by other special evidence S has that justifies his being confident that his seeing is all right after all. It is from one's non-inferential knowledge that one perceives things having certain directly specifiable appearances that all the rest of one's perceptual knowledge must derive. All of one's perceptual knowledge is or comes by memory and inference from one's non-inferential knowledge of appearance-reporting propositions that are such that to understand them is to be able to recognize and discriminate the appearances that they report, to know what those appearances are like.

It should be noted that propositions of this sort are generally *not* ones such that one must be able to *express* them in language if one understands them and knows them to be true. A person may know, hence understand the proposition, that he sees something that looks from his present point of view as would a chartreuse elliptical surface perpendicular to his line of sight a short distance before him in ordinary light without being able to

put that proposition into words. Or, supposing that '*T*' is a description
in English of that shape that has been characteristic of the standard table
telephone, *S* need not be able to formulate '*T*' or any other correct description of that shape in order to know on some occasion that he sees
something that looks from his present point of view as would a black,
solid, *T* object in ordinary light at about arm's reach before him or to
know that *T* is a characteristic shape for table telephones. A person's
behavior may provide evidence of his making visual discriminations that
would show he has the concept of an object's being chartreuse or *T* or
elliptical or about an arm's reach away or at a certain angle to his line of
sight, even if he knows no words for any of these concepts.

To say that *S*'s knowledge of the directly specifiable visual appearances
(from his present point of view) of the things he sees can be non-inferential is to say that there is a set of conditions that minimally suffices for his
knowing that he sees something having a certain directly specified visual
appearance (from his present point of view) and that does not entail that
he has an inferential justification for claiming to know it. A set of conditions that is minimally sufficient, and also necessary, for such non-
inferential knowledge is the following:

> If 'looks as would *y* in *θ*' is a *direct* specification of a visual
> appearance, then *S* knows non-inferentially that he sees
> something that looks from his present point of view as would *y*
> in *θ* if and only if
> (1) *S* sees something that looks from his present point of view
>   as would *y* in *θ*,
> (2) *S* is confident that he sees something that looks from his
>   present point of view as would *y* in *θ*,
> (3) this confidence is supported by the justification that
>   (a) *S* has a visual sensation as if seeing *y* in *θ*,
>   (b) there are no propositions $r_1, \ldots, r_n$ such that *S* has
>   with respect to each of them either a memory-im-
>   pression that r_i or a perceptual sensation as if r_i[11]
>   and his having those memory-impressions or sensa-
>   sations would give him reason (by however elaborate
>   a sequence of inferences) to be unsure that he sees
>   something that looks from his present point of view

as would y in θ despite his sensation as if seeing y in θ, and

(4) there is no truth r such that were S to have justification for believing that r and to retain all of his properties implied by (3) (a) and (b) compatible with his having justification for believing that r then that justification and those properties would be very far from justifying S in being confident that he sees something that looks from his present point of view as would y in θ.

(Note that non-inferential visual knowledge of directly specified visual appearances of things, in my sense of 'visual knowledge' (knowing that one sees such-and-such a thing) will always be visual knowledge in that other sense mentioned in Section 1 (*seeing that* such-and-such a thing is there). That is, if 'looks as would y in θ' is direct, then S knows non-inferentially that he sees something that looks from his present point of view as would y in θ only if S *sees that* what he sees looks from his present point of view as would y in θ. If S knows non-inferentially that he sees something that looks from his present point of view as would a small blue egg shape on a flat brown surface within easy reach before him in ordinary daylight, then what S sees looks *to him* as it looks objectively from his present point of view and he *sees that* there is something that looks as would a small blue egg shape... etc.)

I will argue for the joint sufficiency of the conditions in the analysis just given in Chapter VIII. The necessity of each of them can, I think, be seen fairly quickly. The necessity of (1), (2), and (4) has already been argued in the argument for the general definition of knowledge given in Chapters II–IV. Note that (4) here refers to all of S's properties *implied by (3) (a) and (b)* where (4) in the general definition of knowledge refers to *all* of S's properties, without restriction. This is because here we are giving conditions for S's having a particular sort of knowledge of the fact in question, *non-inferential* knowledge, which is not the only sort of knowledge of that fact that S could have. So we do not want (4) formulated so that it can be true owing to S's also having some inferential justification for confidence in the proposition in question, even though there is a truth r that defeats S's non-inferential justification specified in (3) (a) and (b).

That (3) (a) is necessary for a *non-inferential* justification of a claim to

know the proposition in question follows quickly from things we have
already noted. If S does *not* have a sensation as if seeing y in θ (for example, as if seeing a red square surface perpendicular to his line of sight a
short distance away in ordinary daylight), but instead some recognizable
distortion of that kind of sensation (for example, as if seeing a red surface
with four *concave* sides a short distance away in *dim* light), then what he
sees does not look *to him* as y in θ looks. So he can know that what he
sees nevertheless looks objectively, from his present point of view, as
would y in θ only if he has some other knowledge by which to correct the
belief that should otherwise arise from how it does look to him: if he has
no reason to think that what he sees looks objectively some particular way
that is different from the way it presently looks to him, then he should not
think that it does. But a justification for thinking that it does must, of
course, be inferential.

The necessity of (3) (b) is also easily seen. If, contrary to (3) (b), S has
some memory-impressions or sensations that do give him reason to be
uncertain that he sees something that looks from his present point of view
as would y in θ, despite his having a visual sensation as if seeing y in θ, then
he *should* be uncertain of it and does not have justification for being confident of it and claiming to know it, hence does not know it, *unless* he has
some *other* reason for being confident of it that outweighs these reasons
for doubt and thus, despite them, gives him *inferential* justification for
being confident of that proposition. But his having such other reasons,
outweighing the reasons for doubt ruled out by (3) (b), is not entailed by
(1), (2) or (4); so one who satisfies (1), (2), (4), and (3) (a), but fails to
satisfy (3) (b), will be one who either *has* such other counterbalancing
reasons and thereby has inferential justification for the proposition or
lacks such other counterbalancing reasons and therefore fails to have any
justification for claiming to know the proposition.

In Chapter VIII I will discuss the principles that determine the sorts
of memory-impressions and sensations that (3) (b) rules out. But in the
meantime a few quick illustrations will give a more concrete idea of the
work that (3) (b) does. Suppose S sees and is confident that he sees something that looks from his present point of view as would a turtle resting on a
table within easy reach in good light (so that S satisfies (1), (2), and (3) (a)
if 'y in θ' is replaced with 'a turtle ... etc.'). Now suppose that, contrary
to (3) (b), it seems to S as if he remembers that he saw no turtle on that

table when he looked at it just a moment ago and that he took an hallucinogenic drug a short time before. These memory-impressions give S reason to be unsure that he sees something that from his present point of view looks as would a turtle... etc. and make his confidence that he does unreasonable, even though he has a visual sensation as if seeing a turtle... etc. (and whether or not he believes the deliverances of these memory-impressions), unless these memory-impressions are overborne by other justified beliefs (such as that a friend who has taken no drug has just told him that he too sees what looks like a turtle on the table).

A concurrent perceptual sensation that would give S reason to be unsure that he sees something that from his present point of view looks as would a turtle... etc. (and reason to wonder whether he is having a visual hallucination), despite his having a visual sensation as if seeing a turtle... etc., would be the tactual-kinaesthetic sensation as if feeling with his hand over the entire surface of a table before him (where the table he sees looks to be) and feeling nothing on it. And let us suppose that his visual sensation is as if seeing a turtle on the table and nothing else, no hand. Here the testimony of the two senses conflicts. Each gives reason to doubt the other. If belief in one rather than the other is justified it will be for reasons other than the present deliverances of those senses, and the justification will be inferential.

A final remark in elucidation of the part of (3) that comes before (a): Supposing that S has the non-inferential justification specified in (3) (a) and (b), what makes it the case that S's confidence in (1) is *supported* by this justification? Would it be possible for S's confidence in such a proposition *not* to be supported by such a justification if he has it? Only, I think if S fails to have an adequate grasp of what counts as a reason in one's memory impressions or other sensations for being unsure of (1) despite satisfying (3) (a); so that S would fail to recognize some such reasons as such, if he had them. At least this is the only circumstance that I want 'is supported by' to be taken to rule out here. In some sense, no doubt, confidence in (1) is not supported by (3) (a) and (b) in a subject who has a perfect grasp of such reasons but is willing, out of some motive or other, to maintain confidence in (1) (given (3) (a)) even if such reasons to doubt were to appear without there being any countervailing inferential justification; so that, while satisfying (3) (a) and (b) this subject could truly say that he would still be sure of (1) even if... and then go on to specify a counterfactual circumstance in which (3) (b) would be false and no other justification would be present. But I don't think that we should want on that account to deny that such a subject knows (non-inferentially) that (1) is true. After all, this subject realizes that, though his being confident of (1) in the specified counterfactual situation would defy disinterested reason, it does not do so in the actual situation.

NOTES

[1] As some do. See, for example, Armstrong (1961), p. 191, Hamlyn (1957), p. 110, Hamlyn (1961), p. 196 and Chisholm (1957), p. 3.

[2] This point and ones in the next paragraph were brought home to me by Collins (1967).

[3] For a full and interesting discussion of the conditions of *seeing that p* see Dretske (1969).

[4] See, for example, Armstrong (1961).

[5] Put forward by Berkeley (see *Principles of Human Knowledge*, I: 3, 58) and many philosophers since, for example: J. S. Mill (1865), Ch. 11 and Appendix to Ch. 12, Russell (1914a and 1914b), Lewis (1947), Chs. VI–IX, and Ayer (1947).

[6] In the language of Russell's phenomenalism: one's concept of an external state of affairs is a "logical construction" out of one's concepts of various sorts of sense-data; or in Mill's phrase: an external object is an "enduring possibility of sensation".

[7] Criticisms of phenomenalism similar to those that I have given, and some others as well, are presented in Armstrong (1961), Chs. 5 and 6.

[8] The emphasized phrase represents an *explicit* impurity in that it could be simply deleted, without being replaced by any other phrase with descriptive content, and the resulting description prefixed by 'a visual experience as if one were seeing...' would not be a more general visual-sensation description than one formed by putting that prefix on the scene-description before deletion.

[9] Applied to modes of perception other than the visual, this conclusion means, for instance, that one's knowledge that one hears a dog barking or smells rubber burning or tastes sugar in the tea needs to be grounded on more knowledge than just the knowledge that one hears something that sounds as would a dog barking or that one smells something that smells as would rubber burning or that one tastes something that tastes as would sugar in the tea.

[10] I use 'red' here in its ordinary sense and not in any special 'physical' sense, which it has been alleged to have, in which it is synonymous with some phrase of the form 'reflects light of such-and-such wave-length'. In its ordinary sense 'red' expresses a concept of an objective property that one can grasp fully without knowing anything about the physical theory of color, a concept one must grasp before one can fully understand what that theory explains.

[11] S has a memory-impression that r_i just in case it seems to him as if he remembers that r_i. This does not imply that he does remember that r_i or even that he thinks he remembers it. 'S has a perceptual sensation as if r_i' expresses an intelligible proposition only if 'r_i' expresses a perceptual proposition having S as its subject.

CHAPTER VII

MEMORY KNOWLEDGE

1. Let us say that a *memory fact* about S is a fact expressible by a sentence beginning 'S remembers...' or 'S remembered...'. A memory fact about S is often a *dispositional* fact about S. That is, the fact does not entail that S manifests (at the time at which he remembers...) the fact that he remembers... in any mental or behavioral act, but only that he could or would manifest it given suitable motive to do so. This might well be true, for example, of the fact that one would intend to express by saying 'S still remembers the name of his first grade teacher'. But memory facts are not always dispositional. For instance, the fact reported by 'S remembered in the nick of time that he had a doctor's appointment' is not.

I want to define *memory knowledge* in terms of dispositional memory facts, but not in the way that would be parallel to my definition of perceptual knowledge in terms of perceptual facts. S's memory knowledge is not his knowledge of memory facts about himself. Memory facts are not the *objects* of memory knowledge, but have, rather, to do with its *justification*. S has memory knowledge that p just in case he knows it *because* he remembers it.

It does turn out, on this definition, that S has memory knowledge that p just in case he knows that he remembers that p. So a person's memory knowledge of any fact is equivalent to his knowledge of a certain sort of memory fact about himself. But it is not the case that knowledge of just any sort of memory fact about oneself is equivalent to memory knowledge of some fact, because not every sort of memory fact is equivalent to one of the form 'S remembers that p.' For example, a proposition of the form 'S remembers to V,' where 'V' is a description of some action (for example, 'get milk on the way home') entails more than S's remembering some fact (say, that he has formed the intention to V); it entails that he does V. A proposition of the form 'S remembers V-ing', where 'V-ing' is a description of some past action or perception or subjective experience of S (for example, 'climbing Pinnacle Peak' or 'seeing Franklin Roosevelt in a motorcade'), is always stronger than 'S remembers that he V-ed' or any other proposition of the form '*S* remembers that *p*': one thing that the former entails but the latter does not is that *S* remembers that he *V*-ed *from a time when he V-ed* (a condition I will explain more fully later).

It might seem plausible so say simply that *S* has memory knowledge that *p* if and only if *S* remembers that *p*. It is clear that '*S* remembers that *p*' (though not 'As *S* remembers it, *p*') entails that *p*. And, for many instantiations for '*p*', it is clear that '*S* remembers that *p*' implies that *S* has at some time or other in the past come to know that *p*. The more interesting exceptions to this are those sorts of propositions about his own past experience of which a person may have *original memory knowledge*, which I will discuss in the next section.

(A less interesting sort of exception is the possible case where *S* would have known that *p* but for his *unreasonably* doubting it in the face of his justification for being confident of it. If *S* later becomes more reasonable and, remembering that he was entitled to claim to know that *p*, he claims to remember that *p*, to have come to know that *p*, we should, I think, allow that he then does know that *p*: the only obstacle there was to saying that he came to know it, his unreasonable doubt, has been removed. Strictly speaking this would not be a case of knowledge *retained* from an occasion of original acquisition. On the occasion of his being in an original justifying position for the knowledge claim *S* did not know because he was not confident. Still, in a looser mood, it would be natural to date *S*'s achievement of knowledge from his coming into the original justifying position rather than from his later overcoming his unreasonable doubt while remembering that he had been entitled to claim knowledge. I will ignore the possibility of this sort of case. It could be catered for by replacing 'non-memory knowledge' with 'externally conclusive non-memory justification for confidence' in the definitions to be given at the beginning of Section 3 and at the end of Section 5.)

If *S* came only to believe hesitantly that *p* on rather weak evidence – for example, *S* came to think that probably the checkbook was put in a certain drawer because *R* told *S* that she had a hazy impression but she was not sure that she put it there – then, even if as a result *S* later *thinks* he remembers that *p* (and it happens to be true that *p*), *S* is mistaken. If *S* does remember what his previous basis for thinking that *p* was, then he cannot truthfully say, 'I *remember* that *p*', for that would be to imply that his basis was much stronger than it actually was; nor could anyone else truthfully say this of him, for the same reason. Nor would it seem any more plausible to say that S remembers that p, if every justification S has had for thinking that he knew it failed to be externally conclusive, if in every case it was pretty much a lucky accident that S's justification was justification for a truth.

But the proposed definition, that S has memory knowledge that p if and only if S remembers that p, will nevertheless not do (whatever the instantiation for 'p') because the definiens does not entail condition (2) of the general definition of knowledge: that S is confident that p. It might be true that S remembers that p but false that S knows that p^1 because S's present belief that p is hesitant and uncertain. If for this reason S cannot say that he *knows* that p then no one else can say so either, although it may still be reasonable to say that S does remember that p if it is clear that S's present uncertain belief that p results in the right sort of way (more of this later) from S's having previously come to know that p. (Indeed, S himself may confidently remember that he *used to* know whether or not p: S may be able to say, 'I did know the answer to that and I *think*, but am not sure, I remember that it's p.') If, for example, S were asked what his telephone number was twenty years ago and S comes up with the right number but is extremely uncertain that he has got it right then S does not *know* that this was his telephone number then, but I think we would want to say that S does *remember* his number.

Could we say that S has memory knowledge that p if and only if S remembers that p and is certain that p? No, because the mere conjunction of these conditions does not ensure that the certainty is connected with the remembering in such a way as to make it memory-certainty. Suppose that S came to know that the first five digits of the decimal expansion of π are 3.1415 by having read this in a mathematics textbook. Suppose that some considerable time later S is asked what the first five digits of the decimal expansion of π are and answers (sincerely), 'Well, I'm not certain but I am inclined to think that what I learned was that they are 3.1415, but I am not at all sure of my memory on the last two'. At this point S does *remember* the fact in question (since, we may suppose, his present uncertain belief in it results in the right sort of way from his former knowledge of it) but he does not *know* it (since he is uncertain). Now suppose that S's questioner is a person whom S knows to be a reliable mathematician and the questioner now tells S that what S seems to remember having learned is in fact correct. On the basis of this new expert testimony S now begins to think (correctly) that he knows the fact in question. Now, although he knows it and continues to remember it (as he did just before getting the new testimony), he does not know it *because* he remembers it. His present knowledge of the fact is freshly acquired and not *retained* from a previous acquisition; it is therefore not memory knowledge.

2. These reflections might lead us to say that to have memory knowledge of a fact is just to have retained (in one's memory) knowledge of it that one originally acquired at some past time: it is to know, because one remembers, that one previously came to know it. Such retained knowledge must, of course, be memory knowledge, but not all memory knowledge need be retained from some prior original acquisition of it. There is a certain sort of fact – namely, one about one's own past experience (that is, perception, thought, feeling, action, etc.) – of which one's very first knowledge can (though it need not) be memory knowledge. That is, it can be that whenever one has known a certain fact of that sort one has known it because one remembers it. This, which we may call *original memory knowledge*, can happen in various ways.

It may be that the proposition that p, though it reports a past experience of the subject, is a proposition that he did not understand at the time he had the experience. But after coming to understand the concepts involved in the proposition he remembers that they apply to an experience that he has had. Young children are sometimes able to describe *from memory* experiences they had before they learned any language adequate to describe them. I have heard, for example, of a two-year-old child who, upon seeing a certain building which she had been in only once before when she was under a year old, was able to recall having been inside it and to describe various features of the interior. In this case, for instance, the subject remembers the *experience* from the time when she had it. But she does not remember from that time *that her experience was such-and-such*; that she realizes only later. Still, when she does come to understand that proposition and to know that her previous experience was such-and-such, she knows this because she remembers that it was; therefore this knowledge is, upon its original acquisition, memory knowledge.

(There could be a case of which we would have to say that a subject *remembers* a fact about his own past experience that he *never* knows. Suppose, for instance, that S did not know that he was V-ing (for example, seeing a circuit diagram for a radio, suffering hyperasphyxiation) when he V-ed because S lacked the necessary concepts, and at every time after S comes to possess them S's sincere response to 'Did you ever V?' would have to be 'Well, I've a vague impression that I did once but I can't be sure'.)

A person may also have original memory knowledge of a *generalization* about a period of his past experience of the form 'Never during such-and-such a period did I V'. Generally when a subject knows on the basis of memory such a negative generalization about his past it will not be because he infers it from knowledge retained from each moment during the period in question (even if he did have such present-tense knowledge at each moment during that period). My confidence, for example, that I have not seen anyone enter my study during the few hours that I have been here need not be justified by generalization from a vast number of recollections for each moment within those hours that I was not then seeing anyone enter my study. Nor need it be justified by inference from the proposition that I do not recall seeing anyone enter and I would recall this had I done so. I can *simply recall* that my experience during that period included no such experience, and this will be how I first know that proposition. Simple recall of negative general facts about one's past experience is not limited to short periods in the immediate past. I can simply recall, for example, that during the last twenty years I have never been to a dog show. I can be quite sure of that, on the basis of memory, without being sure of the counterfactual conditional proposition that if I *had* been to a dog show during the last twenty years I would now recall it – a sort of proposition that it is hard to be justified in being sure of. There is no absurdity in saying 'I know that I have not V-ed, though whether or not I would now remember it if I had V-ed I cannot tell'.

The case is often similar with positive generalizations about one's past experience. I believe that my very first knowledge of the generalization about my past that I have several times eaten pickled beets must have been by simply recalling that this was so and not, say, by inference from distinct recollections of several particular occasions on which I had that experience or by inference from the testimony of another. (In fact I do not now remember any particular occasion on which I ate pickled beets but I do remember that I have eaten them quite a number of times). Typically, my original knowledge of such a truth as that I have been reading for quite some time now is also by simple recollection (and not by generalization from a number of recollections about the various moments in the period referred to or by inference from the proposition that I do not recall *not* reading during that period and I would now recall it if I had been not reading then).

Original memory knowledge of generalizations about one's past experience is important in the initial stages of the acquisition of knowledge of one's environment (at least in the actual, normal case, although it is imaginable that it should be otherwise). It is a big help in getting started on perceptual knowledge. For example, a young child may know that he sees a solid cube by inference from the proposition that he sees something that looks from his present point of view as would a solid cube at arm's reach before him in good light plus the generalization that things looking that way from a single point of view (or a limited range of points of view) virtually always are solid cubes; and this generalization the child may know by inference from the generalization about his own experience that he has many times seen something looking like that and subsequently felt it and looked at it on all sides and never (or almost never) did it fail to feel or look solid or cubical on all sides; and *this* the child may know in the manner of original memory knowledge, because he remembers it from his previous experience, without having known on the occasions of previous experience, or even understood the proposition, that he was perceiving something of such-and-such an appearance. The same perceptual experience in the early years, from which the normal person derives his knowledge of many general truths about connections among objective appearances of things, also gives him his grasp of various concepts of directly specifiable appearances, his understanding of various propositions to the effect that he perceives something that appears from his present point of view as would such-and-such (a solid cube or a ball or a person's face, at about arm's reach or further away than that, in good light or relative darkness), since this understanding requires a knowledge of what sorts of further appearances must be perceivable through various sorts of action if what appears as would such-and-such *is* such-and-such. And to think merely that one sees something that *looks* from one's present point of view as would a thing of a certain sort is to think that one is being affected by one's environment in a way that can be counted on, if one moves in certain ways, to produce further perceptions that will have certain

coherent relations to the present perception and accompanying perceptions in other modes (assuming that nothing interferes to break perceptual contact with the environment, such as losing consciousness or mal-
functioning of one's perceptual faculties).

It may be that not all of a normal person's understanding of perceptual
propositions and beliefs about general connections to be expected in his
perceptual experience come about through memory of earlier experience.
It may be that from the beginning of his perceptual experience a normal
infant has some generally correct (if crude and inspecific) beliefs as to
what sorts of things he perceives and what sorts of further perceptual
experience he would have if he moved in certain ways. (Bower (1974)
reports recent experiments on perception in infants that support such an
hypothesis.) If this is so and if the explanation of the normal infant's
having these beliefs that are not derived from experience also explains
why they are generally correct, then it would be natural to count the
correct ones as knowledge, or as close to it as the infant (with his lack of
experience and lack of a concept of justification) can come.

With respect to his beliefs as to the directly specifiable appearances
he sees the inexperienced infant may virtually satisfy the justification
condition (3) in our analysis of non-inferential perceptual knowledge
(as well as the other conditions), all except for the 'supported by' part at
the beginning. And he may have beliefs about general connections to be
expected in perceptual experience that would, when conjoined with his
direct perceptual beliefs, form premises from which some impure perceptual beliefs (such as that he sees a graspable object within arm's reach,
or that he sees a sharp drop-off just ahead of the surface on which he lies,
or that he sees one object go behind another) could be properly inferred
with confidence. The beliefs a very young infant has about general connections to be expected in perceptual experience that are not derived from
earlier experience could be likened to memory-impressions, and the correct ones among them that we might want to count as quasi-knowledge
might be likened to memory knowledge. They are not actually memory-
impressions or memory knowledge, of course, but this comparison becomes plausible (if it isn't already) in light of another: between the infant's
case, as we are supposing it to be, and the fanciful but conceivable case of
the coming into existence full-blown of an adult human being who is much
like one of us in his general beliefs about how the world works and what

sorts or things there are in it but lacks any memory-impressions of particular past experience of his. The inclination to treat such a person's general beliefs as showing impressions on his part that he has come to know certain things, memory-impressions, and to treat the true ones as a sort of knowledge very like our memory knowledge would be very strong, especially if what explains his having them (for example, his brain's having been copied from that of a person who was born and grew up in the real-world way) also explains their being generally correct.[2] Similarly, if the normal infant starts his perceptual experience with some beliefs as to what it is and will be like, and that which explains his having those beliefs (for example, their being genetically determined traits that have important survival value) also explains their being generally correct, then it would not be stretching things far to look at them as, in a way, knowledge and to liken them to memory. Here, and even more plausibly in the case of the newly existent full-blown adult, one might speak of pseudo-memory-impressions and pseudo-memory knowledge (where 'pseudo' modifies 'memory' rather than 'impressions' or 'knowledge').

The two sorts of genuine memory knowledge that I have distinguished – original memory knowledge of one's own past experience and knowledge of any sort of fact retained in the memory from a prior original acquisition – are all the sorts there are. Thus it is true in a sense that one's memory knowledge is always knowledge of one's own past. Or rather: to claim that one knows a fact because one remembers it is always to claim something about one's past: either one implies that one came to know the fact in the past or the fact is itself about one's past experience. This is a significantly weaker sense than that in which many philosophers have taken it to be true that memory is always of the subject's past. Many seem to have thought that to remember something is always really to remember experiencing something.[3] But this is not so. Even to *remember that* one had a certain sort of experience is not necessarily to *remember experiencing* a certain sort of thing. The proposition expressed by 'S remembers V-ing' is much stronger than that expressed by 'S remembers that he V-ed.' S remembers V-ing if and only if he remembers that he V-ed *from* a time when he V-ed and not just from some other time when he acquired knowledge that he V-ed and, further, he remembers, not merely the bare proposition that he V-ed, but also in some detail what V-ing on that occasion was like.

I know that I saw the Chicago World's Fair in 1936, but I do not remember that I saw it *from* the time of my visiting it but rather only from
several accounts of our visit that my parents gave me years later. If
someone now asks me what World's Fairs I have seen, I can truthfully
answer that I remember that I saw the one in Chicago in 1936, but I cannot truthfully say that I *remember seeing* that Fair since I remember
nothing from the original experience itself. Moreover, in order to be able
to say that I remember seeing (attending) that Fair I would have to remember from the time of my seeing it more about that experience than
just the proposition that I did see it: I would need to be able to give some
non-empty answer to the question "What was it like?" that my claim to
remember seeing it is likely to raise: I must be able to describe the experience or picture it to myself in some detail. If I now recall that it is a fact
that I saw the Chicago World's Fair in 1936 but I do not now know
whether I remember that from the original experience and do not recall
any details of the experience, then, even though it should happen that I
do remember that I saw the Fair from the time of the original experience,
I do not remember *seeing* it. The *experience*, as distinguished from the
knowledge that I had an experience satisfying a certain (meager) description, has not stayed with me.

3. Let me turn now to formulating conditions of remembering and memory knowledge. First I shall state several definitions: of remembering
that p, of memory knowledge that p in general, and of each of its two
kinds. Then I will explain and comment on these definitions

> *S remembers* that p if and only if
> (1) S has a (strong or weak) memory-impression that p and
> (2) there was a time t such that either (a) S's memory-im-
> pression that p is memory-connected to his having non-
> memory knowledge that p at t or (b) 'p' is of the form
> 'S V-ed', attributing to S a certain sort of past experience
> (action, perception, or subjective experience), and S's
> memory-impression that p is memory-connected to his
> having V-ed at t.
>
> *S* has *memory knowledge* that p if and only if
> (1) p,

(2) S is confident that p,

(3) this confidence is supported by the justification that

    (a) S has a strong memory-impression that p and

    (b) S has no other memory-impressions or sensations or infallible knowledge that would give S reason to be unsure that p despite his strong memory-impression that p, and

(4) (a) there is no truth r such that were S to have justification for believing that r and retain those properties implied by (3) (a) and (b) that are compatible with his having justification for believing that r then that justification and those properties would be very far from justifying S in being confident that p:

in particular the negation of the following proposition is not a truth:

    (b) either (i) 'p' is of the form 'S V-ed', attributing to S a certain sort of past experience, and there was a time t such that S V-ed at t and S's present strong memory-impression that he V-ed is memory-connected to his having V-ed at t, or (ii) there was a time t such that S had non-memory knowledge that p at t and S's present strong memory-impression that p is memory-connected to his having known that p at t.

S has *retained knowledge* that p if and only if (1), (2), (3), (4) (a), and (4) (b) (ii).

S has *original memory knowledge* that p if and only if (1), (2), (3), (4) (a), and (4) (b) (i).

The definitions of memory-knowledge have, of course, been constructed so as to fit the pattern of the general definition of knowledge given at the beginning of Chapter II. This has the interesting consequence that the crucial feature of memory, namely, the special causal connection that it requires between a present cognitive state and a past experience or cognitive state of the subject, is implied in the fourth, external-conclusiveness condition.

The two species of memory-knowledge are distinguished by the nature of the earlier in the pair of items that this connection connects. In the case where 'p' is of the form 'S V-ed' and attributes to S a certain sort of past experience, what determines whether S's memory knowledge that p is retained knowledge, original memory knowledge, or both (as it could be), is a matter of how (4) (b) is satisfied: it is both if both (i) and (ii) are true; it is only original memory knowledge if (i) but not (ii) is true; and it is only retained knowledge if (ii) but not (i) is true. The justification condition, (3), does not discriminate between these, so S may be justified in claiming to have memory knowledge without being justified in claiming to know that he has one rather than the other or both species of it. In satisfying (3) with respect to a proposition about his own past experience, S may be justified in being confident that (4) (b) is true without being either justified in being confident that (i) is true or justified in being confident that (ii) is true. I may, for example, claim to remember and know that I once saw Franklin Roosevelt in a motorcade without being sure whether I remember this from the occasion of the experience itself or only from later occasions when I was told about it.

Perhaps the most important thing to note about (3), the justification condition, is that it is not inferential: memory knowledge is non-inferential knowledge.

But note that some memory knowledge, namely, retained knowledge, is in another way derivative. Retained knowledge that p derives via the memory-connection from some prior state of non-memory knowledge that p. But one may retain knowledge that p without retaining the justification one previously had for claiming to know that p. Nothing in (3) or (4) (b) (ii) entails that S continues to satisfy the conditions that would have justified S's knowledge claim at the time t from which S retains the knowledge, and this is as it should be. Suppose, for example, that S originally came to know a certain mathematical truth by a certain complex proof that S constructed, but S now remembers confidently only that he did somehow come to know that truth and does not remember at all how he came to know it, not even whether it was by working out a proof or by being told that it was true by a reliable authority. Clearly, S does still know that truth even though S can no longer produce the justification for claiming to know it that S originally could, but only the justification that he does remember that he did (somehow) come to know it. S's retained knowledge in this case will, in a sense, no longer have its original basis, for S no longer satisfies all the conditions that originally made it the case that S knew it. But in another sense S's knowledge does have its original basis for it is *retained from* its acquisition on that basis: without that (or some other) *history* of original justification S's present confidence on the basis of memory would not be retained *knowledge*.

4. Condition (3a) requires that S have a *strong* memory-impression that p. This means that it seems to S that he remembers that p *and* that there is nothing in, so to speak, the way it so seems to give him reason to lack confidence that p. Sometimes when one thinks or is inclined to think that one remembers something, one wants to say something like 'I *seem* to recall that p but I don't *clearly* remember it: my memory on the point is weak (hazy, uncertain)'. This is what I mean by saying that one's memory-impression is weak. 'I *seem* to remember…' or 'It *seems* to me as if I remember…,' with a certain emphasis on 'seems' and a certain tone of hesitation, express this weakness in the memory-impression, suggesting that one's hesitation has to do with the nature of one's memory itself and does not derive entirely from other considerations such as beliefs that fail to cohere with what the memory-impression delivers. But 'seem to remember' can be used without this suggestion of weakness in the memory-impression, as in: 'You say you weren't there at all? How strange. I seem to remember so clearly that you were. It's rare that one *seems* so clearly to remember something that never happened.' The intelligibility of the last sentence shows also that 'seems to remember that p' does not (or at least need not) imply that the subject does not actually remember that p or that he has some reason to doubt that he does. (I take it for granted that 'S remembers that p' implies that p.) That sentence uses 'seems to remember' in that sense in which seeming to remember is not only compatible with remembering but is implied by it.

A *strong* memory-impression is just one that is not weak in the sense explained. It is one whose deliverance its subject will not normally be inclined to doubt except for reasons external to the memory-impression itself, which (3) (b) says he does not have. So one who satisfies both (3) (a) and (3) (b) but lacks confidence that p must be *abnormally* distrustful of his memory (either in general or for some reason having to do with the nature of the proposition that p, for example, that proposition may report something that he very much wants *not* to be the case).

It is possible for one who satisfies (3) (a) and (b) but is abnormally distrustful of his strong memory-impression that p to be confident that p for some *other* sort of reason. This is where the part of (3) *before* (a) and (b) does its work: such a case would not be *memory* knowledge that p. S's confidence that p is supported by the memory-justification specified in (a) and (b) only if S could (provided that he understood the propositions) truthfully say either that he is confident that p *merely* because (a) and (b) or that he would be confident that p merely because (a) and (b) if he had no other reason to be confident that p.

A *memory-impression* (weak or strong) is an enduring sort of dispositional *state* of its subject that may be (and usually is) present when it is not being manifested in any mental or behavioral act. Most of us have at any given time a great many memory-impressions of which we can manifest at that time only a very few. But, of course, whether or not a person has a certain memory-impression is tied to whether or not he *would* manifest it *if* the circumstances were of the right sort. Manifestations of memory-impressions come in a great variety of styles. Contrary to what many philosophers have thought, they need not involve a mental image or other *representation* of the experience or fact remembered.[4] Any act of which we can truly say that in that act the subject relies on his memory that p manifests a memory-impression that p (for example, when asked 'Where did you put the pliers?', simply replying 'the kitchen drawer' or going to the kitchen drawer or pointing to it may suffice to manifest a memory-impression that one put the pliers in the kitchen drawer); any thought that a subject could correctly express by saying 'I recall that p' or 'I seem to remember that p' is a manifestation of a memory-impression that p. We can say that a person has a memory-impression that p, the dispositional state, if he *would* manifest it, at least in the sort of thought just mentioned, were he to consider and try to answer the question whether it seems to him that he remembers that p.

Philosophers who have thought of all remembering as remembering experiencing, have usually also thought of its manifestations as confined to having a mental image of the remembered experience. It seems to have been supposed that producing information from one's memory (remembering it) must be a matter of reading it off from a retained trace or copy of a past experience while feeling the copy to be derived from (a trace of) something past. (Somehow it seems to have been easier to suppose that an experience should produce in its subject later *copies* of itself than that it should produce merely the disposition to assert that it happened or to manifest this belief in some other manner. This tendency may be part of a general tendency to regard any sort of *thinking* of a fact or a possibility as essentially involving a picture or representation of it.[5]) This description of what happens when one remembers has even seemed to be an analysis of what a *memory* impression is, or what a manifestation of one is. But it is no analysis at all: The irreducible element of feeling or being aware that a present mental image refers to a past experience, however it may be described – as there being a feeling of pastness about it, or an aspect about it of seeming left by what has gone before – can be nothing other than *seeming to remember* that one had an experience like what one now pictures. That would have to be the tacit understanding as to how those descriptions – which could have other applications – are to be taken in the context of that analysis.

As far as I can see, the proposition expressed by (3) (a), '*S* has a strong memory-impression that *p*', or the weaker ones expressed by 'it seems to *S* that he remembers that *p*' or 'I seem to remember that *p*', cannot be expressed without the use of 'remember' or some cognate expression (cognate by existing usage or by stipulation). Clearly, 'It seems to *S* that *p*' will not do, since it is obvious that it can seem to *S* that *p* without its seeming to him that he remembers that *p* (for example, he has for the first time just been informed that *p* or come to the conclusion that *p*). Similarly for 'It seems to *S* that he knows that *p*': *S* may just now have come to know that *p* for the first time. The proposition 'It seems to *S* that he previously came to know that *p*.' (or 'It seems to *S* that he *V*-ed') is entailed by, and *in most circumstances* entails, 'It seems to *S* that he remembers that *p*' (or 'It seems to *S* that he remembers that he *V*-ed'). But there is at least one circumstance in which the truth of the former does not require the truth of the latter, namely, when *S* has just now been given what he takes to be good evidence that he previously came to know that *p* (or that he *V*-ed).

Suppose that at some past time *S* came to know that Pluto is about 48 times as far from the sun as the earth and since then has not had occasion to manifest memory of this fact or otherwise to think of it, and suppose that *S* is just now reliably informed that he once came to know that fact. What can now show whether or not it also seems to *S* as if he remembers it? Obviously not merely his thinking it right to say that it seems to him that he has previously come to know it, since that could be explained by his having just now been informed that he previously came to know it. The only criterion that would show it that I can think of is whether or not S thinks it right to say that he *remembers*, or *seems to remember*, it (and he knows the correct use of 'remember'). Suppose someone tells me that he was present the last time I told the joke I have just begun to tell and his doing so *reminds* me of, that is, leads me to remember, that fact. If I am asked how I know that I do *recall* that fact, and do not know of it *only* on the basis of having just been told it, the only thing that I can answer, as far as I can see, is that it just seems to me that I do *remember* it – and, of course, I know how to use 'remember', 'recall', and the like correctly: I know, for example, that it is correct to say '*S* remembers that *p*' when it is the case that *S* previously came to know that *p* and *without* having been introduced in any way to the information again *S* now believes that *p*. Of course, if I were able to supply more detailed information about the previous occasion of my coming to know the fact in question than anything I have since been told about it, that would be convincing evidence that I did remember that fact from that previous occasion. But we cannot require such ability to supply further details as a necessary condition of remembering or seeming to remember, for it is possible to remember about a past occasion only what one has just now been told and no more. As far as I can see, there is no report a subject can give of his present state in other terms, in terms of other things that he thinks it right to say about himself, that will in every circumstance be equivalent to the proposition that he would express by saying 'I seem to remember that *p*'. (From this it follows that, given the unlikely circumstance that *S* is just now informed that he previously came to know that *p* and does *not* know the use of 'remember' or any cognate expression, then the only sort of reason another person could have for saying that it also seems to *S* that he remembers that *p* would be an inductive one: the presence of some condition found to be correlated with seeming to remember in cases where there was present some such clear criterion of seeming to remember as (a) the subject's thinking it right to say that he remembers or seems to remember or (b) its seeming to the subject that he has come to know that *p* when he has *not* just been given good evidence that he came to know that *p*.)

If it were necessary that every memory-impression represent a genuine

memory, impossible that any memory impression be a *memory* delusion –
as distinguished from a memory of some past experience or apparent
acquisition of knowledge that was illusory – then a memory-impression
that *p* could be defined as an impression that *p* that is memory-connected
to a previous acquisition of knowledge that *p* or seeming acquisition of
knowledge that *p* (or, where '*p*' attributes to the subject a certain past experience, to an occasion when the subject had that experience or it seemed
to him that he was having it or he dreamed that he was having it or he
vividly imagined having it or something of the sort). And then we'd need
to consider whether we can explicate memory-connection without using
'remember' or any cognate. But, of course, delusions of memory *are* possible. It is, for instance, possible that a person should seem to remember
skiing (even seem to remember it vividly) but have never actually skied or
had an illusion or dream that he was skiing or engaged in imagining himself skiing or even been informed what skiing was like: though we do not
expect it ever to happen, we can conceive what it would be like for (and
what we would be willing to count as) a person who has never before had
any experience that would have given him any idea of the phenomenon
of skiing to wake up one day with a vivid memory-impression of having
been skiing.

5. Let us consider now the negatively phrased conditions of the definitions,
(3) (b) and (4). There is this relation between them: if a proposition *r* is
incompatible with (4) then *S*'s having justification for believing that *r*,
given him ultimately by his memory-impressions, sensations, or infallible
intuitions, is incompatible with (3) (b). The way in which (4) can be false
to which I wish to give most attention in this chapter is through the falsity
of (4) (b), through the absence of the right *connection* between *S*'s previous knowledge or experience and his present memory-impression that
he had it.

    But there are other ways in which (4) or (3) (b) could be false, which are
compatible with the truth of (4) (b) and also quite compatible with the
truth of (1), (2), and (3) (a). For example, suppose that *S* has just awakened in the morning and let the proposition '*p*' – with respect to which (1),
(2), and (3a) are satisfied – be the proposition that *S* got up in the middle
of the night and closed the bedroom window. A proposition *r* whose truth
would falsify (4a), and *S*'s having justification for believing which would

falsify (3b), would be the following conjunction: the window is now wide open, S's husband did not open it at any time in the night, he is the only other person S has any reason to think was in the house during the night, and dreams while asleep often give rise to false memory-impressions upon awaking. (This proposition is compatible with (1): suppose that S did get up and close the window and that after S went back to sleep a burglar opened it, entered the house, found nothing he wanted to remove and departed without leaving a trace and without closing the window.) Though this r be true, as long as S is ignorant of it, especially the first conjunct, and satisfies both (3) (a) and (3) (b) S is justified in being confident and claiming to know that p; but if this r is true then S does *not know* that p, because if S were to have justification for believing this r (thus failing to satisfy (3) (b)), S's strong memory-impression that p would be too far from justifying her in being confident that p. (This seems to me right, but if it seems not quite so clear to others it will be, I think, because S's coming to have justified belief that r would not cancel altogether the justifying force of her strong memory-impression that p. It would be not unreasonable for S still to think hesitantly, to suspect at least, that her memory is correct and the wide open window has some other explanation now unknown; and, though it would be unreasonable, it would not be quite absurd for S to continue to believe strongly, to insist stubbornly on, what she seems so clearly to remember.)

((3) (b) in the analysis of memory knowledge differs from the corresponding condition in the analysis of non-inferential perceptual knowledge (p. 140) by the addition of reference to S's infallible knowledge as a possible source of reason to doubt the deliverance of his memory-impression. This is necessary in order to exclude the remote possibility that S should have a strong memory-impression of having come to know the contradictory of an *a priori* necessary truth that is now self-evident to him or that he now sees to follow self-evidently from self-evident truths.)

That the negation of (4) (b) is another proposition incompatible with (4) (a) but compatible with (1), (2), and (3) (a) will be clear once it is explained what is meant by its central term 'memory-connection'. This relation is to be defined in such a way that S remembers that p (or that he V-ed) from his having known that p (or his having V-ed) at t if and only if S has a (strong or weak) memory-impression that p (or that he V-ed) that is memory-connected to his having known that p (or his having V-ed) at *t*. To say that a case of seeming to remember is also a case of remembering, that a memory-impression is a bona fide memory, is to say that the memory-impression *results* in the right sort of way from a matching prior experience or state of knowledge.

What is the right sort of way? One answer we could give is this: consider all the ordinary, normal, clear cases of a person's remembering a particular experience or previously acquired piece of knowledge; whatever sort of neurological process it is that in fact links the experiences or the acquisitions of knowledge to the memories in all these clear cases, that in fact provides a true neurological explanation of how experience produces later memory of it (which is not known, as far as I know), is a connection that will suffice to make the memory connection whenever it links a particular experience or acquisition of knowledge and a later matching memory-impression.

Now this seems to be true, provided that there is such a neurological link. But it also seems that we need not go so far as to depend on any such possibly false assumption in order to get a conceptually sufficient condition for the memory connection. We can construct one using the circumstances that define the clear, normal cases of memory, the ones where we look for whatever neurological explanation it may have. It seems to me that these show the notion of the causal connection essentially involved in memory to be a special defeasible concept. Given that a person previously knew that *p* (or *V*-ed) and that he now has a memory-impression that *p* (or that he *V*-ed), the memory-impression *must of course be* the right sort of result of his previous knowledge (or experience) to count as his remembering it *unless* there are certain special facts in the case that defeat that attribution. In the absence of the right special sort of reason to think otherwise, the internal relation between *S*'s memory-impression and his previous knowledge or experience is reason enough to attribute the first to the second as a memory of it.

What sort of fact could defeat this attribution? Only the intervention of something else sufficient to have caused the present memory-impression. This might be an intervening occurrence of something sufficient to give *S* the same piece of knowledge (or an occurrence of the same sort of experience or of something sufficient to inform *S* of his previous experience). Or it might be something more fanciful, such as neurological experimenters applying to *S*'s brain a stimulus designed to give *S* just such a memory-impression. Given that a person on just one occasion acquires a certain piece of knowledge (or has a certain sort of experience) and then later has a matching memory-impression, then the two alternatives, that the impression is a memory of the previously acquired knowledge (or the previous experience) or that it has its source in some other intervening cause (of the sort mentioned), are the only accounts possible. We could not take seriously a third way of regarding such a case, one in which we suppose that neither the matching earlier knowledge (or experience) nor anything since is the cause of it but that it simply has no cause at all and its matching the earlier experience is only coincidence.

This is not because it is inconceivable that something should have no cause (which I disbelieve) but is a matter of our concept of memory. We just do not recognize any basis for doubting that a person's memory-impression is a memory of his matching earlier acquired knowledge (or his matching earlier experience), for suspecting that there is some other connection instead or that the matching is just a coincidence, except the belief or suspicion that the subject would not have that memory-impression had not something else happened that was sufficient to cause it. It would be absurd to suggest *both* that it is a coincidence, an accident, that a person's memory-impression matches his earlier acquired knowledge (or his earlier experience) *and* that the impression has no *other* cause. The first suggestion could be supported only by evidence of the existence of another cause.

This seems to me to hold even for the circumstance where the subject's memory-impressions regarding very similar matters are so much more often wrong than right that the subject could have done as well by guessing: one has good reason to think that someone merely guessing as to the facts on those matters would be right by mere chance as often as this subject's memory-impressions are right.[6] Suppose that in a psychological experiment the subject hears spoken ten three-digit numbers in succession and after a short interval is supposed to write down all of the ten numbers that he can remember having heard, and suppose that one particular subject, claiming sincerely to remember them all, writes down ten numbers. This is repeated, with different sets of ten numbers, several times with the same result each time: this subject confidently offers ten numbers as the ones he remembers having heard. But actually the numbers he writes down coincide with the numbers he has just heard very infrequently, no more frequently over a longish run of trials than those written down by another subject who is asked just to invent sets of ten three-digit numbers. Knowing this about a case would, indeed, make us strongly suspect that those of the subject's memory-impressions regarding the numbers he has just heard that happen to match the facts are not genuine memories, that it is just a coincidence that those memory-impressions are correct. But this would be because what we know about the case gives us reason to suspect equally strongly that those few correct memory impressions, along with the many incorrect ones, have *another cause* unconnected with the subject's hearing the numbers spoken.

Although the absence of any other explanation is *sufficient* to connect the memory-impression to the matching earlier knowledge (or experience) in the right sort of way for the one to be a memory of the other, it is not *necessary*. I may remember that I had a certain sort of experience from the time when I had it, even though something has happened to me in the meantime that was independently sufficient to cause me to have a memory-impression that I had such an experience. Suppose, for example, that I now remember that I once lost control of a car I was driving on a snowy road and skidded into the roadside ditch and that I have remembered this ever since it happened. It is quite compatible with this that on some occasion in the meantime I have had the experience of hearing other occupants of the car tell of the incident in vivid detail and *that* experience *would* have been sufficient to produce in me the same memory impression even if I had before that completely lost my memory of the incident. A sufficient condition for memory connection that is also necessary must not exclude such a case.

Another sufficient condition for memory connection would be simply that since acquiring a certain piece of knowledge (or having a certain sort of experience) the subject has continuously had a memory impression of it. If S came to know that p at t and at all times since t it has seemed to him that he remembers that p, then it cannot be denied that he has never since then forgotten that p, that he remembers that p from t, no matter what else may have happened in the interval. But this too is not necessary for memory connection, since it is possible that a person should totally lose memory of a certain piece of knowledge (or experience) for an interval after which memory of it simply returns without anything *new* impinging on the person that would suffice to produce the memory-impression.[7]

What we can say is this:

> Given a person who at a certain past time t had non-memory knowledge that p (or V-ed) and now has a memory-impression that p (that he V-ed), the latter state has the right sort of connection to the former state to be a memory that p (that he V-ed) from t if and only if, for any time since t at which something impinged upon him sufficient to produce in him a memory-impression that p (that he V-ed), he then already possessed such a memory-impression.

Here 'already' means that his possessing it then was not brought about by what impinged upon him then. This condition is satisfied if upon being told about his past acquisition of knowledge (or his past experience) the person is able to say sincerely or think, 'Ah yes, I remember it now', even if before that a more limited prompting did not succeed in reminding him of it. If he thinks it right to say that, then the prompting, however thorough, does not create the memory-impression but only provides a (perhaps necessary) stimulus to its manifestation. A memory-impression may consist in (among other things) a disposition to be *reminded* when given *sufficient* prompting. However, the only *criterion* for whether a really thorough prompting – an out-and-out telling – reminds the subject or is instead the whole source of the subsequent memory-impression is whether or not, upon being so prompted, the subject thinks it right to say that he is reminded or now remembers or some such thing (and, of course, knows the correct use of such expressions). If the subject, S, does *not* think it right to say some such thing and the reason is that S does not understand any such proposition, then one could speculate that S would think it right if S did understand. This speculation would be supported, for instance, if there were present a neural state that we had good reason, derived from what we have found in clear, unproblematic cases of memory, to think would have resulted in S's so thinking had S possessed the necessary concepts. (The presence of a certain neural state about which we possessed the right sort of information might even support the conjecture that a subject who possesses the necessary concepts but does not think it right to say that he is reminded, even after thorough prompting, nevertheless would have been reminded if some other sort of prompting had been given.) This possibility does not, however, open up any way of specifying what would constitute a subject's possessing an impression that has the memory-connection to that subject's previous coming to know (or experience) without using 'remember' or any cognate expression; and, as far as I can see, there is no way of doing this.

6. If the condition I have given for memory-connection is sufficient, then it follows that the concept of that connection does not require that there be some further causal connection between comings to know (or experiences) and later memories of them that explains the memory-connection in terms of neural mechanisms in the brain; though, of course, neither does it exclude this. In particular, it does not follow that there must be a further causal connection that is spatio-temporally continuous. If the sufficient condition I have given were satisfied by a particular past experience and present memory-impression of a person then, even if there were no intervening continuous chain of states or processes that is the mechanism by which the past experience causes the present memory-impression, the experience would still be the cause of the memory-impression and we would still have a case of memory. In the concept of memory we have a concept of a causal connection that could cross spatio-temporal gaps (though it may not in fact ever do so).[8]

Some philosophers have claimed the contrary. Martin and Deutscher (1966), p. 189, say:

Once we accept the causal model for memory we must also accept the existence of some sort of trace, or structural analogue of what was experienced. Even if someone could overcome the many difficulties of various kinds surrounding the idea of action at a distance, it could not be true to say that someone was remembering an event if his past experience of that event caused him, over a temporal gap, to recount it.

I don't know what difficulties surrounding the idea of action at a distance these authors have in mind. Perhaps one of them could be that it is hard to see how the spatial or temporal parameters would be accommodated in *general laws* governing a causal connection that could cross spatiotemporal gaps of various, and haphazardly determined, sizes. But this is a difficulty only on the assumption that any sort of causal connection requires that there be true causal laws under which its instances are subsumable – that only a law can make a causal connection. But it seems that in the concept of memory we have a counter-example to this assumption, since it seems clear that a particular experience and later matching memory-

impression could satisfy the condition I have given for memory-connection without there being any true nomic generalization of the form 'Whenever a person has such-and-such an experience, and certain further circumstances obtain (then or thereafter), then the person at such-and-such later
time has such-and-such a memory-impression'.

To philosophers strongly influenced by the Humean tradition about
causation, the idea of a causal connection that need not be continuous
or governed by general laws will seem strange. This possibility is perhaps
especially difficult to discern in the case of memory because it is now a
firm belief – at the very least a strongly appealing hypothesis – among
psychologists, neurological investigators, and probably many of the rest
of us, that the phenomena of memory of experience are to be explained
by some specific states or processes which our experiences produce in our
brains and which continue to be or unfold there until they are operative
in producing the manifestations of memory of those experiences. But the
fact that this hypothesis is widely accepted or appealing, perhaps even
strongly indicated by the evidence already turned up by neurological
investigation, should not be confused with the non-fact that the very
concept of memory requires some sort of continuous causal link between
an experience and the memory of it; this is no more the case than the fact
that the hypothesis of an intervening medium to explain the phenomena
of gravitational attraction was once widely appealing (and, some tell me,
still is) indicates that the very concept of gravitational force requires such
an intervening medium through which it is exercised.

If the continuity of the causal connection in memory were a feature
of the concept of memory, and not merely a feature of a dominant
hypothesis that there is a neurological explanation of memory, then, of
course, whether or not memory occurs at all would depend logically on
whether or not there is such a continuous link between experience and
later memory of it. But it seems to be at least logically possible that the
hypothesis of a continuous neurological link in memory might go the way
of the "ether" hypothesis. It might fail to be supported by further investigation. Although there seems to be good evidence that certain kinds of
memories and memory *capacities* depend on the (continuous) absence of
certain kinds of interference with the brain, the search for how a *particular*
experience and a later memory of it are linked by a continuous chain of
brain states and processes specific to that memory could conceivably go

on for a very long time and never turn up any solid answer. It could conceivably give us reason to doubt seriously that there are any such specific continuous brain "traces" for each memory. But it could not, of course, conceivably give us reason to doubt that people actually do remember specific past experiences.

What we have learned about the dependence of particular functions of mind on particular brain states, including the fact that there are such particular dependences on physical states, we have, after all, learned only *a posteriori*; and it is conceivable that we should discover that what has been looking and acting like an ordinary person for a long time – one of us, say – actually has no brain at all inside his skull, nor anything else in him that could be the vehicle of continuous specific causal connections between his experiences and his memories of them. Such a discovery would not demand the conclusion that this apparent person did not really remember his experience (or did not really have experience, or a mind).

Another remark that Martin and Deutscher (1966) direct against the possibility of discontinuity in the memory-connection is this (p. 189):

Furthermore, if our past experience could act directly on us now, there would no longer be any reason to suppose that we could remember only what we had experienced ourselves. If we did not hold [some sort of storage or trace account of memory], why should we not suppose that events which occurred years before we were born could cause us to recount their occurrence?

If my denial that the memory-connection *must* involve a spatio-temporally continuous causal process does have the consequence that it is possible that one person's memory-impressions should have the memory-connection to another person's acquisitions of knowledge (or experiences), it does not much disturb me; for I am strongly inclined to think that interpersonal memory-connection is a logical possibility. Moreover, I cannot see that one is protected from having to admit this possibility by holding that the memory-connection is continuous or involves a continuous trace. As Shoemaker (1970a) points out, if there is a continuous physical connection on which every memory depends, one could surely imagine that this physical process (whatever it may be) might run from one person's experience to another person's later matching memory-impressions, or something sufficiently like it might, so that one would want to say, not perhaps that the second person *remembers* the first person's experience, but at least that he does something very like remember it, he 'quasi-remembers' it (to use Shoemaker's term).

Shoemaker himself suggests a different sort of argument for the spatio-temporal continuity of the causal connection in memory.[9] This argument arises out of his aim (which I endorse) of showing that it is possible to frame a satisfactory sufficient condition of personal identity across time that uses memory as the link and does not require bodily identity. What he appears to suggest is that memory can be the prime factor in *such* a sufficient condition for personal identify only if the causal connection in memory is conceived to be continuous.

Shoemaker's argument has to do with what happens when one provides a sufficient condition for memory connection that is free of the presupposition that the persons connected are identical. And this one must do, of course, if memory-connection is to be of any use in specifying an interesting condition for personal identity. If it is possible at all to formulate a sufficient condition for the memory-connection that does not presuppose the identity of the persons connected and if the condition I have already formulated (*with* that presupposition) is sufficient for memory-connection then it should be possible to formulate a sufficient condition that is free of that presupposition but is like the one already formulated in not entailing a continuous connection.[10] But such a sufficient condition, Shoemaker's argument suggests, will not work as the basis for a memory criterion of personal identity.

This is because such a sufficient condition for memory connection would have a certain feature that must be shared by any plausible candidate for such a condition that does not presuppose the identity of the persons connected: it must entail the possibility that the memory-connection could *branch* or *split*. That is, it must allow it to be possible that similar memory impressions had by two or more distinct persons at time 2 could have the memory connection to a single person's experience up to time 1. Shoemaker's argument finds nothing wrong with this possibility but rather points out that it means that a sufficient condition for identity between person 1 at time 1 and person 2 at time 2 in which this possibly branching memory-relation is central, must also contain a clause that stipulates that there are no "competitors" to person 2's claim to identity with person 1 on the basis of memory-connection that have been produced by branching of that connection. But, says Shoemaker's argument, if discontinuity were permitted in the memory-connection then this required 'no competitors' clause would imply that nowhere in the universe after the time of the extensive experience of person 1 to which person 2's memory-impressions are connected does there exist any *other* person having equally extensive memory connection to person 1. And, says Shoemaker (1970a), p. 274, such a "self-consistent, unrestricted, negative existential claim" is "impossible in principle to establish."

This last claim, on which his argument ultimately rests, Shoemaker seems to think needs no argument. But I see no good reason to accept it. Perhaps Shoemaker's thought is that a spatio-temporally unrestricted negative existential claim ('Nowhere and nowhen is there....') could be established only by inspecting all of space and time, and *that*, I will grant, is impossible in principle. But that is surely not the only way that confidence in such a proposition can be justified. The law of gravity, like any contingent universal generalization, implies some self-consistent, unrestricted negative existential propositions, such as the proposition that nowhere and nowhen is there a body with the same mass as the earth, a body with the same mass as a brick, ten feet of empty space between them, no other bodies within a hundred billion miles, and no motion of the one toward the other. Our justification for being fairly sure of this does not depend on our having inspected all of space and time. Our extremely localized observations and experiments that are grounds for confidence in the law of gravity are grounds for confidence that certain sorts of logically possible states of affairs just do not occur anywhere anytime.

Consider now unrestricted negative claims about duplication. In order to be justly sure that there is nowhere else on the face of the earth a city exactly like New York City in all its details I do not need to have reason to believe that every other part of the face of the earth has been inspected and found to be without a duplicate of New York City. If I have no specific evidence of such a duplicate then I can be sure that there is none simply on the ground that it is just too unlikely, given our experience of the sorts of things of which exact duplicates are found or made. I can be sure on the same basis that there is no complete duplicate of New York City anywhere in our galaxy or in the universe. Adding territory does not significantly increase the likelihood. I have so much reason to think that such massive detailed duplication just does not happen, at all.

It is the same for the possibility that there are two people having exactly the same set of memory-impressions as I now have. Our experience, although restricted to a very limited region of space and time, gives us title, in the absence of specific evidence to the contrary, to be sure that such extensive duplication does not happen. Suppose a person whom we were talking to suddenly vanished without a trace and a few minutes later there suddenly appeared elsewhere in the room 'from out of nowhere' a person possessing all the same memory-impressions as were possessed by the one who vanished (but, let us suppose, having a different bodily appearance). We would naturally think, and would be entitled to think, that the second person's memory-impressions have the same source as did the first person's, namely the previous knowledge and experience of the first. And, as long as we do not observe or hear of *another* person with all those same memory-impressions popping into existence somewhere, we will be entitled to think, as we would think, that the second person is *the same person* as the first, one who has undergone a discontinuous change of spatial and temporal location (along with a discontinuous change of bodily appearance). We would and should not hesitate over the mere logical possibility that somewhere we don't know about there has popped into existence another person with all the same memory-impressions. In the absence of specific evidence to the contrary, we would be entitled to assume that whatever explains the extraordinary vanishing and appearing that has occurred (if anything does) it does not make it more likely than we now find it that more than one person (with a normal sort of totality of memory-impressions) should have all the same memory-impressions.

What if, however, more than one person with the same totality of memory-impressions did suddenly appear after the first one vanished? They could not, of course, both be identical with the person who vanished; and there would be no good reason to say that one rather than the other was, so neither could be. But there would still be sufficient reason for saying that the exactly similar memory-impressions of the suddenly appearing ones are what they are *because* the experience and acquisitions of knowledge of the vanished person were what they were: they quasi-remember *that* previous knowledge and experience. If there is no other causal explanation of the initial memory impressions of the suddenly appearing persons, then the explanation of memory connection, or quasi-memory connection, to the vanished person is far preferable to the hypothesis of sheer coincidence.

NOTES

[1] A possibility that has been denied, for example, by Malcolm, in 'A Definition of Factual Memory' in Malcolm (1963), p. 223.

[2] Unger (1967) brought me to realize how natural it would be to attribute knowledge – perhaps even knowledge of past events – to such a person from his very beginning.

[3] See, for example: Aristotle, *On Memory;* Locke, *Essay Concerning Human Understanding*, Bk. II, Ch. X; Russell, (1921), Lec. IX.

[4] For excellent critiques of this erroneous conception of what must happen when a person manifests that he remembers something (remembers it in the 'occurrent' sense) see Malcolm, (1963), pp. 210–212, Malcolm (1970); Munsat (1966), especially Chs. 4–8; and Shoemaker (1967).

[5] As Malcolm (1970) suggests.

[6] A circumstance that Jose Benardete suggested to me might offer a counterexample to this claim.

[7] This possibility of remembering again after an interval of not remembering or knowing at all seems to be denied by Munsat (1966), p. 34n:

> If I try to remember something at a certain time but cannot, and then later on *can* (do), we say I "knew it all along." And I think that if we now say that I remember that *p*, then we are committed to describing my previous inability to recall that *p* as "not being able to think of it at the time" and *not* as "not knowing at the time (when asked) that *p*."

Apparently Munsat wants to say that, no matter how hard you tried and failed to come up with it, if you ever again remember it (without having been reinformed) then you "knew it all along". It seems to me that this is flatly wrong and that cases of temporary amnesia (though one need not go to such an extreme) are clear counter-examples. We would not say that the temporary amnesiac knew all along the name of the street on which he lives but was just unable to think of it. The blow on his head has, we say, left him temporarily *not knowing* even his own name. The sorts of cases of which we *would* say that, although a person's efforts to recall were not successful, he nevertheless knew it all along are ones in which we think that his not being able to think of it has a special sort of explanation, such as his not trying hard or long enough or distraction or his having a special sort of temporary 'mental block' on that particular matter. There is an analogy here to being *able to do* a certain sort of thing (for example, hit a target, get a tight lid off a jar) though failing to do it when one tries because of interfering external circumstance, or passing jitters, or just not trying hard enough.

[8] This possibility is considered seriously in Russell (1921), Lecture IV.

[9] See Shoemaker (1970a and b). His argument owes something to Wiggins (1967) and ultimately to Williams (1960).

[10] The chief effect of removing the presupposition of identity between the person coming to know (or having the experience) and the person having the later matching memory-impression is that, if the memory-impression is sufficiently limited in the previous knowledge or experience that it delivers, it is no longer impossible, or even implausible, that the matching should be entirely coincidence even if the memory-impression has no other unconnected cause. If person *S* has an otherwise uncaused memory-impression of having come to know that *p*, where '*p*' is some simple proposition that many people have come to know (e.g., that the moon is smaller than the earth), it would be silly to suggest that the latter fact, or any particular person's previous knowledge that

p, has the memory connection to – is the cause of – *S*'s memory-impression. But the more extensive and detailed the match between what *S*'s otherwise uncaused memory-impression delivers and any particular person's previous knowledge or experience, the more plausible it becomes to say that these memory-impressions have their source in that (possibly distinct, possibly identical) person's previous knowledge or experience. It becomes compelling to say this when the extent and detail are so great that we can be justly quite confident that there never have been or will be two distinct people who have acquired all *those* same pieces of knowledge (or had all those same experiences). Here we have a sufficient condition for memory connection that does not presuppose the identity of the people connected or entail that there is a continuous connection between the memory and what is remembered. It is not *necessary*, however, since it is possible that the memory connection should in fact always be explained by a continuous physical chain of a sort that *could* run from a limited, isolated experience of one person to a matching memory impression of another. So any sufficient condition of memory connection that is free of the presupposition of personal identity and is also a plausible candidate for being necessary must be a disjunction of at least these two alternatives. (It might be thought that the non-necessity of the sufficient condition given earlier in this note follows from the fact that the sufficient condition given earlier in the text, for the case where the presupposition of personal identity is satisfied, does not require any such extensive matching of memory-impression with previous knowledge or experience. But this would follow only if the satisfaction of that presupposition did not entail such extensive matching, and whether this is so or not is a difficult question about the criteria of personal identity that I do not want to go into here. My present inclination is to think that personal identity does *not* entail such extensive memory connection.)

CHAPTER VIII

WHEN AND WHY TO TRUST ONE'S SENSES
AND MEMORY

1. One's knowledge of a fact is either inferential or non-inferential, and either fallible or infallible, depending on the sort of externally conclusive justification one has for claiming to know it. All one's inferential knowledge of contingent facts in the world outside one's current state of consciousness is justified ultimately by one's non-inferential knowledge. Although infallible knowledge (of necessary truths and of one's current states of consciousness) comes into it, the principal part of this non-inferential basis of one's knowledge of the 'external' world is formed by one's fallible non-inferential knowledge. This fallible non-inferential knowledge consists of one's non-inferential knowledge of one's current perceptions of directly specifiable appearances of things around one (direct perceptions, let us call them) and of one's memory knowledge (retained and original, of previous perceptions and of other sorts of facts, including general facts).

For each of these two sorts of fallible non-inferential knowledge I have presented four conditions that I claim to be sufficient as well as necessary (for perceptual knowledge on pp. 140–141, for memory knowledge on pp. 153–154). Their sufficiency may strike some as more open to doubt than their necessity. In particular, it may seem that in both analyses the non-inferential justification condition ((3) in each case) is inadequate; and for a reason well worth considering, for doing so will naturally bring us to suggest a general account of the circumstances in which the (b) part of condition (3) holds, an account of when S's sensations or memory- impressions (or infallible knowledge, which needs to be mentioned only in the analysis of memory knowledge) would, and when they would not, give him some reason to be unsure of (1) (the proposition for his knowledge of which I claim (1)–(4) are sufficient) despite his satisfying the (a) part of (3).

Let us concentrate primarily on the conditions I have given for non-inferential perceptual knowledge. (Corresponding things can be said about my conditions for memory knowledge.) It may seem that, in order for S to be justified in his confidence that (1) is true (that is, that he sees something that looks from his present point of view as would y in θ (direct specification)), he must do more than satisfy (3) (that is, have a visual sensation as if seeing y in θ and have no reason in his other sensations or memory-impressions to be unsure that (1)). To support the view that (3) is inadequate, one might try to appeal to reasoning essentially like that I used in Chapter VI, Section 5, to argue that, in order to know that one sees such a thing as a house, one must know more than that one sees something that looks as would a house from one's present point of view. That argument was that, no matter how favorable the viewing circumstances or how much like a house a thing looks, it is possible that things that are not houses but look just the same way in the same circumstances are quite common; hence, one must have reason outside the objective appearance one sees for being sure that what one sees is a house. (Such reason might, for instance, be justified confidence that things having the sort of appearance of a house that one now sees, in the sort of circumstances that one knows to be present, virtually always are houses.)

The parallel argument with respect to my conditions for non-inferential perceptual knowledge would go as follows. It is possible *a priori* that, for some period up to the present, instances where a subject satisfies (3) but (1) is false have occurred very frequently. Hence, besides satisfying (3), S needs some further reason for thinking that the present instance is not of that sort. This must consist in justified confidence in some other proposition from which, along with (3), S could properly infer (1) with confidence. (I am indebted to Richard J. Hall for suggesting this argument.)

2. There are many forms that such another proposition might take. One obviously suitable form would be the following:

(A)   (1) If my (S's) visual sensation as if seeing something that looks from my present point of view as would y in θ is F, then I (S) see something of that appearance; and
(2) my present visual sensation is F.

I do not want to deny, indeed I want to admit, that content can be found for the dummy predicate 'F' in (A) such that it would not be unusual for an S who satisfies (3) (a) to have justification for confidence in that instantiation of (A), and if S did have that justification (and awareness of the self-evident inference rule that (1) can be properly inferred with confi-

dence from the conjunction of (3) (a) and any instantiation of (A)), then
S would have inferential justification for claiming to know that (1) is true.
In fact I shall shortly suggest just such a content for 'F'. But I do not want
to admit that S's having confidence in such an instantiation of the form
(A) – or in any proposition about his subjective sense-experience which
could together with (3) (a) provide the premiss of an inferential justification for (1) – is necessary for S's claim to know the truth of (1) to be
supported by adequate justification. Ryle's point, again, seems to me to
offer a devastating objection to that conclusion: many people, of whom it
would be absurd to say that they have no perceptual knowledge, lack the
concept of subjective perceptual sensations required for understanding
and, hence, for believing any such proposition.

Still, it is obvious that if S did have justification for confidence in some
proposition of the (A) form while satisfying (3) (a) then S would also have
inferential justification for confidence in (1). Now the interesting thing
is that there is an appropriate instantiation of the (A) form such that S has
justification for being confident that it is true if S satisfies both (3) (a) and
(3) (b). The dummy predicate 'F' in (A) can be given a content such that
S must have justification for being confident of the resulting instantiation
of (A) – that is, his directly recognizable position must be such that he
would be justified *if* he were confident of the resulting instantiation –
whenever S has the non-inferential justification for confidence in (1) that
is specified in (3).

A content for 'F' that does, I believe, have this consequence appears
in the following instantiation of (A):

(A*)   (1) If my (S's) visual sensation as if seeing something that
            looks from my present point of view as would y in θ is
            such that its direct deliverance that I see such a thing is,
            according to what my memory-deliverances[1] imply about
            my past direct perceptions,
            (i) *not* ingredient in a history of direct deliverances of my
                 visual and tactual-kinaesthetic senses that fails to be
                 sufficiently coherent, and
            (ii) *not* incoherent with other past or present direct deli-
                 verences of my senses,
            then I do see such a thing; and

(2) my present visual sensation is such that its direct deliverance that I see something that looks from my present
point of view as would y in θ is, according to what my
memory-deliverances imply about my past direct perceptions, (i) and (ii) [as above].

3. The meaning of (i) and (ii) in (A*), particularly the meaning of 'coherent' in (i) and 'incoherent' in (ii), needs explanation. Let's start with (i).
A history of direct deliverances of a subject's visual and tactual-kinaesthetic senses *is* sufficiently coherent, in the sense of (i), just in case it satisfies
the following two conditions:

(a) The shape-appearances that each sense has delivered have been
stable and regular enough in their pattern of changes to permit selecting
of places (among the perceived things) relative to which more or less
enduring fixed spatial locations can be identified. This would not be
possible if the spatially continuous changes that the shape-appearances
underwent over temporally continuous periods of sensation were too
rapid, widespread, or irregular, or if there were spatially discontinuous
changes that were too frequent, widespread, or irregular: if, in other
words, the pattern of changes has been too chaotic to present a coherent
external space.

(b) The shape-appearances delivered by the visual sense have been
sufficiently congruent, and sufficiently free of incongruence, with those
delivered by the tactual-kinaesthetic sense. The two senses deliver *congruent* shape appearances when at the same time they deliver the same shape
at the same place. They deliver *incongruent* shape-appearances when at
the same time either they deliver different shapes at the same place or one
delivers absence of any shape where the other delivers a certain shape.
Thus when I both see and feel a telephone receiver in my hand, or when
climbing stairs I both see the rising steps before me and feel them with my
feet and legs, then congruent shape-appearances are being delivered by
the two senses. But if I were to have a visual sensation as if seeing a telephone but no hands on a table immediately before me while at the same
time having a tactual-kinaesthetic sensation as if running my hands over
the surface of a table immediately before me and feeling nothing on it at
all, then the two senses would be delivering incongruent shape-appearances.

One sense can and often does deliver a shape-appearance that is neither congruent nor incongruent with any delivered by the other sense, as when I see a distant tree or feel an object behind me. So by no means total congruence, but only enough of it, is required if the history of direct deliverances of the two senses is to be sufficiently coherent in respect (b). Nor, for that matter, is total lack of incongruence required.

I have only an extremely vague idea of what is sufficient coherence in respects (a) and (b) for the purposes of (i) in (A*). I do not see how it can be made more precise. It can, however, be characterized in another way. It is the same as my extremely vague idea of what is sufficient coherence in what a person remembers or expects about his visual and tactual-kinaesthetic experience for him to have the concepts of seeing and feeling external things. That is to say: sufficient coherence in respect (a), in the deliverances of a sequence of visual/tactual-kinaesthetic sensations (which is long enough for the notion to apply at all), is a degree of it at least as great as that degree such that only if the deliverances of a person's memory or expectations (or both) imply that whatever past or future visual/tactual kinaesthetic history he has is coherent in respect (a) at least to that degree, can that person have a concept of what it is to see/feel things of this or that appearance (things in space). Sufficient coherence in respect (b), between the deliverances of a sequence of visual sensations and the deliverances of a concurrent sequence of tactual-kinaesthetic sensations, each of which is sufficiently coherent in respect (a), is a degree of it at least as great as that degree such that a person who has a concept of what it is to feel things in space can have a concept of what it is to see them only if what the deliverances of his memory or expectations imply about his past or future visual experience is coherent in respect (b) at least to that degree with what they imply about his concurrent past or future tactual-kinaesthetic experience.

A person who has only a very short, isolated visual or tactual-kina-esthetic sensation, of whatever kind, and has no idea at all, even in imagi-nation, of a more extensive visual or tactual-kinaesthetic experience that was sufficiently coherent in respect (a) and included such a sensation, clearly can have no idea of what it could be to see or feel objects in space.

And if it were only in his imagination, and not in the deliverances of his memory or expectations about himself, that he had the idea of a more extensive, coherent visual or tactual-kinaesthetic history, then he would have only imagined possible sorts of perceiving. He would not have a concept of what visual or tactual-kinaesthetic perception is. He could not say, 'This is what it is like, subjectively, to see such-and-such' but, at most, 'This is what it could be like, in some possible world, to perceive a certain sort of thing in a certain sort of way'. A person who has always been blind might, conceivably, be able to imagine a visual experience that is what it is in fact like, subjectively, to have many of the various sorts of visual perceptions that we are familiar with or have concepts of. But if this person did not know that this was what he was doing (as perhaps he could not), he would not have succeeded in coming by imagination alone to a concept of what seeing this or that sort of thing is like. If he did not know that what he imagines is in fact like, or systematically related in the right sort of way to, the experience that people actually have when they see, he could not say, 'Now I know what it is (or would be) like to see such-and-such'. The most he could say would be 'This that I imagine is what it could be like to see such-and-such'. (Similarly, some normally sighted person might be able to imagine a sensory experience in which touching different surfaces causes different sorts of special tactual sensations according to the color of the surface touched. This would not be to conceive what it is like to feel colors, or what instances of feeling color would have to be like if they were to occur, but only what feeling colors could be like in a world different from the actual one in certain ways. There is no concrete concept of feeling color in this world (yet anyway) and the concrete content of that concept for one non-actual possible world may be different from what it is for another. It may be possible to imagine a world for which the concrete content of the concept of seeing things having certain shape appearances would be very different from what it is in the actual world.)

A perceptual history sufficiently extended and coherent in respects (a) and (b) for the memory of it to permit its subject concepts of seeing and feeling things could contain an occasional visual-tactual incongruence, for this could be regarded either as a perceptual malfunction (an hallucination or severe distortion by one of the senses) or as a perception by one sense of something that was imperceptible to the other sense. But if there were too much visual-tactual-kinaesthetic incongruence, or too little visual-tactual-kinaesthetic congruence, then only the sensations on the tactual-kinaesthetic side could, in the absence of the subject's some-

how expecting whatever visual-tactual-kinaesthetic future he has to be
much more coherent in this respect, permit a concept of objective perception or give rise to perceptual beliefs (provided that the tactual-kinaesthetic deliverances were sufficiently extensive and coherent in respect (a)).
The sensations on the visual side could be thought of by their subject as
no more than merely subjective mental phenomena, like the play of an
exceptionally vivid and uncontrolled visual imagination but without the
subject's thinking that he is imagining *seeing* various things. They could
not even give rise to the idea of seeming to see, or visually hallucinating,
various external things, and they could certainly not be regarded as any
sort of guide to the contents of the environment.

    This primacy of tactual-kinaesthetic perception can be seen, I think, if
one asks oneself how one would regard one's visual and tactual-kinaesthetic experiences if the two were to diverge totally with respect to congruence over a fairly long period. Suppose that you awoke sometime to
find that the environment being delivered by the one sense is completely
different from that being simultaneously delivered by the other. For
example, you have tactual-kinaesthetic sensations as if feeling yourself
stretched out on the floor with your children piling on you and wrestling
with you, and you have the sort of visual sensations you would have if
first sitting in a chair then getting up and going into the kitchen and
making coffee and in the process seeing no other persons. After a while of
such complete divergence you would, I think, begin to think of your
visual experience as a subjective picture show, a fantasy, that distracts
you from attending to your commerce with the actual environment by
touch and motion.[2]

    The explanation for this probably lies in such facts as the following.
My tactual-kinaesthetic perceptions, but not my visual perceptions, of
the movements of my own body are intimately connected with the fact that
it is *my* body that is moving. I cannot have a kinaesthetic awareness of
someone else's body doing sit-ups. The subjective experience ingredient
in my tactual-kinaesthetic perception of my body walking forward over a
level surface can be ingredient only in a perception of my, the *perceiver's*,
body doing this; whereas the very same visual sensation ingredient in my
seeing my feet moving forward one after the other could have been ingredient in my seeing someone else's feet moving. Also my will to move my
body in a certain way is a part of my tactual-kinaesthetic perception, but

not of my visual perception, of a voluntary movement of my body. My impression that my body moves because I will it, that *I am moving* my body, is an inseparable aspect of the subjective experience I mean when I speak of the tactual-kinaesthetic experience as if I were moving my body in such-and-such a way; this experience differs from the tactual-kinaesthetic experience as if my body were being moved in that way by something other than me. To have an illusion of raising my arm (voluntarily) would necessarily require a putative kinaesthetic perception of doing so, but not necessarily any putative visual perception. Finally, my tactual-kinaesthetic, but not my visual, perceptions include those painful (or pleasant) sensations that deliver the most directly forceful and alarming (or appealing) perceptions of actions of other things on my body. My seeing a vice slowly flattening my hand, unaccompanied by any tactual-kinaesthetic perception of it, could fail to arouse in me any *active* concern (I might not even realize that it was my hand); but the same could not be said for my tactual-kinaesthetic perception of the same thing unaccompanied by any visual perception of it.[3] So, in a case of prolonged extreme divergence between one's visual experience and one's tactual-kinaesthetic experience, even if one tried to believe in the visual environment and disbelieve the tactual-kinaesthetic one, the attempt would be constantly undermined by one's dispositions to bodily action and reaction (without which actions and reactions one's tactual-kinaesthetic experience would in any case be very impoverished and very different from the familiar sort). (It should be noted that what I've said does not imply or give support to the suggestion that in any instance of visual-tactual-kinaesthetic incongruence, however short-lived and whatever the other perceptual experience of the subject, the subject's presumption would or should be in favor of the veridicality of the tactual-kinaesthetic side: if I see something moving my right hand towards my right where I seem to see an active buzz saw (and where I previously thought I saw and felt a buzz saw), but it feels to me as if my right hand is being moved to the left, I will doubtless try to stop the apparent movement to the right and scoff at any questioning of the reasonableness of doing so.)

4. Condition (ii) of (A*) speaks of incoherence among different direct deliverances of the subject's sensations. One thing that is meant by this is the sort of incongruence between visual and tactual-kinaesthetic shape-

appearances discussed above. But there are other sorts of incoherence, in the sense needed in (ii), that are not the opposites of any of the sorts of coherence so far explained. They have to do with a given deliverance or combination of deliverances possessing what is a severely *anomalous* feature in light of, against the background of, all that is implied about the subject's past perceptions by his memory-deliverances. (One can, of course, remember what was a general connection or frequent feature in one's past perceptual experience without remembering many, or even any, particular instances of it.)

A feature of some direct perceptual deliverance or combination of direct perceptual deliverances is a severe anomaly within the totality of the past and present direct perceptual deliverances of a person's sensations if it is a feature that in the light of the totality would definitely be expected not to occur, whose non-occurrence could be inferred with considerable confidence from the other features of the totality. Against the background of a normal sort of sensation history among us, severe anomaly would be offered by spatio-temporal discontinuity in the changing of the shape-appearances delivered (for example, from something looking as would a large oak in an open field abruptly to something looking as would a wall full of books close at hand), or by certain bizarre sorts of continuous changes (for example, what looks as would walking, gesturing furniture or what looks as would a filing cabinet gradually changing into a man), or by certain bizarre combinations of shapes or of shapes and colors (for example, what looks as would wings on a purple cow). Deliverances of different, non-continuous segments of a person's sensation-history could, taken together, constitute a severe anomaly: given the background of a sort of sensation-history normal for us, it would be severely anomalous if a person had visual sensations as if seeing through a window a violent windstorm come along and uproot some fair-sized trees and then, no more than an hour or so later (in the meantime having had perceptual experience only of indoor scenes), he had visual experience as if seeing through the same window the same trees firmly planted and showing no signs of unusual disturbance.

In general, whether or not, and to what degree, a given feature of a perceptual deliverance or sequence or combination of deliverances would be anomalous in light of the whole of a person's perceptual deliverances is a matter of the strength with which its contradictory could be properly inferred from the totality minus that feature and is thus a matter of logic broadly conceived (mainly non-deductive), a study into which we are not entering here.

Not every sort of possible anomaly in the direct deliverances of one's senses would be severe enough to produce incoherence in the sense I mean in (ii). A feature will be severely anomalous enough just in case a person whose sense- and memory-deliverances imply it thereby has reason to be unsure that the deliverance or sequence or combination of deliverances it embraces is true. I doubt that any more informative general criterion for what degree of anomaly is enough can be given: it is anomalous enough when it becomes unclear that confidently accepting the delivered anomaly is preferable to accepting the anomaly that at least some part of the perceptual deliverances of one's senses or memory is false. It is clear that, against the sort of background of perceptions implied by a normal totality of concurrent memory-deliverances, thorough spatial discontinuity in the changing of the shape-appearances delivered by the subject's visual sense would be anomalous enough, whereas what looks as would a man twice as tall as normal would not be. A chartreuse moose deliverance is perhaps not clear one way or the other – assuming that the subject has no evidence that he sees a moose that has been dyed or painted chartreuse or illuminated by special light which reflects chartreuse from the moose, for if he had then his seeing something that looks as would a chartreuse moose in ordinary light need not be at all anomalous in light of the totality of perceptual deliverances that his memory delivers. But one could add to a chartreuse-moose deliverance to get a combination that would be more clearly anomalous enough: add, for instance, deliverances that are strong evidence that the subject has taken a drug that typically causes visual hallucinations of bizarre-looking animals.

A sufficiently anomalous sequence or combination of deliverances might (though it need not) be made up of parts each of which is not anomalous in itself, so that the anomaly of the combination or sequence lies in the relation of these parts to each other. In such a case, the extrinsically anomalous parts can be said to be incoherent with each other (in the sense intended in (ii)). (In a case where a perception delivered by the senses or memory is intrinsically severely anomalous, that is, it is severely anomalous and can*not* be divided into separate non-anomalous perceptions (such as one's seeing a big red bear with large white wings), the perceptual

deliverance can be said to be incoherent with all the other perceptual or
perception-implying deliverances of the subject's senses or memory that
provide the evidence in light of which it is severely anomalous, but *they*
are not incoherent with *it*.) Among the possible cases of anomalous combinations or sequences that divide into non-anomalous parts, one kind
would be visual-tactual-kinaesthetic incongruence and another would be
a sharp, thoroughgoing break in the continuities of shape delivered by
a temporally continuous sequence of visual sensations (in a totality of
perceptual deliverances that is otherwise like what is normal).

Another kind of possibility is illustrated by the example given earlier
of the uprooted and restored trees. This example differs from the two just
mentioned in that the anomaly of the direct deliverances in the uprooted-
trees example can be comprehended only by understanding that they are
evidence for another, unperceived anomaly (a very quick restoration or
replacement of the trees). If certain direct deliverances are evidence for an
anomaly in the world then they must themselves be anomalous against
the background of the whole of the subject's perceptual deliverances:
if what I have perceived is evidence for something that I have a right to
regard as anomalous then I have a right to regard what I have perceived
as anomalous. Another sort of case that would have this feature even
more strikingly (again assuming a sort of background of perceptual deliverances that is otherwise fairly normal) would be deliverances that are
strong evidence of an incongruence between a perception by the subject
and a perception by another person. That is, the senses or memory of the
subject deliver his perceiving something of a certain appearance at a
certain place and they deliver also strong evidence that another person has
perceived something of a quite different appearance, or nothing at all, at
the same place and time.

Another possible case of incoherence through extrinsic anomaly is this:
one's senses deliver or have delivered strong evidence that a particular
one (or ones) among one's perceptual sensations, whose deliverances
would otherwise be non-anomalous, has been caused in such a way as
to make it hallucinatory in some respect(s). For example, it could be that
I clearly seem to remember having observed or conducted or participated
in or saw reliable testimony concerning experiments that showed that
electrically stimulating a person's brain in a certain way causes him to have
a visual hallucination of a vulture, and I also seem clearly to remember

my being told a short while ago by the same experimenters that my brain would shortly be stimulated in that way, and now I have a visual experience as if seeing something that from my present point of view looks as would a vulture sitting on the ledge outside the laboratory window. This direct perceptual deliverance and those implied by the memory-deliverances must form an anomalous combination; otherwise, those implied by the memory-deliverances could not be evidence that the present visual sensation is at least partly hallucinatory, that is, false in its direct deliverance.

In a case of a perceptual deliverance that is non-anomalous in itself but has an anomalous relation to others of the subject's perceptual deliverances, it could happen that, even though the anomaly is severe enough of its kind to give the subject some reason to be unsure of that deliverance, the subject has countervailing reason in other parts of his total perceptual deliverance for being confident of the deliverance despite its anomaly, reason that outweighs the reason for doubt, that restores the confidence that the incoherence would otherwise destroy. Suppose, for example, that, as his visual sense delivers it, a person is one moment (what looks as would) sitting in his study at his typewriter and the next moment (what looks as would) flying over fields and woods like a bird (without the aid of any device, as if swimming in the air). Here the subject's confidence in his (memory-delivered) perceptions of having been in his study at his typewriter might be justly restored, despite the anomalous abrupt switch to outdoor flying, in light of the fact that the earlier perception is continuous with so much more in his past and the fact that the flying perception is intrinsically anomalous, as well as being abruptly and thoroughly discontinuous with the preceding perceptions. And if the flying perception were followed by an abrupt switch back to the study and typewriter, it would be doubly anomalous extrinsically. All this might justify the subject in regarding the flying perception as hallucinatory and restoring his confidence in the preceding and following mundane perceptions.

Or consider the example where my senses deliver strong evidence that another person has had a visual perception that is incongruent with one of my own. My confidence in my own might be restored by my having evidence in other perceptions that the other person's visual perception is intrinsically or extrinsically anomalous within his perceptual deliverances (and apart from comparison with mine), or by my having equally strong evidence that several other subjects have perceptions that are congruent with mine but incongruent with his. Or in the example where the deliverance of my current sensation is incoherent with the deliverances of some of my past ones (as implied by my memory deliverances) because those past ones deliver evidence that the current one has had a hallucination-producing cause, the fact that so much of my putative perceptual history is tied up in or continuous with those past putative perceptions as compared with the current perception might justify restoring confidence in all those past perceptual deliverances despite their incoherence with the present one: they massively outweigh it.

In all such cases the subject's justification for being confident of a perceptual deliverance despite its incoherence with others is inferential. The justification has the form: 'Although my perceptual deliverance P is incoherent with my perceptual deliverance(s) Q, P is surely true but Q may not be, since P and Q have such-and-such relations to others of my (non-anomalous) perceptions or to each other.' But we are now concerned with non-inferential justification for claims to know direct perceptual propositions about oneself, and with the notion of a reason for being unsure that weighs against such a non-inferential justification. The explication of this notion need not take account of the kinds of factors that can inferentially restore confidence despite anomaly, but can simply rely on the kinds of incoherence that I have been explaining.

5. Turning to memory-knowledge of one's perceptual past, we can construct a proposition parallel to (A*) such that a claim parallel to the one I am making about (A*) vis-à-vis the conditions of non-inferential perceptual knowledge – namely, that one who satisfies condition (3) has justification for being confident of (A*) – can equally well be made about this parallel proposition vis-à-vis condition (3) of memory knowledge for the specific case where p (the proposition of which the subject has memory knowledge) is a past-tense direct perceptual proposition about the subject.

(A*m)   (1) If I (S) have a strong memory-impression that I have seen something of such-and-such an appearance (direct specification) and this perceptual deliverance is, according to what my memory-deliverances imply about my other past direct perceptions, (i) and (ii) [same as in (A*)], then I have seen such a thing; and

(2) [as in (A*), (2) is the same proposition as the antecedent of (1)].

The parallel claim that holds concerning (A*m) is this: if S satisfies condition (3) of memory knowledge with respect to the proposition that he has seen something of such-and-such a directly specified appearance – that is, he has a strong memory-impression that he has and his other memory-impressions or sensations give him no reason to be unsure that he has despite his strong memory-impressions that he has – then S would be justified in being confident that (A*m).[4]

Note incidentally that there is just one sort of case where the incoherence of a perceptual memory-deliverance (or a perceptual implication of a memory-deliverance) with other perceptual deliverances of a subject's memory or senses is such as to give the subject reason to suspect that it is his ostensible memory, rather than the putative perception ostensibly remembered, that is playing him false. This is the case where the incoherence is a matter of the other perceptual deliverances being strong evidence that this memory-impression has been caused in such a way as to make it delusory. Otherwise, any reason the subject has for preferring one suspicion to the other must consist in further facts about his sense- and memory-deliverances than the incoherence in question.

6. Let us return to the claim I am making about (A*) vis-à-vis (3) of the conditions of non-inferential perceptual knowledge (which were stated on pp. 140–141, namely, that a subject who satisfies (3) thereby has the makings of a justification for being confident that (A*) (which was stated on pp. 176–177).

My claim can be made out in two parts: first, how it is that such a subject has justification for confidence that (A*) (2) is true and second, how such a subject has justification for confidence that (A*) (1) is true. (A parallel argument could be given for the corresponding claim about (A*m) vis-à-vis (3) of the conditions of memory knowledge given in Chapter VII, Section 3.) The first is fairly obvious, the second I will take up in Sections 8 and 9.

A person who has the visual sensation specified in (3) (a) will have justification for being confident that (A*) (2) holds of that sensation if he satisfies (3) (b). Whatever would make it false that the specified direct deliverance of that sensation, according to what S's memory-deliverances imply about his past perceptions, satisfies (i) and (ii) – would make (A*) (2) false – would also, clearly, be a reason, offered by S's memory-impressions or other sensations, for S to withhold non-inferential trust in that direct visual deliverance. And, as far as I can see, that sort of thing is the only such (sense- or memory-delivered) reason a person could have for withholding non-inferential confidence in a direct deliverance of his senses. My explication of coherence in the sense of (i) and incoherence in the sense of (ii) has also been an explication of (3) (b), of the circumstances under which non-inferential trust in the current direct deliverances of one's senses is justified.

It does not follow from any of my claims, nor do I think it true, that a subject can be justified in suspecting the truth of some of the perceptual deliverances of his senses or memory only if he confidently accepts the truth of others, as some philosophers seem to have suggested.[5] What is true, rather, is that a doubt about any of one's perceptual deliverances must arise from the nature of the rest and cannot be grounded on something outside that, such as the mere logical possibility that all the perceptual deliverances of one's memory and senses, no matter what their nature, are false. It is pretty clear that if the totality of the visual and tactual-kinaesthetic deliverances of a subject's senses and memory (at a given time) fail to be coherent in the minimal sense of (i) then that subject ought not to be confident of any of them (supposing he somehow had the understanding of perceptual propositions necessary for believing them). But even if that totality satisfied (i), the nature of the totality of the perceptual deliverances of the subject's senses and memory could still be such that none of them satisfy (ii) and the subject should on that account be less than confident of any of them.

One way in which this latter possibility might be realized is this: at a certain time a person whose sense- and memory-deliverances up to then have been perfectly normal and coherent throughout, suddenly experiences a radical and thorough discontinuity in his perceived environment, of the sort described earlier. For example, one moment the person is in his study at his typewriter and the next he is in a canoe moving down a wooded stream. At first, it may be plausible to suppose, his memories of his experience prior to the break in continuity would be sufficiently more extensive than the new sense-experience to restore his confidence

in the former (but not the latter). But, if his post-break experience continues long enough in coherent fashion and is retained well enough in his
memory (and brings no strong evidence that he did undergo a discontinuous change of place, such as testimony of others that they saw him
disappear in the one place and suddenly appear in the other), then perhaps
there could come a time when neither the deliverances of his memory concerning his pre-break experience nor those concerning his post-break
experience are sufficiently more extensive than the others to restore confidence in either set. They might come into a kind of balance in which the
subject would not be unreasonable if he were to be uncertain whether to
trust the one or the other or both or neither of the internally coherent
parts of the incoherent whole. (All of the putative perceptual experience
prior to the break is incoherent with all of that after the break because the
thoroughgoing discontinuity, the feature that is severely anomalous in
light of the totality of the totality of the subject's perceptual deliverances
(as he remembers them), is a relation between two different sequences of
the subject's putative perceptions and it would be arbitrary to exclude
from either sequence any putative perceptions that are either continuous
(in respect to the perceiver's location in space and the perceived environment) or give no evidence of discontinuity (in either respect) with what is
already included in that sequence.)

A somewhat different sort of example of a feature that would make the
totality of the perceptual deliverances of a subject's senses and memory
incoherent, and would, therefore, make it reasonable for the subject to
have confidence in none of them, is the following. The subject has strong
memory-impressions of a life in which he has become a neuro-physiolo-
gist and, by much study and experiment and with the help of colleagues,
he has discovered and demonstrated that certain complex, delicate operations on a normal adult human brain will cause its possessor to have, over
a certain period, memory-impressions and sensations whose perceptual
deliverances, though extensive and coherent, are all false. They are even
able to cause a delusive but coherent set of sense- and memory-deliverances that justify a subject in being confident that he has been a neuro-
physiologist who has developed the means to cause people to have extensively delusory sensations and memory-impressions. This person now
seems to perceive himself lying in a hospital room and feels as if he has
just awakened from deep sleep, and he has a strong memory-impression that

the last thing that he experienced before becoming unconscious was that
his fellow-neurologists strapped him to an operating table and told him
that they were about to perform on him the same sort of total-delusion-
causing operation that they had performed on others. Here, the perceptual
deliverances of the subject's memory and senses that support the proposition that such an experiment has indeed been performed on him might be
so extensive and continuous with others of his perceptual deliverances that
it would be arbitrary to doubt only those and maintain confidence in all
the rest. Yet, for him to be confident of those would, paradoxically, be
for him to have reason to doubt them all, including those. It seems that as
reasonable a response as any to such a situation would be a sweeping
uncertainty, a feeling that he cannot be sure of anything, at least as far as
concerns his past and present perceptions and propositions inferred
therefrom.

7. Here is as good a place as any to remark upon an intuition concerning
perceptual deliverances that I share with some other philosophers. For
some among those perceptual deliverances of a normal person's senses
and memory at a given time that are not, in what they imply about the
subject's direct perceptions, incoherent with any others, the justification
of confidence is even stronger than it is for others (where it is still justification for confidence). Malcolm (1952) has argued that one may know
such truths as that one sees an ink bottle before one in an especially
"strong sense". In one place he explains this claim in this way: "When I
use 'know' in the strong sense.... I do not concede that anything whatsoever
could *prove* me mistaken" (p. 64,[6] my emphasis). This suggests that, given
an S who knows that p and knows that q, where p and q are perceptual
deliverances of S's memory or senses, one way in which the subject's
justification for claiming to know that p could be stronger than S's justification for claiming to know that q is this: the totality of the perceptual
deliverances of S's senses and memory is such that the most that any
possible further addition to those deliverances (with no loss) could do by
way of weakening S's justification for confidence that p would be to
create a position in which S should be uncertain or doubt or withhold
belief that p; whereas some conceivable further addition without any loss
would create a position in which S would be justified in being confident,
or at least believing, that q is false.

It does seem that, although I seem to remember seeing recently what looked as would a large tree growing in the middle of a certain yard, if my seeing today at the same spot nothing that looks as would a tree or the remains of one, my wife's testimony that she passed the same spot a few days ago and saw nothing looking like a tree in that yard, plus, if you like, the testimony of the residents of the houses on that street that they have never seen anything in that yard looking like a tree, if all this (or the strongest possible perceptual evidence of it) were over a period added to the perceptual deliverances of my memory, and nothing were taken away, I would then have a totality of perceptual deliverances that would justify me in being sure that I did not recently see something that looks as would a tree in that street, despite my continuing memory-impression that I did. Whereas, it does seem that no matter what happens, as long as I retain the very extensive memory-impressions I now have of having seen what look like trees, I can be justified at most in doubting, being uncertain of, my memory's deliverance that I have seen such things. No possible mere addition, without loss, to the present totality of my memory-impressions could make one that would justify my being confident that I have never seen things that looked like trees despite the great mass of my contrary memory-impressions.

I doubt that any perceptual proposition tied to a limited time period could have this sort of security from being *shown* false. For what seems to give a memory-deliverance this status is the fact that if it were false then a large amount of the direct perceptual deliverances of the subject's memory would either have to be false or else have to have an explanation against which his memory and senses deliver massive evidence. (I must, however, confess to an intuition that one's confidence in a *present* tense perceptual proposition is naturally more insistent, or less easily shaken, than one's confidence in a comparable past-tense perceptual proposition, even where both are completely coherent with all the rest of the perceptual deliverances of one's senses and memory. For example, though I am entitled to be confident and claim to know that I saw yesterday what looked as would large blooms on a lilac bush immediately before me, I seem to be even more strongly justified in claiming to know that I now see what look as would large blooms on a lilac bush immediately before me. I would feel more justified in maintaining confidence in the face of certain sorts of contrary evidence (for example, testimony of others) in the latter case than

I would in the former. Two things occur to me that might make this plausible: (1) there are more alternative ways in which my memory-impression
that I saw what looked as would... etc. could conceivably be delivering
falsely: it could be either my memory that is at fault or else the original
putative perception and not my memory; whereas my present perceptual
sensation is not thus doubly vulnerable to error in its deliverance; (2) since
a deliverance of a present perceptual sensation concerning one's present
environment ordinarily would have a greater bearing on one's current
practical concerns than a comparable memory-deliverance concerning
one's past environment, it is easier to alter or weaken one's conviction
about the latter: doing so ordinarily entails less practical concern or
adjustment than would altering one's conviction with regard to one's
present environment.)

In another place Malcolm gives his "strong sense" of 'know' a stronger
explanation. He says that a person who thinks he knows that *p* in the
strong sense "would look upon nothing whatever as evidence that *p* is
false" (p. 62) and would not admit "that any future investigation *could*
refute it or *cast doubt on it*" (p. 64, last emphasis mine). This suggests that
a perceptual deliverance might be such that no possible addition without
loss to the totality of perceptions delivered by the subject's senses and
memory could even weaken his position to the point where it would no
longer justify confidence in that deliverance.[7] I very much doubt that a
person can ever be *so* strongly justified in claiming to know a contingent,
perception-implying deliverance of his memory or senses.

Consider my memory's deliverance that I have seen things looking like
trees. It is perhaps true that if one other person were now (when I happen
to be perceiving nothing looking like a tree) to tell me, with apparent
sincerity, that he has never seen anything looking the way I describe and
draw trees as looking, that bit of testimony will be overwhelmingly out-
weighed by the extent of my memory-impressions of having countless times
seen what looked like trees. But suppose that I then go outdoors and the
environment I seem to perceive is very different from what I seem to
remember perceiving the last time I was outdoors, in that no matter where
I look there is nothing that looks as would a tree; every person I seem to
see and to ask 'What happened to the trees?' seems to look blank and
say, 'Trees? What do you mean by 'trees'?'; and , when I describe or draw
for them how trees look, seems to say, "I have never seen any such thing".

Then I ought to wonder whether (though not to believe that) my memories of having seen trees are all delusory, to be less than certain that I have seen such things. (Indeed, this may be another example where I should not fully trust any of the perceptual deliverances of my senses or memory, since perceptions of trees have been so pervasive in my previous experience as I remember it.) If we can imagine future developments in my experience that would (even though I continue to remember the experience I remember now) put me in a position where I ought to lack confidence in the proposition that I have seen things that look as would trees, then surely we could do it for any perceptual deliverance of my memory or any deliverance whose original justification would have to have been by inference from perception.

8. In Section 6 I pointed out that a person who satisfies (3) of the conditions of non-inferential perceptual knowledge (p. 140) has justification for being confident that (A*) (2) (pp. 176–177) is true of him. I hope it is equally clear that a parallel claim holds concerning condition (3) of memory knowledge (p. 154) and (A*m) (2) (p. 187).

The remaining part of my claim regarding (A*) (or (A*m)) is that a person who satisfies the conditions of non-inferential perceptual knowledge (or memory knowledge) has justification for being confident that the conditional (A*) (1) (or (A*m) (1)) is true of him. This holds because a person *always* has justification for being confident of that conditional no matter what the current deliverances of his senses and memory. Justification for confidence that (A*) (1) (or (A*-m) (1)) holds in one's own case is something that one has non-inferentially and *a priori*. How else could one have it?

Not by any sort of inference ultimately from what one's perceptions are or have been, since it seems clear that as long as it is in question whether (A*) (1) (or (A*-m) (1)) holds of oneself it will also be in question whether any of the perceptual deliverances of one's memory or senses are true. It would seem highly arbitrary to pick some of those that satisfy the antecedent of (A*) (1) (or (A*-m) (1)) and not others in which to place one's confidence. What could justify the selection? And it would seem even more perverse to select only some that do *not* satisfy that antecedent. Why do that?

Nor could one's confidence in (A*) (1) (or (A*m) (1)) arise from *a* *priori* demonstration, since it is not a necessary truth. Its consequent does not follow from its antecedent, nor from any other proposition merely about the intrinsic nature of one's current memory-impressions and sensations (nor from any other fact directly recognizable to one). No matter what sort of totality of sense- and memory-deliverances we suppose a person to have, it is conceivable that all their perceptual members (or perceptual implications) should be false. It is conceivable, for example, that a person should suddenly, at one stroke, lose entirely his memories of earlier experience and acquire new but delusory memory-impressions as to what his experience has been. If the memory-delusion were extensive and coherent enough and were retained while he went on to have total perceptual hallucination for a period, it would then be the case throughout that period that all of the perceptual implications of his sense- and memory-deliverances were false but he would have no reason to suspect any falsity in them at all.

One might think that such an extensive, comprehensive, coherent delusion, undetectable to its victim is not possible. One might think that its impossibility follows from certain considerations about what is necessary in order for a person's belief or expression or thought to have reference to the past. Malcolm argues that a person's having memory-beliefs or memory-impressions requires that he be able to express beliefs or make statements about the past and his ability to do this presupposes that the statements he makes by uttering ostensibly past-tense sentences are mainly true when so interpreted.[8] According to Shoemaker, it is a necessary truth that a person's memory *beliefs* are generally true and also necessary that his *sincere* memory *statements* are generally true.[9]

Behind these various and somewhat unclear claims[10] there is a sound idea that I would put as follows. Any way of selecting a set of behavioral and mental acts in the life of a person as the set of all the formulations of propositions about the past that he ever makes (whatever his epistemic attitude towards the propositions at the time of formulating them) must yield the result that some significant portion (not necessarily most) of the proposition formulated in all those acts, or the propositions implied by those propositions, are true of the past. Otherwise there could be no basis for construing those acts as intended by their subject to have reference to the past. But from this principle we cannot get the consequence that a person's memory-impressions at a given time could not be entirely (though coherently) delusory with respect to what their deliverances imply about the subject's past perceptions. It is easy to conceive cases of wholesale memory and perceptual delusion that do not violate the above principle (but do violate, and therefore constitute counterexamples to, Malcolm's and Shoemaker's stronger principles).

Consider the following three cases, in order of the increasing extent of the subject's memory-delusion.

(1) A normal adult whose native language is English suffers a severe blow on the head. For a considerable period after he regains consciousness the utterances he makes sound like English but if they are so construed they are all false in their first-person present- or past-tense perceptual implications. In addition his non-verbal behavior is appropriate, not to his actual environment, but to one such as is implied by the propositions that are expressed by his apparently English utterances if they are English. It would be reasonable to say of such a person, on the basis of his behavior and circumstances both before and after the blow, that the only knowledge (or true belief) of his that has survived the blow on his head is his knowledge of how to speak English and some very general knowledge as to what sorts of things are to be found in the world. His beliefs as to what particular things he has perceived or is perceiving are all false. He now has an extensive and coherent delusion about his past and present environment which he has no reason to suspect to be such.

(2) A normal adult whose native language is German and who has never encountered any other language receives a blow on the head even stranger in its effects: his behavior upon recovering consciousness exactly fits the description of post-blow behavior that we gave in case (1). That is, this person makes utterances which all sound like English and which, if so construed, express assertions that imply a coherent set of false beliefs about his past experience and what he presently perceives, which false beliefs seem to fit with the subject's non-verbal behavior which is inappropriate to his actual environment. Here the only true memory-beliefs expressed by the subject's acts (or that are implicit in beliefs his acts express) have to do with general facts about the sorts of things that are to be found in the world. The correct memory of how English is spoken, attributable in case (1), drops out in this case (though the subject has correct beliefs as to how it is spoken).

(3) A human being, looking like a normal adult, simply materializes

before our eyes, from out of nowhere – or perhaps he is synthesized by a
highly advanced biological technology – and proceeds to behave in a way
that satisfies the description of post-blow behavior given in case (1). Of
such a creature we can say that at his unusual beginning, though he has
true beliefs as to how English is spoken and as to what sorts of things
there are in the world, he has no true memory-beliefs at all but only false
ones, since he has no past whatever to remember. All the memory-impressions that he formulates in his behavioral or mental acts, impressions
that he has done or experienced or come to know various things, must be
delusory. But how then could any of his behavior or mental acts near his
beginning express memory-beliefs? What could there be that would show
that any of his (internal or external) acts near his beginning were *intended*
to refer to the past? Perhaps nothing that is there at his beginning. Maybe
it would have to be such things as how his *later* use of what are ostensibly
English past-tense utterances correlates, when so construed, with the
hallucinatory perceptual experience that he has previously seemed to be
expressing and with the interpretation of it implied by the memory-beliefs
he has seemed to be expressing. If a suitably significant portion of the later
utterances construed as English expressions of memory-beliefs (or of his
mental acts construed as expressions of memory-beliefs) turn out to
express or imply or pre-suppose truths as to what his earlier sense-deliverances and his inferences drawn therefrom have apparently been, then
there is a basis for saying that he generally uses (is disposed to use) the
ostensibly English past-tense locutions that he utters in the same way that
they are used in English (or he uses the symbols involved in his mental
acts in the way implied by the construal of them as expressions of thoughts
or beliefs about his past) and was so using them at his beginning. And thus
there is a basis for saying that he began his existence with true beliefs
about the correct use of English and with an extensive set of delusory
memory-impressions.

So that which is necessary to make mental or behavioral acts formulate
propositions that refer to the past is compatible with the possibility that
a subject might have a normal sort of totality of memory- and sense-
deliverances that are entirely or mostly false, at least in their perceptual
implications. That this is a possibility means that the consequent of (A*)
(1) (or of (A*m) (1)) cannot follow from any proposition, like its antecedent, that is merely about the intrinsic nature of the subject's memory-

impressions and sensations. It also means that there can be no *a priori* demonstration that it is necessary that the consequent is highly probable relative to the antecedent, that is, necessary that the vast majority of those of a person's perceptual deliverances that satisfy the antecedent must be true. There simply are contrary logical possibilities.

We have, of course, plenty of *a posteriori* evidence that such wholesale perceptual and memory-delusion does not occur and would be practically impossible to cause, and also that what perceptual hallucination does occur, being the result of rather haphazard interference of physical and psychological forces in the normal process that correlates sensation with environment in a regular way, almost always delivers perceptions that are severely anomalous. And we can see *a priori* that in one's own case it would be impossible to have *a posteriori* (perceptual) evidence of the falsity of anything but incoherent (anomalous) parts of one's perceptual deliverances (past and present).

9. Could the justification for (A*) (1) (or (A*m) (1)) be by non-deductive inference from some other intrinsic features of the totality of one's sense and memory-deliverances? I don't see how. What other features could make the consequent of (A*) (1) (or of (A*m) (1)) a more attractive proposition than those specified in its antecedent? I cannot see any (aside from mere size of the total ostensibly remembered history of perceptual deliverances referred to in the antecedent: perhaps the larger that is the more attractive is the consequent, up to a point that any normal non-infant person has passed).

There is nothing left but the *intrinsic appeal* of (A*) (1) (or of (A*-m) (1)). When a perceptual deliverance of one's memory or senses is as attractive as the intrinsic features of the totality of the perceptual deliverances of one's memory and senses can make it (which is to say, as attractive as one's directly recognizable position can make it) – that is, when it satisfies the antecedent of (A*) (1) (or of (A*-m) (1)), is a member of the coherent part relative to the totality – then it is so attractive as to 'win hands down' over any competing logically possible alternative.

We who understand the proposition that is the consequent of (A*) (1) have a fundamental impulse, a *desire*, to respond to the situation specified in the antecedent with confidence in that proposition. This is a desire that does not derive from any other desire for a further end; it is brute.

Some philosophers have suggested that there are further features of a proposition like (A*) (1), that explain or justify its cognitive appeal.

It is something like this proposition (that the coherent part of the totality of his perceptual deliverances is true) concerning which Descartes maintains (in the *Sixth Meditation*) that, given his strong natural inclination to believe it, if it were false then God must have intended to deceive him. I maintain that, even if his premiss as to its divine cause were taken away, Descartes could still appeal to this strong inclination.

Brandt (1955) suggests that such a proposition (plus further propositions about the world that can be properly inferred from it) offers by far the best explanation we have thought of for one's memory-impressions and sensations being what they are. I suppose that this is true, but even if one were to work out in detail a wholly contrary hypothesis that would explain the nature of one's memory-impressions and sensations equally well (perhaps even by kinds of mechanisms we know of) it would not have anything like the same appeal; it would in fact be no more appealing than the hypothesis that all of one's memory-impressions and sensations at a given time are just brute facts that have no explanation in terms of facts beyond them. (Of course, no contrary hypothesis could be devised that explains one's sensations and memory-impressions equally well if 'explains equally well' requires that it have as much intrinsic appeal to our intellects.)

Slote (1970) suggests that belief in the external world delivered by the coherent part of one's perceptual deliverances, rather than any contrary hypothesis, is recommended by what he calls the "Principle of Unlimited Inquiry'. This is "the principle (a) that it is scientifically *unreasonable* for someone to *accept* what (he sees or has reason to believe) is for him at that time an inquiry-limiting [i.e., further-explanation-blocking] explanation in favour of an acceptable non-inquiry-limiting explanation of a certain phenomenon, other things being equal; and (b) that there is *reason* for such a person to *reject* such an explanation in favour of an acceptable non-inquiry-limiting explanation of the phenomenon in question, if he can find one." (p. 67). I doubt that its giving more scope for finding further explanations is really the reason for the greater appeal of the hypothesis that one perceives an external world (at least in the coherent part of one's perceptual deliverances); because, though it is far from clear to me that no possible contrary hypothesis could offer the same scope for further explanations, it is clear to me that if some contrary hypothesis did do so it would still not begin to have the appeal of the ordinary 'hypothesis'. It also seems clear that people who markedly lack interest in scientific explanation of the world that we all perceive would nevertheless find it impossible to believe some wholly contrary hypothesis that would be no more frustrating to *their* desire for further explanation.

The compelling and over-riding appeal of the ordinary 'hypothesis,' represented by (A*) (1), even as compared with contrary alternatives that would explain one's memory-impressions and sensations equally well or would offer the same scope for further explanation is, as far as I can see, a fact with no further, deeper explanation or justification. In its bruteness it is like the appeal of *simplicity* in theories and explanations: we just prefer the simpler of competing explanations or theories, other things (like explanatory power and scope for further explanation) being equal, and we have no more ultimate preference that is our reason for doing so. The justification of our liking what we like, in matters of belief as in other matters, has to end somewhere.

In any case, I think that what needs to be pointed out is not so much what features of the ordinary 'hypothesis' give it the overwhelming appeal it has, as compared with any possible contrary one, as that this appeal *justifies* our unquestioning confidence in it. To refrain generally from confidence in the sort of perceptual proposition that is the consequent of (A*) (1) when in the sort of situation specified in the antecedent would be too intolerably frustrating to be borne and in practice impossible. To refrain occasionally or even once would be no mean feat and would be no less lacking in motive. This is the situation in which we find ourselves, or the nature that we find in ourselves, which we can do nothing about and for which we are not responsible. Given a normal sort of totality of perceptual memory- and sense-deliverances, one wants a strong motive to resist the strong appeal to one's belief of any of them; and we find such a motive only in the conflict of other such appeals, in other perceptual deliverances being incoherent with it. We do not find it in the mere realization that something contrary is logically compatible with our directly recognizable position, which by itself gives the hypothesis of something contrary no belief-appeal at all.

I would not deny that disbelief in the ordinary 'hypothesis', or even belief in some contrary hypothesis, in one who has a normal sort of

totality of perceptual deliverances of his memory and senses, may
be possible. Such a thing might even be motivated, conceivably,
by some specious philosophical reasoning. Nor should it be denied
that belief in *some* of the hypotheses thoroughly contrary to the ordinary
one might (although completely unjustified and crazy) make no practical
difference in the subject's behavior. If I were to believe that all the perceptual deliverances of my senses and memory are false but also that they
have been and, no matter how I will to move my ostensible body, will
continue to be coherent and of the sort I am used to, then presumably I
will make my bodily volitions (which I must regard as producing only
hallucinations of the effects that in making them I pretend to bring about)
the same as I would if I had normal convictions. Still, this belief that none
of what my senses or memory delivers is genuine perception, if I really
have it and do not merely occasionally entertain the proposition with a
certain philosophical seriousness, would have to make a radical and pervasive difference to my *thinking*, to my *attitude* towards my experience.
Indeed, the difference would be so great that I am unable to imagine what
it would be like. It would, I suppose, be something like, only much more
extreme than, having the insane conviction that the dominant motive
guiding everyone else's actions is to harass and fool me in subtle and devi-
ous ways and, of course, to conceal this intention from me (which is, after
all, a logical possibility compatible with all my actual direct perceptions),
and at the same time following the policy of never letting others suspect
that I know of their malevolent aim.

I would deny, however, that we can make sense of the suggestion that
there might be a person who understands all the same perceptual propositions we do, has had and remembers a normal sort of history of perceptual sensations for an adult human being, but has always completely
lacked any impulse to believe the consequent of (A*) (1) when satisfying
its antecedent. The lack of any impulse to perceptual belief in those circumstances would mean the absence of the criteria that we employ for
the kinds of perceptual sensation that a subject has, criteria that determine
our concepts of those kinds. As I have argued elsewhere,[11] following
Wittgenstein, our concepts of kinds of anything must have criteria, and
our concepts of kinds of sensations must have criteria that lie in the subjects' reactions to their sensations or in what their reactions would be if
other conditions were present. The subjects themselves can appeal to no

other sort of criteria for the kinds of their sensations. The kinds into which a subject's sensations fall are *essentially* linked to such (possibly conditional) reaction-criteria. As was pointed out earlier, in Chapter V, Section 3, the reactions that are in fact our criteria for kinds of perceptual sensations – the only reactions we make that could serve the purpose of discriminating and identifying all the kinds that we do discriminate and identify – are our direct perceptual beliefs (our beliefs that we perceive things of certain directly specifiable appearances) or our inclinations thereto. If a person has a sensation but in no circumstance whatever would he be disposed to react to it by having at least an inclination to believe that he was seeing, say, something that looks as would a square red surface a short distance away against a blue background in good light (or at least the thought that as far as his visual sensation goes it is possible that he is seeing that), not even the circumstance that he understands that perceptual proposition, then that person cannot possibly be having the kind of sensation that we specify by speaking of a visual sensation as if seeing a square red surface... etc. We have stipulated the absence of the only fact that could make it that kind of sensation. The kind of visual sensation that we can specify with some particular phrase of the form 'as if seeing y in θ' (direct specification) is necessarily the kind to which a subject would react, if he satisfied the antecedent of (A*) (1), with at least an impulse to believe that he sees something that looks as would y in θ (if he understands that proposition). So a person who has and remembers a normal sort of totality of perceptual sensations and understands what would be the ordinary 'hypothesis' about it must have at least an impulse to believe this hypothesis.

In fact, of course, we all continually feel sure of such propositions as the consequent of (A*) (1) (or of (A*m) (1)). And what prompts us to do so is a directly recognizable position that satisfies the antecedent, the fact that that sense-deliverance (or perceptual memory-deliverance) belongs to the coherent majority of the totality of direct perceptions delivered or implied by our senses and memory. The disposition to be prompted to that attitude by that situation amounts to being confident of (A*) (1) (or of (A*-m) (1)) in one who understands it. It is tantamount to being confident of it in one who does not understand it, falling short only by that lack of understanding. Everyone acts and thinks in a way that manifests confidence in (A*) (1) (or in (A*m) (1)) or would manifest confidence in it if he understood it.

It is not that we want to be confident of (A*) (1) (or of its consequent when we satisfy its antecedent) because we want it to be true in order that certain further desires of ours will be satisfied. Our justification for confidence in (A*) (1) is not an *interested* one. We simply want to be confident of it.

'Want' is too weak a word. Our wanting to react to the situation specified in the antecedent of (A*) (1) by being confident of its consequent – our wanting to act confidently as if (A*) (1) is true – is like wanting to react to touching an extremely hot surface by qucikly drawing the hand away, only more so. A powerful motive is needed even for slight restraint. And even if, by some crazy, Herculean effort, one could resist, why *should* one? Certainly not because we recognize that it is logically possible that the consequent be false even when the antecedent is true. That recognition simply will not move us in that way, any more than the recognition that it does not follow with logical necessity from anything that has happened in the past that I would suffer pain if I were now to thrust this letter opener into my hand moves me in the slightest to doubt that I would. We just do extend our confidence to propositions that go beyond what our justifying positions, the facts directly recognizable to us, can *entail* and we find no real inducement to refrain from doing so.

One should trust the direct deliverances of one's senses, or the direct perceptual deliverances of one's memory, when they belong to the part that is coherent relative to all that their deliverances imply about one's direct perceptions. *Why* should one do this? Why not?

NOTES

[1] 'I see *d*' is a perceptual *deliverance* of my visual sensation just in case that sensation is as if seeing *d*, and it is a *direct* perceptual deliverance just in case it reports a direct perception. '*p*' is one of my *memory-deliverances* just in case I have a strong memory-impression that *p*.

[2] Compare Berkeley's idea, in *Essay Towards a New Theory of Vision,* that the perceptions of touch are the real perceptions of external objects and the ideas of sight come to be mistakenly regarded as perceptions of objects in space only through their correlation with, and hence reliability as indicators of, available perceptions of touch.

[3] Berkeley remarks (in *Essay Towards a New Theory of Vision,* sec. 59):

> We regard the objects that environ us in proportion as they are adapted to benefit or injure our own bodies, and thereby produce in our minds the sensations of pleasure or pain. Now, bodies operating on our organs by an immediate application, and the hurt or advantage arising there-

from depending altogether on the tangible, and not at all on the visible, qualities of any object: This is a plain reason why those should be regarded by us much more than these.

[4] Further complications would be required to obtain a proposition that would have the same relation to the conditions for memory knowledge *in general* (of any sort of proposition) that (A*) has to the conditions for direct perceptual knowledge. The relation of incoherence would have to be understood to include logical incompatibility (a relation that could not obtain between the direct perceptual deliverances of different sensations). The class of propositions to which the relation of incoherence applies would include, besides direct perceptual deliverances, (a) memory-deliverances that merely imply something, however vague and inspecific, about what the subject's perceptions have been (such as the deliverance that he has come to know a certain general proposition through experience or through reading it somewhere), (b) memory-deliverances that knowledge of certain necessary truths has been obtained by *a priori* demonstration, (c) self-evident truths of which the subject has infallible knowledge, and (d) truths about his current conscious mental states or acts and memory-deliverances as to what his conscious mental states or acts have been. The incoherence of members of (a) would be a matter either of their logical incompatibility with other deliverances or of their perceptual implications being incoherent in other ways with perceptual implications of other deliverances. Only the memory-deliverance members of (d) could be incoherent and incoherence of them would be a matter of evidence from other deliverances of memory-delusion. Members of (c) could not be incoherent at all, and if a memory-deliverance were self-evidently incompatible with a necessary truth self-evident to the subject then that memory-deliverance would be intrinsically anomalous.

There is some similarity (and this is not, I believe, an accident) between the criterion I am suggesting for non-inferential trustworthiness of a memory-deliverance and the rule suggested in Brandt (1955) for determining "justifiable attitudes towards our memory beliefs." Brandt's rule (p. 88):

> (a) Accept as a basis for action and for accepting other beliefs all your clear recollections except those (but not more than a few) of which the system (laws, theories, etc.) of beliefs supported by the vast majority of your recollections requires rejection or makes rejection convenient.
> (b) Believe (disbelieve) any particular recollection *more* firmly and confidently corresponding to the degree of support by (seriousness of conflict with) the system which can be erected on the base consisting of the vast majority of your recollections.

[5] Ayer (1956), p. 38, says, "... no judgments of perception would be specially open to distrust unless some were trustworthy". He goes on, pp. 38–39, "but this is not a proof that we cannot be mistaken in trusting those that we do.... From the fact that our rejection of some of them is grounded on our acceptance of others it does not follow that those that we accept are true. Nevertheless the argument does show that these general forms of skepticism can find no justification in experience."

[6] My page references in this paragraph and in note 7 are to the reprinted text in Malcolm (1963).

[7] This is what Malcolm's remark suggests but I am not sure that this is what he meant. I am puzzled by his further remark (p. 68):

> In saying that I should regard nothing as evidence that there is no ink-bottle here now, I am not *predicting* what I should do if various astonish-

ing things happened.... That assertion describes my *present* attitude
towards the statement that here is an ink-bottle. It does not prophesy
what my attitude would be if various things happened... no imaginable
future occurrence would be considered by me *now* as proving that there
is not an ink-bottle here.

Either these remarks have no implications at all for the crucial epistemological question
of what the attitude of one who claims to know in the strong sense *ought* to be if and
when various things were to happen; or they imply (what I think false) that sometimes
a subject would be justified in taking the attitude described, whatever attitude he
actually does take; or else they are impenetrable to me, seeing a difference that I cannot see between saying that I am justified *now* in thinking 'No matter what sensations
and memory-impressions are in the future added to those I now have I will not be in a
position to be uncertain that p' and saying that no matter what sensations and memory-
impressions are in the future added to those I now have I will not *then,* with that new
lot, be justified in thinking 'It is uncertain that p'.

8 Malcolm (1963), 'Memory and the Past', pp. 195–198.

9 Shoemaker (1963), pp. 201, 230, 235.

10 Malcolm's claim that a person's *past-tense* statements must be mainly true is stronger
than Shoemaker's claim that most of a person's *sincere memory* statements must be
true. A child who persistently tries to kid us about the past, who thinks that making obviously false assertions about the past is a very funny thing to do, might satisfy
Shoemaker's requirement while failing to satisfy Malcolm's. And Shoemaker's claim
that most of a person's sincere memory *statements* must be true is not equivalent to his
claim that most of his memory *beliefs* must be true. An extremely taciturn person who
verbally expresses very few of his memory beliefs and these happen to be mainly false
ones might satisfy the second requirement while failing to satisfy the first. In all these
claims there is a lack of precision as to just what class of statements, or sincere statements, or beliefs, must be mainly true if all members of the class are to be past-referring
memory statements or beliefs. Is it all the past-tense statements *so far* made by a
person at any point in his existence, or all that he ever makes? Is it all his memory
beliefs at a given time, or up to a given time, or throughout his entire existence?

11 Ginet (1968).

BIBLIOGRAPHY

Alston, W. P.: 1971, 'Varieties of Privileged Access', *American Philosophical Quarterly* **8**, 223–241.

Armstrong, D. M.: 1961, *Perception and the Physical World*, London.

Armstrong, D. M.: 1973, *Belief Truth and Knowledge*, Cambridge.

Austin, J. L.: 1962, *Sense and Sensibilia*, Oxford.

Ayer, A. J.: 1947, 'Phenomenalism', *Proceedings of the Aristotelian Society* **47**,163–196. Reprinted in Ayer: 1954, *Philosophical Essays*, London.

Ayer, A. J.: 1956, *The Problem of Knowledge*, Harmondsworth, Middlesex.

Bennett, J.: 1964, *Rationality*, London.

Berkeley, G.: 1709, *An Essay Towards a New Theory of Vision*, Dublin.

Berkeley, G.: 1710, *A Treatise Concerning the Principles of Human Knowledge*, Dublin.

Berkeley, G.: 1713, *Three Dialogues Between Hylas and Philonous*, London.

Bower, T. G. R.: 1974, *Development in Infancy*, San Francisco.

Brandt, R. B.: 1955, 'The Epistemological Status of Memory Beliefs', *Philosophical Review* **64**, 78–95.

Brown, D. G.: 1970, 'Knowing How and Knowing That, What', in G. Pitcher and O. P. Wood (eds.), *Ryle: A Collection of Critical Essays*, Garden City, N. Y., pp. 213–248.

Cartwright, R.: 1966, 'Propositions', in R. Butler (ed.), *Analytical Philosophy, First Series*, Oxford, pp. 81–103.

Castaneda, H. (ed.): 1967, *Intentionality, Minds, and Perception*, Detroit.

Caton, C.: 1967, 'Comments' [on Firth (1967)], in Castaneda (1967), pp. 383–394.

Champawat, N. and Saunders, J. T.: 1964, 'Mr. Clark's Definition of "Knowledge"', *Analysis* **25**, 8–9.

Chisholm, R.: 1957, *Perceiving: A Philosophical Study*, Ithaca, N.Y.

Collins, A. W.: 1967, 'The Epistemological Status of the Concept of Perception', *Philosophical Review* **76**, 436–459.

Deutscher, M. and Martin, C. B.: 1966, 'Remembering', *Philosophical Review* **75**, 161–196.

Dretske, F. I.: 1969, *Seeing and Knowing*, London.

Dretske, F. I.: 1970, 'Epistemic Operators', *Journal of Philosophy* **67**, 1007–1023.

Ducasse, C. J.: 1951, *Nature, Mind, and Death*, La Salle, Ill.

Firth, R.: 1967, 'The Men Themselves; or the Role of Causation in Our Concept of Seeing', in Castaneda (1967), pp. 357–382.

Gettier, E.: 1963, 'Is Justified True Belief Knowledge?', *Analysis* **23**, 121–123.

Gibson, J.: 1950, *The Perception of the Visual World*, Boston.

Gibson, J.: 1966, *The Senses Considered as Perceptual Systems*, Boston.

Gibson, J.: 1967, 'New Reasons for Realism', *Synthese* **17**, 162–172.

Gibson, J.: 1972, 'Outline of a Theory of Direct Visual Perception', in J. Royce and W. Rozeboom (eds.), *Second Banff Conference on Theoretical Psychology, 1969: the Psychology of Knowing*, New York.

Ginet, C.: 1968, 'How Words Mean Kinds of Sensations', *Philosophical Review* **76**, 3–23.

Ginet, C.: 1970, 'What Must Be Added to Knowing to Obtain Knowing that One Knows?', *Synthese* **21**, 163–186.

Grice, H. P.: 1961, 'The Causal Theory of Perception', *Proceedings of the Aristotelian Society* (Supplementary vol.) **35**, 121–168. Reprinted in Swartz (1965).

Grice, H. P.: 1974, 'The Logic of Conversation', in D. Davidson and G. Harman (eds.), *The Logic of Grammar,* Encino, Calif.

Griffiths, A. P. (ed.): 1967, *Knowledge and Belief,* Oxford.

Hamlyn, D. W.: 1957, *The Psychology of Perception,* London.

Hamlyn, D. W.: 1961, *Sensation and Perception,* London.

Harrison, J.: 1962, 'Knowing and Promising', *Mind* **71**, 443–457. Reprinted in Griffiths (1967).

Hilpinen, R.: 1968, *Rules of Acceptance and Inductive Logic* (Acta Philosophica Fennica, Fasc. 22), Amsterdam.

Hilpinen, R. and Hintikka, J.: 1965, 'Knowledge, Acceptance, and Inductive Logic', in J. Hintikka and P. Suppes (eds.), *Aspects of Inductive Logic,* Amsterdam, pp. 1–20.

Hintikka, J. and Hilpinen, R.: [same as preceding item].

Kelley, J. L.: 1955, *General Topology,* Princeton.

Kemp-Smith, N. (ed. and transl.): 1952, *Descartes' Philosophical Writings,* London.

Kirk, R.: 1967, 'Rationality without Language', *Mind* **76**, 369–486.

Kyburg, H. E. Jr.: 1965, 'Probability, Rationality, and a Rule of Detachment', in Bar-Hillel (ed.), *Proceedings of the 1964 Congress for Logic, Methodology, and Philosophy of Science,* Amsterdam, pp. 301–310.

Kyburg, H. E. Jr.: 1970, 'Conjunctivitis', in Swain (1970b), pp. 55–82.

Lehrer, K.: 1968, 'Belief and Knowledge', *Philosophical Review* **77**, 491–499.

Lehrer, K.: 1970, 'Justification, Explanation, and Induction', in Swain (1970b), pp. 100–133.

Lehrer, K. and Paxson, T.: 1969, 'Knowledge: Undefeated Justified True Belief', *Journal of Philosophy* **66**, 225–237.

Lewis, C. I.: 1947, *An Analysis of Knowledge and Valuation,* La Salle, Ill.

Lewis, H. D. (ed.): 1956, *Contemporary British Philosophy, Third Series,* London.

Locke, J.: 1690, *An Essay Concerning Human Understanding,* London.

Macdonald, M. (ed.): 1954, *Philosophy and Analysis,* Oxford.

Malcolm, N.: 1950, 'The Verification Argument', in M. Black (ed.), *Philosophical Analysis,* Englewood Cliffs, N.J., 229–279. Reprinted in Malcolm (1963).

Malcolm, N.: 1952a 'Moore and Ordinary Language', in Schilpp (1952), pp. 343–368.

Malcolm, N.: 1952b, 'Knowledge and Belief', *Mind* **61**, 178–189. Reprinted in Malcolm (1963).

Malcolm, N.: 1963, *Knowledge and Certainty,* Englewood Cliffs, N.J.

Malcolm, N.: 1970, 'Memory and Representation', *Noûs* **4**, 59–70.

Martin, C. B. and Deutscher, M.: 1966, 'Remembering', *Philosophical Review* **75**, 161–196.

Mill, J. S.: 1865, *An Examination of Sir William Hamilton's Philosophy,* London.

Moore, G. E.: 1914, 'The Status of Sense-Data', *Proceedings of the Aristotelian Society* **14**, 355–380.

Moore, G. E.: 1952, 'A Reply to My Critics', in Schilpp (1952), pp. 535–677.

Moore, G. E.: 1953, *Some Main Problems of Philosophy,* London.

Moore, G. E.: 1962, *Commonplace Book 1919–1953* (ed. by C. Lewy), London.

Munsat, S.: 1966, *The Concept of Memory,* New York.
Paxson, T. and Lehrer, K.: 1969, 'Knowledge: Undefeated Justified True Belief', *Journal of Philosophy* 66, 225–237.
Pitcher, G.: 1971, *A Theory of Perception,* Princeton.
Price, H. H.: 1932, *Perception,* London.
Prichard, H. A.: 1950, *Knowledge and Perception,* Oxford.
Quine, W. V. O.: 1953, 'Reference and Modality', in *From a Logical Point of View,* Cambridge, Mass., pp. 139–159.
Quinton, A. M.: 1955, 'The Problem of Perception', *Mind* 64, 28–51.
Radford, C.: 1966, 'Knowledge – By Examples', *Analysis* 27, 1–11.
Ross, W. D. (ed.): 1915, *The Work's of Aristotle Translated into English,* Oxford.
Russell, B.: 1914a, *Our Knowledge of the External World,* Chicago.
Russell, B.: 1914b, 'The Relation of Sense Data to Physics', *Scientia* 4. Reprinted in Russell: 1918, *Mysticism and Logic,* New York.
Russell, B.: 1921, *The Analysis of Mind,* London.
Ryle, G.: 1949, *The Concept of Mind,* London.
Ryle, G.: 1956, 'Sensations', in Lewis (1956), pp. 425–443.
Saunders, J. T. and Champawat, N.: 1964, 'Mr. Clark's Definition of "Knowledge"', *Analysis* 25, 8–9.
Schilpp, P. A. (ed.): 1952, *The Philosophy of G. E. Moore,* New York.
Searle, J.: 1969, *Speech Acts,* Cambridge.
Sellars, W.: 1963, *Science, Perception, and Reality,* London.
Sellars, W.: 1968, *Science and Metaphysics,* London.
Shoemaker, S.: 1963, *Self-Knowledge and Self-Identity,* Ithaca, N.Y.
Shoemaker, S.: 1967, Article on Memory in P. Edwards (ed.), *The Encyclopedia of Philosophy,* Vol. 5, New York, pp. 265–274.
Shoemaker, S.: 1970a, 'Persons and Their Pasts', *American Philosophical Quarterly* 7, 269–285.
Shoemaker, S.: 1970b, 'Wiggins on Identity', *Philosophical Review* 74, 529–544.
Slote, M.: 1970, *Reason and Skepticism,* London.
Swain, M.: 1970a, 'The Consistency of Rational Belief' in Swain (1970b), pp. 27–54.
Swain, M.: 1970b, *Induction, Acceptance, and Rational Belief,* Dordrecht.
Swartz, R. J. (ed.): 1965, *Perceiving, Sensing, and Knowing,* New York.
Unger, P.: 1967, 'Experience and Factual Knowledge', *Journal of Philosophy* 64, 152–173.
Unger, P.: 1968, 'An Analysis of Factual Knowledge', *Journal of Philosophy* 65, 157–170.
Vendler, Z.: 1972, *Res Cogitans: An Essay in Rational Psychology,* Ithaca, N.Y.
Waismann, F.: 1945, 'Verifiability', *Proceedings of the Aristotelian Society* (Supplementary Vol.) 19, 119–150.
Wiggins, D.: 1967, *Identity and Spatio-Temporal Continuity,* Oxford.
Williams, B.: 1957, 'Personal Identity and Individuation', *Proceedings of the Aristotelian Society* 57, 229–252. Reprinted in Williams: 1973, *Problems of the Self,* Cambridge, pp. 1–18.
Wittgenstein, L. W.: 1953, *Philosophical Investigations,* New York.
Wittgenstein, L. W.: 1958, *The Blue and Brown Books,* Oxford.
Wittgenstein, L. W.: 1969, *On Certainty,* Oxford.
Woozley, A. D.: 1952, 'Knowing and Not Knowing', *Proceedings of the Aristotelian Society* 53, 151–172. Reprinted in Griffiths (1967).

INDEX OF NAMES

Slote, M. 198
Swain, M. 64–65 (n. 9)

Unger, P. 80 (n. 2), 171–172 (n. 2)

Vendler, Z. 26, (n. 4)

Waismann, F. 115, 116 (n. 14)
Wiggins, D. 172 (n. 9)
Williams, B. 172 (n. 9)
Wittgenstein, L. W. 11 (n. 2), 23, 27 (n. 7, 8)
Woozley, A. D. 26 (n. 1)

INDEX OF SUBJECTS